THINKING POLITICS

CHATHAM HOUSE STUDIES IN POLITICAL THINKING
SERIES EDITOR: George J. Graham, Jr.
Vanderbilt University

THINKING POLITICS
Perspectives in Ancient, Modern, and Postmodern Political Theory

Leslie Paul Thiele
University of Florida

Chatham House Publishers, Inc.
Chatham, New Jersey

Thinking Politics: Perspectives in Ancient,
Modern, and Postmodern Political Theory

Chatham House Publishers, Inc.
Post Office Box One
Chatham, New Jersey 07928

Publisher: Edward Artinian
Cover design: Lawrence Ratzkin
Production supervisor: Katharine Miller
Composition: Bang, Motley, Olufsen
Printing and binding: R.R. Donnelley and Sons Company

Library of Congress Cataloging-in-Publication Data

Thiele, Leslie Paul, 1959–
    Thinking politics : perspectives in ancient, modern, and
    postmodern political theory / Leslie Paul Thiele
    p.   cm.
    Includes bibliographical references and index.
    ISBN 1-56643-000-x (pbk.)
    1. BOGUS   I. Title
BOGUS JK271.A37   1997
BOGUS 320.973—dc20   96-00000
                                                                 CIP

Printed in the United States of America
10   9   8   7   6   5   4   3   2   1

To my mother, Wilfrida Maria Thiele,
and to the memory of my father,
Jacob Zachary Thiele

Contents

Preface

This book was originally conceived as a standard introduction to political theory. Demonstrating the continuity and change within the long and venerable tradition of political thought was a pleasant prospect. I quickly discovered, however, that I was not well suited to writing a stock survey text. I could not bring myself to strip from political theory that which, for me, has always been its most redeeming quality, namely, its capacity to stretch the mind, induce critical inquiry, and bring worldly problems to bear—often in a disquieting way—on the aspiring theorist. The result is a book that, I hope, will intellectually, practically, and personally challenge its readers. This, I believe, is the best means to cultivate a love for the discipline.

The chapters of this book integrate the insights of ancient, modern, and postmodern political thought. At the end of each chapter, I have offered suggestions for further reading. Many of these works, particularly the classic texts, are available in more than one satisfactory edition. I have for this reason abbreviated bibliographical information. Most of the suggested readings are also found in the endnotes, where readers can identify the editions that I have used. The endnotes themselves are wholly bibliographical and need not be consulted unless references for citations are desired.

For making this book's arguments more compelling and its writing more readable, I would like to thank Al Damico, Luke Garrott, George Graham, Albert Matheny, Hillard Pouncy, and Donna Waller. Special thanks are due to Paul Wapner, Ted Schatzki, and Susan Thiele. Paul has engaged me, over many years of friendship and travel, in a critical dialogue about the integration of philosophic concerns and political life. Without that dialogue, this book, and my life, would be much poorer. Ted's critical commentary on the penultimate draft of this manuscript was so reassuringly thorough that I am tempted, contrary to tradition, to make him responsible for any confusions and oversights that remain. Finally, Susan provided much critical insight and a perspicacious editing of the entire manuscript. She also gave unflagging encouragement and abiding support.

Introduction

Political theory is deliberation about the proper organization of collective human existence. It is concerned with understanding political life as it is defined by the public use of power. This investigation of things political has traditionally been understood as an inquiry into the nature of "the good life." Since ancient times, the good life has been characterized as a life of reason, shared with others in liberty and grounded in justice. Political theorists describe the components of this life, speculate on its requirements, evaluate its potential, and argue for its achievement.

The tradition of political theory, while rich in historical insight, conceptual refinement, ethical debate, and philosophic reflection, is poor in eternal truths and practical implementations. It follows that the art and craft of political theory is less a learning of set principles, technical procedures, or concrete applications than an exercise in critical thought. To teach political theory is to introduce students to a tradition of thought so that they might interact creatively with it. To teach political theory is to aid in the acquisition and development of the analytic and interpretive skills, the moral and philosophic judgment, and the social and historical knowledge needed to appreciate a tradition of thought, to contest its claims, and to make good use of its insights.

Developing this skill, judgment, and knowledge is an exciting but arduous task. Returns on investments of time and effort are seldom certain. This is partly because political theory has always been, and remains today, a field uncertain of its objectives, unsettled in its procedures, and self-consciously critical of its own identity. Political theory might be described as an unending dance staged between skeptical reserve and the epic effort to achieve methodological rigor, conceptual stability, and moral certainty about things political. *Thinking Politics* introduces the reader to this form of dance.

Only that which has no history is truly definable. Historical phenomena may be described in detail, but their meanings cannot be affixed once and for all. The discussion of political theory in this book occasionally takes on the pretense of being definitive. Political theory, however, is a historical product. Its multiple origins and ongoing evolution make it a topic for rich description but not for conclusive definition. As in times past, political theory today means different things to different people. The history of political theory is often circumscribed within a canon of thinkers that originates in classical antiquity and proceeds through medieval and modern periods to contemporary times. This roster of theorists is assumed to constitute a distinctive, self-contained tradition of Western political thought. Yet the canon is largely a retrospective construction. Most of its representative figures did not identify themselves as contributors to a singular tradition. Nonetheless, the voices that animate the history of political theory have produced a sustained, if unruly, conversation over the ages. It is a conversation well worth entering.

This book sets out the scope and methods of political theory, understood as a tradition of historical, normative, interpretive, and analytic thought whose concern, most broadly speaking, is the nature of collective human life. The aim of this text is not encyclopedic. Rather than provide a survey of the discipline and its major figures, it approaches the tradition from various points of view in an effort to engage readers in *thinking politics*. This somewhat unusual term requires an explanation.

The project of thinking politics means three things. It means, first, *thinking about politics* as this phrase is commonly employed. To think about politics is to think about the means and ends of political life. It entails exploring the nature and charting the limits of politics. Thinking about politics is primarily an analytical and historical enterprise.

Thinking politics also means *thinking through politics*. To think through politics is to acknowledge that one's own attitudes, beliefs, and values are themselves products of a political life. To think through politics is, self-consciously, to think through the medium of one's participation in a collective existence. Thinking through politics, then, is a consideration of the various political forces that stimulate and constrain thought and action in greater and lesser degrees. This is largely a self-reflective and interpretive project.

Finally, thinking politics means *thinking politically*. To think politically is to think explicitly about one's opinions and behavior in reference to common standards, rights, and responsibilities. To think politically is to think as a member of political society, rather than as a particular individual with particular interests. It requires that one step outside oneself and into the shoes of others. It demands one's judgment as a citizen among citizens. The task of thinking politically is largely normative and critical in nature.

Political theorists and political theory texts often give pride of place to one of these three projects: the analytical and historical, the self-reflective and interpretive, or the normative and critical. Yet these three aspects of thinking politics remain inextricably entwined within the tradition of political thought. Thinking politics integrates these three fundamental features of political thought and life. The presumption is that they are best exercised together.

This text distinguishes itself from standard introductions to political theory in important ways. First, many introductory works offer historical or conceptual overviews of the tradition. They supply glosses on an extensive roster of figures and political ideas. Such glosses are informative. In painting the theoretical canvas with such broad strokes, however, few lasting impressions are made. The reader receives a smattering of information about a canon of figures, texts, and concepts for which he or she gains little appreciation. Often the reader ends up with a laundry list of definitions and descriptions that are memorized only soon to be forgotten. Such survey texts court the danger of undercutting what should arguably be their most important service: prompting the reader to engage in independent, critical political thought.

Rather than reproduce such efforts, this text explores the art and craft of political theory. To this end, not only the nature of politics but also the nature of theory are discussed extensively. What it means to theorize, and to theorize well, is a central focus. The aim is to develop both an understanding of the domain of politics and a sensibility to the ways in which this domain may be intellectually and morally engaged. The text relies on the exemplary fashion in which certain theorists within the history of political thought have constructed and evaluated the domain of politics. These references to canonical figures, however, are meant less to celebrate past achievements or invoke authorities than to stimulate and guide the reader's own political thinking. While standard definitions of key political concepts are provided, these definitions are also frequently challenged. In turn, more original and controversial perspectives are explored. The aim is to encourage the reader not only to learn about political theory but to learn how to think theoretically about politics. This goal is best pursued by exploring how various political quandaries have been intellectually and morally approached and reapproached over time, and by underlining the reader's responsibility creatively to work through such quandaries.

The second distinguishing characteristic of this text is its integration of contemporary theoretical and political concerns. The American anthropologist Clifford Geertz has observed a blurring of genres in the humanities and social sciences in recent decades.[1] Since ancient times, political theory has crossed paths with philosophy. Today, however, it also borrows from and lends to such fields as anthropology, biology, ecology, economics, history, literary criticism, psychology, and sociology. This ongoing cross-fertilization has stimulated a renaissance in political theory. It has also challenged the stability and identity of the discipline. With this in mind, the text integrates these kindred disciplines into discussion.

The book is also significantly informed by postmodern concerns. Introductory texts in political theory tend to traverse the tradition in retrospect. Historical overview has much to recommend it and is an indispensable component of political theory. But students also need to be grounded in the present and to cast a glance to the future. To study political theory today and ignore postmodern thought is to neglect one of its more creative forces. Yet students can find few manageable introductions to postmodern thought that successfully integrate it with the tradition of political theory. Hence an important contemporary trend among political theorists has remained unproductively isolated and obscure.

While postmodern theory occupies a territory different from ancient and modern theory, the border between them follows a zigzag course over the rough terrain of politics. Occasionally, with particular thinkers or issues, this border slips from sight altogether, and an uneasy convergence takes place. Determining if and how the border between the ancient, modern, and postmodern should be drawn is a demanding task. This text demonstrates that border crossings can make for good theory.

Most contemporary political theorists think of themselves as standing at the edge of modernity or perhaps straddling the modern and the postmodern. Instead of proposing postmodern orientations as superseding more traditional ones, this text encourages the simultaneous exploration of ancient, modern, and postmodern theoretical perspectives. It brings postmodern thought to bear on traditional political issues by integrating the postmodern concern with the social construction of identity, the modern concern with the regulation of social interaction, and the ancient concern with the cultivation of virtue and the formation of character. In this way, postmodern thought is made theoretically accessible and politically relevant.

The book is divided into seven chapters, each of which approaches the task of understanding political life from a different point of view. Chapter 1, "Theory and Vision," explores the nature of theory. The chapter suggests that theories are best understood as conceptual lenses that furnish focused visions of the world. It discusses similarities and differences between interpretive political theory and scientific theory. In turn, the chapter examines the normative nature of political theory as well as its key methods of historical and conceptual analysis.

Chapter 2, "The Question of Human Nature," argues that human beings are unique because they are political animals and that the question of human nature must be broached before the question of politics can be adequately addressed. Many of the greatest achievements in the tradition of political theory are grounded on specific understandings of human nature. With these exemplars in mind, current knowledge of human biology and genetics is brought to bear on political and theoretical concerns.

Chapter 3, "Politics, Power, and the Public Good," explores the meaning of politics. It defines politics as the public use of power. An extensive investigation of the means and ends of power provides an important distinction between power and force. Subsequently, the chapter explores the ambiguous boundaries of public life. Because politics is pervasive, it becomes necessary to distinguish between actions, events, and institutions that are more and less political in nature.

Chapter 4, "Modernity and Postmodernity," approaches postmodern understandings of politics by way of their modern predecessors. The chapter begins with a historical analysis of modernism. It proceeds with an overview of structuralist, poststructuralist, and postmodern thought. It then contrasts the modern concern with the governmental regulation of social interaction and allocation of scarce resources with the postmodern concern with the social construction of individual and collective identities. The chapter highlights the political nature of postmodern theory by contrasting it to modern behaviorism.

Chapter 5, "Identity and Difference," examines various ways in which individual and collective identities are forged and contested. It investigates the political significance of racial, religious, gender, and economic identities. In each case, the text prompts the reader to explore whether, how, and to what extent his or her own identity is a social construct and how identities thus constructed respond and relate to difference.

Chapter 6, "Statecraft and Soulcraft," begins by exploring the linkage between postmodern concerns and the concerns of classical theorists. It compares the ancient Greek effort to craft virtuous souls through education and legislation with the postmodern focus on the social construction of identity. It links the relationship between statecraft and soulcraft, politics and identity, to the valorization of key political concepts in the tradition of political theory, such as justice, liberty, and reason.

Chapter 7, "Ideology and Irony," examines the history of ideology from the coining of the word in the eighteenth century through the putative "end of ideology" in our times. The chapter introduces irony, a kind of skeptical reserve, as a counteractive force to ideology. Political theories tend to balance themselves between the use of ironic and ideological lenses. These lenses expand or contract the theorist's breadth of vision and impetus for action. The chapter encourages readers to weigh the merits and demerits of both ideological and ironic lenses, to identify their uses within the history of political thought, and to explore the nature of an appropriate balance.

I

Theory and Vision

In subsequent chapters we investigate the nature of politics and political life. Before doing so, however, it is useful to explore our proposed method of investigation. That is to say, we first need to explore the nature of theory itself and the various ways of theorizing.

The best way to conceive of theory is to think of it as a kind of lens. We all have natural lenses in our eyes that focus light on our retinas. Many people also wear optical lenses made of glass or plastic that cor ect poor vision. These artificial, external lenses aid the eye in focusing light so that it produces clear images, rather than blurs and blotches. Microscopes and telescopes are also constructed from optical lenses. These magnifying lenses bend light in particular ways, allowing a focused image of very small or very distant objects.

Theories also aid us in putting the world in focus. What optical lenses do for our vision, theories do for our understanding. Whereas optical lenses improve our sight, theories improve our insight. Theories are conceptual lenses. They help us produce clearly focused mental views.

We might define a theory as a cognitive scheme or conceptual system that brings a part of the world into clearer focus and allows it to be better understood. Most of us can see the world quite well without the artificial lenses found in telescopes, microscopes, or even eyeglasses. Our unaided vision suffices. Likewise, most of us can get along in the world quite well without engaging in formal theorizing. Our unaided intellect, common sense, and traditional cultural viewpoints prove adequate. Nevertheless, like the lenses we make out of glass or plastic to see more clearly, the theories we fashion out of concepts allow us to understand the world more thoroughly and profoundly. They provide alternative viewpoints to those filtered through our personal or cultural predispositions. They also provide magnified views of features of our world that otherwise would go unnoticed.

By allowing us greater insight, theories take us beyond superficial overviews. Instead of merely redescribing what we see from customary viewpoints with the unaided intellect, theories allow us to get beneath the surface. Theories, in short, allow *radical* insight. The word "radical" derives from the Latin word for "root." Theories give us greater access to the roots of our concerns.

We could certainly survive without the intricate conceptual schemes that constitute theories. But we would have to give up much that we have come to take for granted. Science would end, as would philosophy. Our cultural life would become severely impoverished. Many of our most practical affairs, such as agriculture and education, would cease to develop or would revert to quite primitive levels. A world without theory would be very different from the world we now inhabit.

To be sure, theorizing also has its darker side. Theories of Aryan supremacy helped Hitler pitch Germany into a murderous war. Einstein's brilliant theories of particle physics eventually led to the development of thermonuclear bombs. A complex combination of economic, scientific, and social theories have aided in the unrestrained growth of industry and population that gravely threatens our environment. Still, the greatness of humankind has evolved largely out of the power of the human mind, and the engines of theory generated much of this power.

Quite likely, some very basic form of theorizing occurs whenever humans focus their attention on particular parts of the world or come to perceive the world in particular ways. To look up into the night sky and ponder the stars—whether they are assumed to manifest the hand of God, are appreciated solely for their aesthetic qualities or are charted as astrological signs dictating our fates, whether they are investigated as distant suns burning atomic fuel or are employed as navigational tools to guide our earthly travels—each of these perceptions has been structured by some form of cognitive scheme or conceptual system. These schemes and systems all evidence theoretical insight. The French thinker Auguste Comte (1798–1857) was perhaps the first modern social scientist to insist that "no real observation of any kind of phenomenon is possible, except in as far as it is first directed, and finally interpreted, by some theory."[1] Theory, in one form or other, channels most if not all of our perceptions, attitudes, opinions, values, judgments, and actions. Theories do not simply chart reality; they aid us in constructing it.

To say that our most basic perceptions are directed and finally interpreted by theory is not to suggest that there is no reality out there apart from our theoretical constructions of it. Indeed, the problem we face as theorists is not an absence of such worldly facts but an overabundance of them. Theories, Comte was saying, are the conceptual lenses we need to sort through the plethora of facts that daily confront us. Theories organize the multiple facets of reality into a comprehensible order. Without theories of a very rudimentary kind, we would not be able to tell which facets of reality are important and which are insignificant or how some correspond to others. Indeed, without theories we might not even be able to identify something as a fact at all.

Setting Our Sights

No lens can bring everything into focus all at once. As anyone who has worked with optical lenses knows, bringing particular things into clear view means that other things, which lie closer or farther away, necessarily remain out of focus. The same principle holds for images formed by our own eyes. If after gazing for a time on some distant object one quickly glances back at the pages of this book, a moment of blurry vision occurs. The lenses in one's eyes then rapidly change their shape to make the written words legible. Photographers exchange one lens for another or alter the distance between lenses to produce clear images. Our eyes simply change the shape of their lenses. The results are the same. Specific lenses, or specific shapes of lenses, allow us to see certain things at certain distances. The rest of the world is necessarily left in a haze.

Theoretical lenses likewise either limit the depth of our vision in order to focus on the foreground or they forego close-up views in order to capture the background. In other words, by focusing our attention on particular clumps of reality, theories cause us to ignore other clumps that lie nearer or farther away. An economic theory that seeks to explain present levels of unemployment may, for instance, focus expansively on the history of industrial cycles. To do so, however, it would have to sacrifice an in-depth psychological investigation of the reputed breakdown of the work ethic. Likewise, a biological theory might suggest the inevitability of war based on the effects of certain human hormones that induce aggression. To do so, however, it would ignore arguments for the potential eradication of collective violence through the cultivation of religious faith. By organizing ideas, principles, and facts into systematic, conceptual accounts and explanations, theories give us insight into a part of the world that otherwise would remain too complex and too chaotic to comprehend. In producing this focused image, theories necessarily leave much out of the picture.

Lenses bend light reflected from things to create focused images. Not all available light is used. The apertures of cameras and the irises perforated by the pupils in our eyes serve the purpose of restricting the amount of light that passes through the lens. Too much light leads to overexposure, with much detail lost in the glare. Too little light leads to underexposure, with much detail lost in the gloom. As anyone who has walked into a dark theater from a well-lit lobby and out of a matinee performance into the brilliant afternoon sunshine knows, one can be blinded not only by darkness but also by light.

Theories have analogous characteristics. Theories work well only when they effectively regulate the amount of data we receive and the conceptual networks we form. Too little data or a dearth of conceptual linkages lead to dim, underexposed, and impoverished images of the world. Without sufficient information, we have no foundation on which to build knowledge. This relationship is generally well understood. Yet too much data and a glut of conceptual linkages are no better. They produce confusing, overexposed images of the world. We are confronted with a busy hodgepodge of phenomena that is impossible to decipher. We have the proverbial problem of not being able to see the forest for the trees. In order to produce a clear image, shadows are as necessary as well-lit surfaces. By attempting to shed light on everything, nothing is thoroughly revealed. If theories are to yield good vision, certain things must remain in the dark.

Conceptual lenses, like optical lenses, influence not only the kind of images we perceive but also the manner in which our observation takes place. Like all tools, theories demand, or at least suggest, specific targets and specific ways of being handled. Those armed only with telescopes have to work outside on cloudless nights. Those armed only with microscopes generally work indoors during the day. The tools of their trade make the former unlikely to examine bacteria and the latter unlikely to chart planetary motion. Our conceptual lenses also prompt us to examine certain phenomena in certain ways. Theories not only influence *what* we see, but also *how* we see it. They provide a framework for our investigations of the world. Theories, like particular types of lenses, have their own methods of use or methodologies.

In political science, statistical analysis of survey data provides us with a kind of telescopic lens that may be used to furnish an overview of the body politic. In-depth psychological analysis, in contrast, provides us with a microscopic lens that reveals the intricate inner workings of individual political actors. Statistical and psychological theories supply their own particular methodologies that influence where and how we look for political knowledge. A person skilled at survey statistics is generally convinced of the importance of aggregated opinions and behaviors. Political knowledge is produced through the analysis of the variance and correlation of these opinions and behaviors within large populations. It is captured in terms of descriptive and inferential statistics. A person skilled at psychological analysis is generally convinced of the importance of individual desires or unconscious drives. Political knowledge is produced through the analysis of life histories and personality characteristics. In selecting our methodology, then, we are implicitly if not explicitly suggesting which things are and which things are not significant objects of knowledge. It is said that the person whose only tool is a hammer confronts every problem as if it were a nail. For this reason, methodologies may be seen as ways of "shaping the mind."[2] It repays us to be conscious and critical of how our chosen methods shape our perceptions and theories no less than how our perceptions and theories shape our methods.

Parsimony, Accuracy, Elegance, and Significance

How does one choose the correct aperture for conceptual lenses, finding the middle ground between underexposed and overexposed images? How does one choose the correct shape for these lenses, determining which images will come into focus and which will remain obscure? Finally, how does one decide the direction in which to point conceptual lenses in the first place? In short, what makes for good theorizing?

The answer to these important questions is that it all depends on what one wants to accomplish. Like photographers, theorists choose different lenses to do different jobs. There are no hard and fast rules. Still, certain general statements can be made about the features of a good theory.

The first theoretical virtue is *parsimony*. Parsimony means frugality. To be theoretically parsimonious is to forgo unnecessary speculation and confusing detail. Theories must be straightforward and condensed enough to offer an advantage over an extended, unsystematic description of the world. Simplicity is crucial. A good theorist is thrifty in employing concepts and outlining relationships. Interpretations, descriptions, explanations, or predictions must not be cluttered with unnecessary facts or assumptions.

Theorizing, in this sense, is like map making. Maps offer us condensed outlines. The more details included in these outlines, the more accurately they represent the geography. But theories should not represent reality in too much detail. If we create a map that contains all the recognizable features of a territory, it will approximate the size of the land that it charts. Lewis Carroll, the whimsical author of *Alice in Wonderland,* once told of a map of the German countryside that had a scale of one to one. It was, of course, a wonderfully detailed representation. But it could not be used because when unfolded it covered all the crops. Theories should not be so cumbersome that they cannot fruitfully be employed.

Good maps have clear legends or explanatory captions. They maintain the same scale throughout and do not randomly change their format. Likewise, to remain parsimonious, a theory must be relatively uniform in its structure. Parsimonious theories are consistent; their rules do not tolerate many, if any, exceptions. They are straightforward to grasp and easy to use. Parsimonious theories have relatively few phenomena within their jurisdiction that are left without an interpretation, description, explanation, or prediction. The chunk of the world they portray does not contain large areas of unexplored territory.

The pursuit of simplicity goes too far, however, if it makes a theory simplistic. Parsimony must not sacrifice too much detail. To ensure that reality is sufficiently represented, theorists claim *accuracy* as their second key virtue. If the map we create is overly reduced in size, if it is simplified to the point where crucial details are lost, then it will fail to aid us in finding our way about. A map of a country that reveals mountain ranges and major bodies of water but leaves out all highways and thoroughfares may be wonderfully compact, but it will be of little use to us in finding our way from place to place. Theories must be sufficiently detailed to allow for accurate assessments or explanations of the world.

If a theory is both sufficiently parsimonious and sufficiently accurate, then we may say that it demonstrates the virtue of *elegance.* An elegant theory simply yet precisely interprets, describes, explains, or predicts some aspect of the world. An elegant theory simplifies reality enough to make it comprehensible but remains accurate enough in its representations to avoid unnecessary ambiguity. The particular balance struck between parsimony and accuracy will, of course, vary according to the circumstances. Generally speaking, the more complex the reality one seeks to understand, the more complex the theory needed to capture it, the less parsimonious that theory will be.

There is a final virtue for which theorists of all sorts strive: *significance.* To be significant, a theory must be of interest. Significant theories illuminate an important part of the world. If we create maps of places no one ever visits, wants to visit, or ever will visit, we theorize in vain. However parsimonious and accurate our theories are, if they fail to offer important insights, they fail to be good theories. We must point our theoretical lenses at interesting parts of the world, otherwise there is not much point in looking through them.

There are, generally speaking, two threats to significance. The first is tautology. To say that all bachelors are unmarried is to speak tautologically. It is simply to state a definition. Likewise, a theory becomes tautological when it offers nothing more than a reiteration of terms. It says the same thing using different words. A stated definition, rather than a process of reasoning, speculation, or experimentation, does all the important work. A complex theory that boils down to the prediction that all political science majors will, at some point during their college careers, enroll in political science classes is tautological. By "political science major" we mean precisely a student taking courses in political science. This theory does not interpret, describe, explain, or predict. It simply defines.

Tautological theories are nonfalsifiable. That is to say, no evidence could be presented that would repudiate their claims. No gathering of new facts, no elucidation of principles or ideas, and no subsequent reasoning can undermine a tautological theory. A tautological theory may provide a set of useful definitions that simply and accurately label things. Like any good set of definitions, tautological theories may provide conceptual clarity, and this is no small accomplishment. The reasoning that holds the component parts of a tautological theory together, however, is completely circular and self-enclosed. Unless its definitions challenge or reorganize our common ways of understanding the world, unless it reinterprets the world in an original way, tautological theory will be of no more significance than a list of related entries in a dictionary.

To avoid tautology, a set of propositions and arguments must take the chance of being refuted or falsified.[3] Good theories must be open to challenge, either from argument or evidence. One should be able to construct or at least imagine an argument or empirical test that would disconfirm the theory. A theory that produces the assertion that the moon is made of green cheese, for example, is falsifiable. We can disconfirm it by gathering empirical evidence. We might employ spectral analysis or bring back bits of the moon for chemical analysis. Even before we had spectrometers or could send astronauts to the moon, however, the kind of evidence needed to falsify the theory was imaginable. Far from constituting a shortcoming, being susceptible to refutation or falsification is a prerequisite for good theory. If a theory is not susceptible to contestation by reasoned argument, gathered evidence, or repeated experimentation, then it is not so much a theory as a dogma, which is to say, an article of faith wrapped up in a circular series of definitions. Indeed, theories are never really proven. They are simply confirmed and reconfirmed by overcoming every attempt to refute them.

The second threat to significance occurs if our theory becomes trite. Something is trite when it is commonplace or self-evident. Trite propositions or theories fail to interest us because they simply state the obvious. To suggest that every student, regardless of race or gender, will take a breath within the first few minutes of a lecture is to say something completely trite. Because the statement could be falsified by a very determined breath-holder, it is not tautologous. But we do not need a sophisticated theory of race, gender, education, or physiology to make such a banal statement. Indeed, we do not need a theory at all. Simple observation and common sense tells us as much. To avoid triteness, theories must contribute to the task of better understanding a complex world. These theoretical illuminations need not be overly intricate or obscure. Nonetheless, they must be original and enlightening.

Scientific Theory and Political Theory

The virtues of parsimony, accuracy, and significance are elements of any good argument and hence are useful in describing the elements of all theories. They are most appropriately identified as virtues of scientific theories. Scientific theories describe the laws or regularities that account for the behavior of things. Originally, the word "science," from the Latin *scientia*, simply meant knowledge. Science eventually came to mean knowledge of a certain sort, namely, a body of related physical laws combined with trusted methods for obtaining and testing such laws. These laws pertain to the regular, recurrent, and ideally invariant associations between and among events and things within the natural world.

The natural sciences serve as a paradigm for scientific theory. Natural scientific theories explain the way things behave with such parsimony and accuracy that prediction about the way they will behave in the future becomes possible. Thus a scientific theory is a set of hypotheses with predictive force. Certain sciences, such as geology and evolutionary biology, effectively predict events that have already transpired, producing theories that explain what happened in the distant past. These theories may eventually come to be confirmed or disconfirmed by subsequent discoveries, say, of geological formations or fossils.

Explanations and predictions always stand in need of verification. The typical method of verification in the natural sciences is the methodologically rigorous replication of the experimental process. This entails very precise forms of measurement. If, for instance, I can explain the amount of a chemical produced when certain amounts of two other chemicals are mixed together at certain temperatures, then I should be able to predict that this same reaction will reoccur and produce the same results given the same mixture of chemicals at the same temperature. In turn, someone else should be able to verify my results, thus validating my theory's explanations and predictions, by repeating the same experiment with the same methodological rigor.

Certain social sciences (also known as behavioral sciences), including some areas of political science, strive for this level of parsimony, accuracy, and methodological rigor. They aim to duplicate in the study of culture what has been achieved in the study of nature. They aim to produce theories capable of predicting human behavior, theories that are testable through repeated observation and precise measurement if not repeated experimentation.

One of the first people to advocate this scientization of the study of politics was the French social philosopher Claude Henri de Saint-Simon (1760–1825). Saint-Simon wrote:

> Hitherto, the method of the sciences of observation has not been introduced into political questions; every man has imported his point of view, method of reasoning and judging, and hence there is not yet any precision in the answers, or universality in the results. The time has come when this infancy of the science should cease, and certainly it is desirable it should cease, for the troubles of the social order arise from the obscurities in political theory.[4]

Likewise, the English political theorist and philosopher John Stuart Mill (1806–73) wrote in his *System of Logic* that "the backward state of the moral sciences can only be remedied by applying to them the methods of physical science, duly extended and generalized."[5] Saint-Simon's and Mill's vision is shared by certain social scientists today who believe that "we are in the political sciences where the natural sciences were two hundred years ago." The task at hand is to "apply scientific methods to the management of society as we have been learning to apply them in the natural world."[6] Most social scientists admit that they will never attain the explanatory or predictive power currently enjoyed by natural scientists. Nonetheless, many social scientists mimic the methods of natural science as closely as possible in an effort to achieve greater explanatory and predictive power.

Do we have any reason to believe that social science will ever produce laws that have the predictive and explanatory power of, say, the laws of physics or chemistry? Attempts have certainly been made. While these attempts have all fallen short of the mark, their achievements have not been negligible. The political sociologist Robert Michels (1876–1936), for instance, developed the famous "iron law of oligarchy" after studying political parties in Europe at the turn of the century. Oligarchy means rule by the few. The iron law of oligarchy states that "an essential characteristic" of all human collectivities is a hierarchical structure wherein a minority exercises most of the power and effectively rules over a majority.

Michels maintains that all human organizations bear this characteristic. He writes: "It is organization which gives birth to the dominion of the elected over the electors, of the mandataries over the mandators, of the delegates over the delegators. Who says organization, says oligarchy."[7] Michels's law, like scientific law, is predictive and testable. Given the formation of an organization (and particularly the formation of a political party), we may predict the formation of an oligarchy. We may then test, by way of observation, whether an oligarchy indeed exists. Like most "laws" of social science, however, Michels's iron law of oligarchy is not very precise. The law supplies us with no way of knowing, or even guessing, how soon an oligarchy will form, how strong an oligarchy will become once it forms, how long it will last, or how and why it will decrease in strength, dissipate, or change form. Unlike, say, Isaac Newton's law of physics, which states that force is equal to mass multiplied by acceleration ($F = ma$), the iron law of oligarchy is not a precise equation. Unlike Newton's law, which allows for quite exact measurements, calculations, and predictions, Michels's law can yield only very general statements about the way the social world works. Moreover, Michels's law does not apply equally to all organizations. Small organizations whose members have close, friendly relations are frequent exceptions.

One reason why social science falls short of achieving the parsimony, accuracy, explanatory and predictive power of natural science is that the methods of scientific theory building are not easily adapted to social and political concerns. Outside the scientific laboratory, too many uncontrolled and unforeseen forces affect social and political life to allow for rigorous scientific observation and measurement. Yet the observation and analysis of political society cannot be done in controlled laboratory conditions. In the social sciences, experimentation, let alone repeated experimentation, is very difficult if not impossible to arrange. Often it would be morally unacceptable even if it could be arranged. We might adequately observe the reaction of a democratic people to a coup d'état and subsequently develop a theory to account for their behavior. Yet it would be ethically unacceptable to stage a second coup d'état under similar circumstances so as to verify our results.

Social and political practices, therefore, are seldom if ever replicable. Comparative studies between different people, different countries, or the same people at different times can be very enlightening. But they fail to duplicate the precise experimental conditions of the natural sciences. Humans learn from history and from each other. Hence repeated observations of social reality are not observations of exactly the same reality. The actors involved have in all likelihood thought about themselves and their world in the meantime and have developed or otherwise changed their behavior or conditions as a result.

Experimental observation allows for the construction of scientific theory because the objects of study, being either biological or mechanical, operate in relatively fixed patterns and display regularities according to ascertainable physical laws. For the political theorist, in contrast, the objects of study are self-conscious agents, that is, thinking human beings who reflect on themselves, their worldly conditions, and their actions. This self-reflexivity makes human behavior far more irregular and unpredictable than the behavior of other forms of life or of inorganic forms of matter. Self-reflection changes how we understand ourselves and our world and hence how we act in the world. Human actors may even learn of social scientific explanations and predictions and change their behavior to invalidate those explanations and predictions.

In the light of these difficulties, some argue that social scientists should not try to mimic the natural sciences. They should instead develop their own standards and procedures. The German economist and sociologist Max Weber (1864–1920) maintained that social scientists ought not search for laws that determine and predict human behavior. Instead, they should limit themselves to describing historical correlations and tendencies. Following Wilhelm Dilthey, Weber suggested that social scientists strive to understand human behavior rather than attempt to predict it.[8]

Human history, Weber maintained, is best described as a concurrence of events, not a system of ascertainable laws. In coming to terms with this concurrence, social scientists ought to remain sensitive to cultural factors. They should chart the subtle interaction between historical or social influences and the material or physical causes of behavior. Despite his reluctance to mimic the natural sciences, Weber was opposed to any historical description of events that made no systematic attempt at explanation. He suggested that explanatory theories be developed and actively employed in the social sciences. These social scientific theories, however, having no predictive laws on which to ground themselves, could be based only on the observed correlations of human events, institutions, attitudes, and values.

Weber called these correlations "ideal types." An ideal type is not a moral category but a conceptual construct that, by accentuating particular features of social phenomena, manages to explain these phenomena more efficiently and elegantly. One might, for instance, accentuate the role played by the president or prime minister of a country in order to make better sense of that country's foreign policy. Perhaps a strong correlation can be found between a country's foreign policy and its top executive's psychological type, personal history, or ideological orientation. This theoretical framework may allow us to explain foreign policy neatly, leaving the waters unmuddied by complicated analyses of the role played by advisers, institutions and bureaucracies, the economic climate, or the election cycle.

Ideal types put historical events, institutions, or (sets of) attitudes and values into their "most consistent and logical forms."[9] Achieving this consistency and logic, Weber admitted, entails doing a certain amount of "violence to historical reality."[10] Political life is seldom, if ever, as neat and tidy an affair as the social scientist might desire. Ideal types are, by definition, "one-sided." Without the construction of ideal types to simplify matters, however, the social scientist could not understand or portray the complex interplay of cultural and material forces that produce human history. Ideal types are like the conceptual lenses that create focused images of social reality. In producing clear images, ideal types necessarily truncate a larger reality, violating its integrity. The task at hand, according to Weber, was to do as little violence as possible to a complex reality while still developing a theory powerful enough to explain it.

The Interpretive Nature of Political Theory

To the extent that human beings may be studied as mechanical objects or biological organisms, they are subject to scientific theorizing. Much modern medical research, for example, proceeds under these conditions. After all, the laws of physics, chemistry and biology apply to human beings no less than to rocks, trees, and other animals. Nevertheless, the farther we move away from being interested in, say, the basic chemistry, physiology, or genetics of human life, the farther we move away from being able to theorize it scientifically.

Employing physiological and evolutionary theories, we may with great accuracy explain why and predict how a person will cry out and pull away if suddenly jabbed with a sharp pencil. With somewhat less accuracy, employing economic theories and accounting for cultural traits, we may be able to explain why and predict how a person will react if offered $1,000 to break a pencil in two. Here the laws of physiology find an approximate analog in the demands of economic life that stimulate people to react according to the perceived costs and benefits of their opportunities. While economic incentives do not produce as predictable a reaction as acute physical pain, certain broad regularities are nonetheless observable. But the strictly scientific observer has no accurate predictions to make about the way a person will react when given a pencil and paper and asked to respond to the question "How should the exercise of individual liberty in a political community be balanced with the pursuit of social equality?" Only vague generalities could be mustered.

Being self-reflective, humans consciously distinguish themselves from their environment, make themselves and others objects of thought, and even turn these thoughts about themselves and others into objects of further thought. This spiral of self-reflection has no predictable end point. The question about balancing the values of freedom and equality demands a response based on self-reflective experience. In answering this question, one would not simply react, as one does physiologically to pencil pricks. Nor would one behave in ways conforming to easily ascertained regularities, as one often does in response to economic incentives. Instead, one would first have to think about the world and one's place in it and then respond on the basis of these reflections. Faced with this reality, the political theorist does not seek to predict responses. The political theorist *interprets* responses in a way that is illuminating and promotes understanding.

This brings us to a major difference between scientific theory and political theory. Scientific theory strives for objectivity. The scientific theorist is supposed to be a neutral observer whose feelings and biases are left outside the door of the laboratory. The scientist is detached from her* subject matter, approaching it only by means of impersonal tools of analysis and measurement that anyone with similar skills could employ. Only in this way can repeated experimentation confirm theory, since any other scientist, employing the same procedures under the same conditions, will arrive at the same results.

For theorists of social and political life, in contrast, the ability to

---

* In order to facilitate a gender-neutral approach and minimize awkward language, the chapters of the book alternate in their use of gender-specific terminology, with exceptions made only to ensure historical accuracy.

feel and think in ways similar to the object of study is a crucial component of their task. The analysis of responses to the question about the
appropriate balance between liberty and equality, for example, is necessarily grounded in the theorist's own reflective experience of these political values. Without such resonance between the theorist and the theorized, little of interest can be said. Humans, unlike plants and rocks,
self-reflectively interpret themselves. To understand a self-interpreting
animal, one must be a self-interpreting animal. To do political theory,
in other words, one must interpret others based on one's own self-inter-
pretations.

A central task of political theory is to understand how humans understand themselves and their world. The concern, in other words, is
with meaning. Meaning is grounded not in objective laws but in shared
or intersubjective understandings. The value of a political theory, therefore, is based not on its ability to generate verifiable predictions but on
its ability meaningfully to inform political life. In turn, political theories are not so much proven true or false as they are shown to be helpful or unhelpful in understanding collective existence, an existence that
is rife with meaning but short on truth.

To say that political theory is an interpretive rather than strictly
scientific enterprise is to say something about *what* political theorists
perceive when they look at the world as well as *how* they perceive it.
Interpretive theory seeks to gain understanding of political life through
self-reflective study. It is validated not by experimental verification but
by its meaningfulness, that is, by the resonance it produces with its self-
interpretive audience. This resonance may be gauged by the extent to
which a theory informs or illuminates experience.[11]

Political theorists vary greatly in the degree to which they tend toward the interpretive or scientific end of the social science spectrum.
Some, like Weber, try to steer a middle course, taking what they can
from science and balancing it with interpretive insight. Strict social scientists are often critical of interpretive theorists for producing ambiguous descriptions and lofty but largely useless concepts. The charge is
that the interpretive approach is too speculative and too subjective to
aid us in explaining, predicting, or controlling concrete reality. For
their part, interpretive political theorists are often critical of their social
scientific colleagues for misunderstanding the nature of political life
and the task of those who study it. They claim that social scientists too
often view citizens as objects to be measured and efficiently managed
instead of as subjects to be critically understood and morally engaged.

Often it is appropriate to measure and manage people—when they
are commuters on busy highways, for instance. Measuring the habits of

automobile drivers and controlling the cumulative effect of their behavior is crucial to avoiding congestion and ensuring efficient traffic regulation. But measuring and efficiently managing automobile drivers does not unduly detract from, and may eventually enhance, their experience of driving. Measuring and most efficiently managing citizens, interpretive theorists argue, may not be so benign. If, as the ancient Greek philosopher Aristotle (384–322 B.C.) suggests, politics is a realm of freedom in which citizens mutually coordinate their activities in pursuit of the good life, then what remains most significant about citizens, namely, their autonomy and moral purpose, is not susceptible to precise measurement and may be threatened by too efficient control. For these reasons, political theorists approach political events and actors more like works of art or literature in need of interpretation rather than chemical reactions in need of explanation, prediction, or control.

In short, interpretive theory, like scientific theory, attempts simply, accurately, and significantly to account for worldly phenomena. Yet it does so without making lawlike pronouncements that are subject to experimental confirmation. Instead, if offers suggestive conceptual insights that are subject to self-reflective commentary and critique.

Hermeneutics and Intersubjectivity

A brief look at the origins of the word *theory* will help to illustrate the nature of interpretation. The word "theory" comes from the Greek word *theoros*. The *theoros* was originally an emissary sent on behalf of the state to consult an oracle (something like a fortune-teller) or to perform a religious rite. Later, the *theoros* took on the role of an envoy or spectator of foreign religious and cultural events who would report back to his native city. In time, *theoria,* the activity of the *theoros,* came to mean a form of contemplation, a kind of internal spectating. The terms *theoria* and *theoros* stem from *thea,* which means to look upon or view. Thus the fundamental relationship between theory and mental vision was already established in ancient Greece, where, it turns out, Western political theory began.

How do you suppose the early Greek *theoros* gave reports of his voyages? How would he describe and explain to his compatriots the religious and cultural spectacles he had witnessed in other lands? Very likely, the *theoros* would make sense of these events, and make them understood to others, by remarking on their similarities to and differences from events with which he and his fellow citizens were familiar. For example, he might inform his compatriots that in the splendid Egyptian festival of the goddesses, the worship of Isis was similar in its form to the worship in Greece of the goddess Demeter. Drawing on the similarities between these two agricultural deities, the *theoros* would then be able to highlight some differences in the respective festivals and perhaps speculate on their origins and purposes. To be able to understand the Egyptian worship of Isis, in other words, the *theoros* would have to make meaningful comparisons.

To make sense out of a form of behavior, one must understand the motivations that underlie it. To understand these motivations, one must have experienced similar sorts of motivations. In order to comprehend the concerns and passions that underlie the Egyptian religious practice, the *theoros* would have to have experienced similar concerns and passions. When what one is studying is less an objective event, like a chemical reaction, than a network of motivations and self-reflective attitudes and beliefs, then comprehension entails having certain experiences in common. Interpretive theory, it follows, aims less at an objective account than an intersubjective understanding. Any account of the world that interpretive theory produces is grounded in shared experiences.

This is not to say that one cannot theorize about events without having participated in these same events or that one cannot understand someone's beliefs, feelings, or behavior without having had identical beliefs and feelings or without having engaged in the same behavior. Sometimes, because distance allows broader insight or because emotions do not cloud vision, a detached observer might even understand a person's motivations or attitudes better than that person herself. The detached observer could not do so, however, if she had never experienced similar motivations or attitudes. I can understand a child's belief in Santa Claus without currently believing, or even ever having believed, in Santa Claus. Nevertheless, I cannot well understand the nature of a child's belief in Santa Claus without ever having believed anything based on hope and hearsay myself.

In the same vein, trying to describe love to someone who has never experienced love would be like trying to describe a mountain panorama to someone who was born blind, or trying to describe a Beethoven symphony to someone who was born deaf. Where would one start? How would one proceed? It follows that the theoretical task of understanding the characteristics of political life, say, the love of justice, or the struggle to balance liberty with equality that largely defines the love of justice, is only possible for those who have experienced these features of political life in some form, however attenuated or restricted their experiences may have been. In turn, the theoretical task of describing and explaining political life is based on the assumption that the theorist's audience has shared similar experiences.

The interpretive theorist seeks to understand other human beings as the thinking, feeling, believing, self-reflective, and socially integrated beings they are. The theorist would be at a severe disadvantage were she somehow to discard all her own values and commitments so as to approach this task as a detached observer. Of course, she must guard against allowing her idiosyncratic likes and dislikes, prejudices and predilections, to undermine or pervert her understanding of others. Without a palette of shared experiences to draw on, the theorist could not adequately paint pictures of political reality that others could understand. Nonetheless, that does not mean that the theorist should paint pictures that always and only display her favorite colors.

Owing to its intersubjective nature, political theory is often considered a *hermeneutic* exercise. Hermeneuts were people employed by the early Christian church to interpret the religious service and scripture to worshippers who spoke a different language. (The word *hermeneut* derives from the name of the Greek god Hermes, who was the patron deity of speech and writing.) In the nineteenth century, hermeneutics developed as a method of interpreting biblical texts and later other legal and literary documents. The German philosopher Wilhelm Dilthey (1833–1911) further expanded hermeneutics to encompass the interpretation of human experience in general, the historical text of human life. Dilthey argued that nature provided a field for explanation but that humanity provided a field for *understanding*, in German, *Verstehen*. Explanation is based on external observation. Understanding is based on what Dilthey called "lived experience." Dilthey wrote that "understanding of other people and their expressions is developed on the basis of experience and self-understanding and the constant interaction between them."[12] In other words, we understand people, their behavior and expressions, because we share with them the experience of certain thoughts, beliefs, emotions, behaviors, and capacities.

Political theorists are hermeneuts who interpret things political. Like the biblical hermeneuts who interpreted religious services and scripture for those who shared the same faith, political theorists share certain attitudes and experiences with the members of their audience. Not all attitudes and experiences are evenly shared. If they were, there would be little for the theorist to communicate and nothing for her to argue. Even if the members of the theorist's audience do not speak different languages or come from different cultures, they undoubtedly will have different conceptual schemes, beliefs, and values. Building bridges of political understanding on the foundations of shared experience is a central task of political theory.

Political theory often puts its hermeneutic analysis to work in the interpretation of texts. Much political theory today consists of such critical commentary on the great texts of political thought written throughout the ages. Plato's *Republic*, Aristotle's *Politics*, St. Augustine's *City of God*, Niccolò Machiavelli's *The Prince*, Thomas Hobbes's *Leviathan*, John Locke's *Second Treatise of Government*, Jean-Jacques Rousseau's *The Social Contract*, John Stuart Mill's *On Liberty*, and John Rawls's *Theory of Justice*, among many others, have each been subject to hundreds of detailed interpretive analyses. These analyses may seek to clarify or criticize a text's arguments, describe the intent of its author, or establish its practical import.

Political theory may also focus on political attitudes and behavior rather than formal political writing. Indeed, we may view people's political beliefs and practices as texts that have been transcribed into speech and action. In either case, a crucial component of the theorist's task is to interpret political thoughts, words, and deeds. We should keep in mind that active political life is also a text in need of close and critical reading.

The interpretation of politics could not get off the ground without the theorist's relying on her own experiences and evaluations. The conceptual lenses of theory are shaped by the emotions, desires, motivations, beliefs, judgments, interests, and values of the theorist. Scientific theorists who aim at objective observation and validation strive to eliminate all such biases. Interpretive theorists who seek intersubjective understanding and meaning accept these biases as inevitable and indispensable, however troublesome they prove to be. Hans-Georg Gadamer, a contemporary German philosopher, observes that "to try to eliminate one's own concepts in interpretation is not only impossible, but manifestly absurd. To interpret means precisely to use one's own preconceptions so that the meaning of the text can really be made to speak for us."[13] Gadamer, who is well known for his hermeneutic analyses, insists that whenever we attempt to understand a text we are always "projecting" our own "fore-conceptions" and "fore-meanings" on it.

The goal for the interpretive theorist is not to eliminate foreconceptions. These prejudices, Gadamer writes, "constitute the initial directedness of our whole ability to experience.... They are simply conditions whereby we experience something—whereby what we encounter says something to us."[14] Prejudice is to be understood less as a distortion that mars the purity of understanding than as the initial condition under which understanding first becomes possible. Preconceptions make for friction between the theorist and the text. They cause the theorist to move slowly and pay attention. But friction also makes movement possible. Attempting to theorize in the absence of preconceptions would be like attempting to move in the absence of friction. It would be like running on sheer ice with flat shoes. There would be nothing against which one could push off, nothing that would allow one to get started.

The point is not blindly or uncritically to promote one's prejudices. Their retention is certainly not the goal. One's attitudes, beliefs, and values simply provide a starting point. "The important thing," Gadamer writes, "is to be aware of one's own bias, so that the text may present itself in all its newness and thus be able to assert its own truth against one's own fore-meanings."[15] Good interpretation constantly seeks to replace initial preconceptions with more suitable ones as the reading of the text progresses.

Knowing oneself is a condition of knowing and interpreting others. The obverse relation is also true. Knowing and interpreting others is a condition of knowing oneself. Gadamer calls this intersubjective understanding the theorist achieves with a text a "fusion of horizons."[16] To fuse horizons is not to agree with everything another person thinks, believes, or feels. To fuse horizons is not to fuse entire selves. Instead, it refers to the development, from initially divergent positions, of a sufficient level of understanding such that meaningful conversation can take place. Meaningful conversations do not necessarily produce agreement about the answers to the questions they address. They do entail a basic agreement about the importance of the questions being asked, the merit of pursuing the conversation as a means of addressing these questions, and the need for appropriate answers.

The act of interpretation effectively extends the theorist onto common ground with others. It demands that the theorist become porous, capable of absorbing and integrating previously foreign perceptions and insights. This extension of the self leaves one vulnerable but also poised for growth. As Gadamer writes:

> Understanding is an adventure and, like any other adventure, is dangerous.... Hermeneutical experience has a far less degree of certainty than that attained by the methods of the natural sciences. But when one realizes that understanding is an adventure, this implies that it affords unique opportunities as well. It is capable of contributing in a special way to the broadening of our human experiences, our self-knowledge, and our horizon.[17]

To do political theory is not so much to confirm one's preconceptions and prejudices as to challenge them. In order to challenge one's preconceptions and prejudices one must first acknowledge having them. Then one must leave them open to modification by way of an interpretive encounter with other texts and other people.

In studying political theory, one necessarily begins with one's own lenses. These conceptual tools are intended to be used as a means of discovering and understanding other viewpoints, of gaining glimpses through the lenses of other political thinkers or actors. On occasion, one may choose to adopt another's point of view as one's own. For the most part, the task of the theorist is more limited and yet more demanding. One studies political theory to gain a sufficient understanding of other conceptual schemes to facilitate constructive and critical engagements with them.

The Normative Nature of Theory

Political theory is inherently critical. To criticize means to judge. To judge means to measure something against certain standards. The inherently critical nature of political theory derives from its concern for norms. For this reason interpretive political theory is often simply called *normative theory*. A norm is an authoritative rule or standard. The word "norm" comes from the Latin word *norma*, which means a carpenter's square. Normative theory is concerned with the way things measure up. It seeks to understand not simply the way things *are* but also the way things *ought to be*.

The political theorist investigates the standards guiding or regulating political life. These standards are grounded in self-understandings and intersubjective understandings and hence are available for interpretive analysis. If the theorist primarily focuses on the way people ought to act or behave, then she will concern herself with the realm of *ethics*. Normative political theory, in this sense, is ethical or moral theory. The normative theorist concerns herself with moral principles. She advocates some particular principle as a standard in accordance with which political life ought to be fashioned. She may, for instance, construct a standard of distributive justice that stipulates how individuals within a community ought to allocate benefits and share burdens. Alternatively, she might construct a standard of civil rights that stipulates the extent to which the liberty of citizens may not be restricted by the society or state.

The normative political theorist may be less concerned with the way people act or behave and more concerned with the rules and standards guiding the way people think, learn, or believe. Such a theorist would be primarily interested in *epistemology*, that is, in the study of the foundations of knowledge. The norms of the epistemologically oriented theorist are judgments about the merit of particular ways of understanding the world. Certain feminist theorists, for instance, argue that women tend to have different standards for (acquiring or generating) knowledge and these standards should not be judged inadequate simply because they are unlike those of their masculine counterparts. Similar arguments have been made for the different epistemological standards evidenced within various cultures. (We investigate these claims further in chapter 4.)

Since words and deeds, thinking and acting generally go together in political life, political theorists are usually interested in both epistemology and ethics. Indeed, the distinction between epistemology and ethics is often rather tenuous. We tend to act on the basis of our beliefs and understandings. We tend to form our beliefs and understandings on the basis of our actual engagements and experiences. To analyze or formulate the norms that regulate political life, therefore, is to enter into the overlapping fields of epistemology and ethics.

For many political theorists, making normative judgments about the political world is an essential part of their enterprise. Political philosopher Leo Strauss (1899–1973) writes:

> It is impossible to study social phenomena, i.e., all important social phenomena, without making value judgments. A man who sees no reason for not despising people whose horizon is limited to their consumption of food and their digestion may be a tolerable econometrist; he cannot say anything relevant about the character of human society. A man who refuses to distinguish between great statesmen, mediocrities, and insane impostors may be a good biographer; he cannot say anything relevant about politics and political history.... Generally speaking, it is impossible to understand thought or action or work without evaluating it. If we are unable to evaluate adequately, as we very frequently are, we have not yet succeeded in understanding adequately.[18]

The normative theorist is necessarily concerned with the standards of political life. This is not to say, however, that she seeks to impose her beliefs and values upon others.

Indeed, the norms the theorist studies and advocates— particularly if they are oriented to democracy, diversity, fair play, individual liberties and rights, and the principle of tolerance—may strongly militate against the imposition of morality or the heavy-handed regulation of behavior. Nonetheless, engaging in the defense of ideals such as democracy, diversity, fair play, individual liberties and rights, and the principle of tolerance remains very much a normative enterprise. "I know of no safe depository of the ultimate powers of the society but the people themselves," Thomas Jefferson wrote, "and if we think them not enlightened enough to exercise their control with a wholesome discretion, the remedy is not to take it from them, but to inform their discretion."[19] Informing people's discretion and otherwise engaging in political education is an eminently normative enterprise. Yet it remains grounded in the moral autonomy of citizens and constitutes a crucial feature of democracy.

Some normative theorists argue for very specific beliefs or values. Others shun the explicit advocacy of particular moral positions. They remain more broadly concerned with understanding the means and processes by which diverse attitudes and interests become articulated and integrated into political life. Nonetheless, every political theory facilitates the pursuit of some but not all courses of action and some but not all beliefs, attitudes, interests, and values. Thus all political theory prompts us to accept certain aspects of our world and to change others that are judged to be deficient. As such, every political theory is normative in some degree.

Conceptual and Historical Analysis

The two primary means employed by the theorist to examine political norms and understandings are *conceptual analysis* and *historical analysis*. To analyze is to divide a whole into its constituent parts. Conceptual analysis takes a complex concept or system of ideas and examines its components to determine their meaning, the relationships they form with each other, and whether they constitute a coherent whole. For instance, one might analyze the concept of the *nation-state* by first dividing it into its constituent parts of geographic territory, a sovereign government that administers this territory, and an independent citizenry over which the government rules. Subsequently, one would investigate the meaning of these three terms and examine the nature of the relationships they form. Sovereign government might be defined as the formal institutions through which binding decisions are made for a society. Governments are formed by election or appointment (the gaining of political power), and engage in lawmaking (the legislative exercise of political power) and administration (the executive exercise of political power). Of course, each of these elements could become the object of further conceptual analysis. Then one might apply one's understanding to specific cases. In liberal democratic nation-states, for example, the citizenry elects representatives who form a government that presides by rule of law within constitutional limits.

Engaging in conceptual analysis is like using a microscopic lens to investigate the texture and integrity of things. Engaging in historical analysis, in contrast, is like using a telescopic lens that allows one to see objects at a distance in the context of what precedes and follows them. The objects of historical analysis may be political events or institutions of previous times. Alternatively, the objects of historical study may the political writings of theorists from earlier eras. In either case, the point is not only to gain knowledge of the past. The larger goal is to gain knowledge of contemporary times by viewing it afresh through historical lenses. Much historically oriented political theory effectively constitutes a history of the present.

Historical analysis demonstrates that many features of political life that are currently taken for granted developed at particular times for particular purposes. The nation-state, for instance, is less than 400 years old. One might date its rise to prominence from the Peace of Westphalia in 1648, at the end of the Thirty Years War. The nation-state system developed, in part, as a means of alleviating the bloody religious and imperial conflicts that had afflicted Europe at this time. Previously the chief political units were empires, kingdoms and city-states. Thus historical study prompts us to acknowledge that the nation-state is not an indelible feature of political life and may not be the chief political unit in the future. Quentin Skinner, an English political theorist, writes that studying the history of thought demonstrates

> the extent to which those features of our own arrangements which we may be disposed to accept as traditional or even 'timeless' truths may in fact be the merest contingencies of our particular history and social structure.... Our society places unrecognizable constraints upon our imaginations.... The historical study of the ideas of other societies should be undertaken as an indispensable and irreplaceable means of placing limits on these constraints.... To learn from the past—and we cannot otherwise learn it at all—the distinction between what is necessary and what is the product merely of our own contingent arrangements, is to learn the key to self-awareness itself.[20]

For the political theorist, study of the past often provides the best means of understanding the present.

Normative concerns can never be completely eliminated from historical and conceptual analysis. While many theorists may not openly advocate a particular moral position, the very topics chosen for historical or conceptual analysis are, by dint of being chosen, deemed of particular interest, importance, and value. In turn, the manner in which they are approached will highlight certain features and obscure others. These unavoidable choices of subject matter and methodology harbor implicit normative valuations. If, in analyzing the state, one focuses predominantly on the government administration rather than the citizenry, for example, one may give credence to a top-down view of politics that undermines the inherent value of democratic processes. The decision to make particular phenomena worthy of study and the decision to study them in particular ways are inherently normative decisions.

Conceptual and historical analyses are frequently not ends in themselves but serve as the forestage to syntheses, the piecing back together of conceptual systems or historical narratives. The constructive effort to provide a holistic view of things political, even more so than the analysis of its constituent parts, creates a standard or norm for understanding and action. In supplying better ways of understanding politics we are implicitly suggesting that there are better ways of acting politically based on our improved understandings. To supply a right way of knowing, one might argue, is to imply a right way of acting.

The *Republic* written by the ancient Greek philosopher Plato (c. 427–347 B.C.) provides a good example of this point. The *Republic* is widely recognized as the first major work of political theory. It remains to this day, by many estimates, the most important. For this reason, Plato's *Republic* has itself been subjected to countless analyses, both conceptual and historical. Both sorts of analyses have served to increase our understanding of politics and to inform our political practice.

Plato's text certainly lends itself to these two related tasks. The *Republic* examines the concept of justice by way of an extended discussion between Socrates (469–399 B.C.), Plato's teacher, and a small number of other Athenians, mostly young men. A key component of Plato's argument is that once one figures out how best to understand justice, one has also figured out how to act justly. Indeed, the stronger claim is made that *to know* the just is also *to be* just. For Plato, knowledge is virtue. One only acts viciously out of ignorance. Epistemology and ethics not only go hand in hand, they are one and the same. Sustained philosophical analysis carried out earnestly in the pursuit of truth, Plato maintains, is the only route to creating adequate political norms and securing the good life.

By no means do all political theorists agree with Plato on this point. Even Plato's most famous student, Aristotle, contested his teacher's claim that knowledge constitutes virtue. Nonetheless, Aristotle, like most political theorists today, acknowledges the important connection between thinking and acting, epistemology and ethics. It may be true that knowledge is not always virtue, or even that virtue presupposes firm knowledge. One might be able to know what justice is without acting justly, and perhaps also act justly without well knowing—or being able to articulate—what justice is. Nonetheless, in suggesting how we best understand political life, the political theorist is implicitly if not explicitly suggesting how political affairs ought to be put in order.

The kinds of conceptual lenses one employs influences what one sees and how one sees it. This applies to ancient thinkers like Plato no less than to contemporary theorists. Plato chose rather rigid lenses that produced immutable, well-defined images. On the portals of Plato's school, called the Academy, were inscribed the words: "Let no one unacquainted with geometry enter here." Plato's students were trained in geometry because evaluating forms in the mathematical world was believed to be the proper intellectual preparation for the ethical evaluations demanded of one in the political world. Plato suggests that moral and political truths are of the same eternal and unchanging nature as mathematical truth. The ideals that his political realm are designed to replicate on earth are already to be found—eternal and invariable—in the heavens.

These ideals can be apprehended by humans, but only through the intellect rather than through the senses. Plato depreciates sensory experience because it cannot lead to knowledge of unchanging truths, called the Ideas or Forms. Through our senses we never experience true circles or triangles, for instance, but only approximations of them sketched on paper or in sand. To apprehend absolute circularity or triangularity, we must reach beyond our senses to perceive the Idea or Form of the circle or triangle with our intellect. Only an abstract, intellectual apprehension allows these categories to be truly known. Likewise, Plato suggests that political categories such as justice can never be adequately grasped by our senses. They are apprehended only through philosophical intellection. Once political categories are defined as eternal truths that remain uninformed by our sensory experiences, they become as inflexible and immutable as geometric categories and definitions. A circle is a circle is a circle. And justice is justice for Plato, regardless of the circumstances. The rigidity of Plato's social caste system, of which we hear more later, reflects the rigidity of this geometric vision.

Aristotle criticizes Plato for trying to reduce the diverse, evolving political community to an unchanging, unitary state. Geometric measures and truths, Aristotle argues, are not the sort of standards by which human affairs can or should be ordered. Aristotle aptly observes that when measuring things political, it is best to use a ruler that is flexible. In his *Nichomachean Ethics,* Aristotle states that we should not attempt to fashion our epistemological or ethical standards in politics with the precision of the carpenter's square. Politics is a diffuse and variable affair. The level of exactness we pursue in our political assessments should not exceed that allowed by the subject matter.

Aristotle holds that the measuring rod for politics ought to be pliable. It should resemble the measuring rod made of soft lead that was developed in his time by the architects and masons on the island of Lesbos. A leaden rule can measure things of various shapes better than a rigid square because it can bend to conform to these shapes. Likewise, the norms appropriate for assessing the world of politics need to be flexible. In order to account for a world filled with unpredictable irregularities and ambiguities, our conceptual schemes must not be so rigid as to make them unfit for use. To buttress his point, Aristotle records the varieties of political life encountered in other lands and in other times. He demonstrates that comparative investigations, by broadening our perspective, may give our conceptual analysis the flexibility appropriate to the study of politics.

To illustrate the need for this theoretical flexibility we might recall the ancient Greek myth of Procrustes. Procrustes was a famous robber known for mutilating his victims. He would stretch or cut off the legs of people so that they would fit snugly into his bed. To call something Procrustean is to suggest that it produces uniformity and exactness by rough or violent methods. Political theorists must be wary of their Procrustean impulses. In an effort to make the political world fit neatly into their conceptual schemes, theorists may be tempted to lop off all those parts that prove unwieldy. If we try to make the world of politics reflect uniform, geometric visions, we are likely to do much violence to it.

The mark of a good education, Aristotle insists, is knowing which fields of study allow for certainty and exactitude and which do not. Politics, he observes, is not an exact science. Its study depends less on precise measurement than on contextual understanding grounded in shared experience. By developing their own conceptual lenses while remaining receptive to the different viewpoints of others, interpreters of political life may strike an appropriate balance between the intellectual demands of theory and the practical and moral demands of an ambiguous, complex, and unruly world.

Suggested Readings

Fred Dallmayr and Thomas McCarthy, eds. *Understanding and Social Inquiry*

Hans-Georg Gadamer. *Reason in the Age of Science*

Clifford Geertz. *The Interpretation of Cultures*

John Gunnell. *Political Theory*

Thomas Kuhn. *The Structure of Scientific Revolutions*

Karl Popper. *The Logic of Scientific Discovery*

George Sabine. *A History of Political Theory*

Leo Strauss. *What Is Political Philosophy and Other Studies*

Eric Voegelin. *The New Science of Politics*

Max Weber. *The Methodology of the Social Sciences*

Sheldon Wolin. *Politics and Vision*

2

The Question of Human Nature

hat makes human beings different from other animals? Humans have developed technology. Humans make and employ tools and machines. But that is not an unqualified distinction. Other animals, such as elephants, many primates, and certain birds, use primitive tools, like sticks, to get food or scratch themselves. Chimpanzees use rocks and bones as weapons, and certain ants have domesticated plants and animals for the production of their own food, excelling in the crafts of cultivating yeasts and fungi and farming and "milking" aphids. While other species may use tools, however, they do not actually "make" tools, certainly not complex tools or machines. The sophistication of human technology is unique. Perhaps, however, we can discover a less qualified distinction.

One might suggest that human beings are unique because humans alone have language. But the case here is similar to that of technology (not surprisingly perhaps, since language is, in one sense, a tool). Many other animals use symbolic gestures to communicate. Honeybees engage in an elaborate "waggle dance" to let their fellow bees know precisely where sources of food are to be found. Dolphins, porpoises, and whales employ a complex series of high-pitched tones to communicate, effectively singing their messages to each other. Vervet monkeys can warn each other whether snakes or eagles or leopards are approaching with distinct sounds that clearly identify each type of predator. Chimpanzees, gorillas, and orangutans have even been trained to communicate with rudimentary elements of human sign language. Often these animals not only respond to questions in sign language but also initiate communication and make basic requests.[1]

Still, no other species has achieved the sophistication and creativity of language use that humans have. More specifically, no other species seems capable of using original combinations of words in a rule-governed fashion, employing a grammar or syntax. Yet this skill comes naturally to human beings. Most of us speak grammatically in relatively complex sentences from the time we are three or four years old without any formal training.

The complexity of human language allows for the development of reason. Reason might be defined as the capacity to think logically, to deliberate coherently, and to infer consistently. Reason allows one to separate, contrast, and combine thoughts so as to establish sustained chains and patterns of ideas. Language, in combination with reason, vastly extends our mental reach. This intellectual extension, and the creative and analytical power it allows, accounts for the development of our technology. Our sophisticated technological capacity is largely derivative of our capacity for language and reason. Our linguistic and rational capacities make us unique among animals. Aristotle made a similar claim over two millennia ago. He defined human being as a *zoon logon echon,* a rational, speaking animal.

Aristotle is better known for a different definition of human being. He defined human being as a *zoon politikon,* a political animal. His two definitions are mutually supportive. The two key features of a human being—a linguistic, rational nature and a political nature—go hand in hand. One might say that we are political because we have language and reason, and we have language and reason because we are political.

In calling the human being a political animal, Aristotle suggests that what makes humans different from the rest of the animal kingdom is their capacity to live together in a manner that other animals do not and cannot. He observes that we live politically, whereas other animals that sleep, travel, forage, or hunt in groups only live collectively. Animal collectivities are often hierarchically ordered, with distinct leaders and followers and quite sophisticated divisions of labor. What differentiates human societies from animal colonies, packs, and herds, therefore, is not that humans organize themselves nor that this organization results in hierarchically ordered, collective units. Certain animals, like ants and bees, create societies that exhibit a much greater degree of order with much less disruption than human societies achieve. Still, human society is unique, Aristotle claims, and uniquely political.

The reason, one might hypothesize, is that humans understand themselves to be distinct individuals—unprecedented and unrepeatable beings—who exist within a community made up of other distinct individuals. Some animals, like bees or ants, are fully collective beings. Some animals, like spiders, snakes, and bears, are mostly solitary creatures. Some animals may engage in both a solitary and collective existence, like dogs and wolves, which live at times as loners and as members of packs. Yet no other animal thinks, speaks, or acts self-consciously as an individual within a community. Certain human cultures celebrate the individual, while others emphasize the importance of the community. Yet all political cultures evidence a conscious tension between individuality and community.

To live politically, it follows, one must be able to conceive oneself as an individual within a community of individuals. To do this, one must be capable of abstract thought. More specifically, one must be capable of reflecting on the meaning of individuality as something that one shares with other human beings and yet makes one a unique entity. Only abstract thought allows us to understand ourselves as such unique parts within a complex whole.

Abstract thought is possible only if one can distance oneself from a singular stream of consciousness. Abstract thought requires a temporary and at least partial escape from all-consuming desires, feelings, and inclinations. One must escape one's impulses long enough to be able to glance back on oneself, to see oneself as some distinct *thing* that is available for evaluation and judgment. In other words, to think abstractly one must become self-conscious. As a self-conscious being, one not only wills something but understands oneself to be willing. One not only desires or ponders something but understands oneself to be desiring or pondering. To think abstractly is to extend one's mind through language and reason, achieving a distance from one's inner drives that demonstrates self-consciousness.

Human beings, unlike other animals, not only desire and act but also evaluate their desires and actions rationally and self-reflectively. They can consequently indulge, deny, postpone, or reroute their desires and actions, having judged them from a more encompassing vantage point that allows present inclinations and behavior to be weighed against more abstract or distant concerns. They may learn from the past and prepare for the future not out of instinct but from thoughtful projection. They can learn to care for others not only through emotional attachment but also from a sense of duty.

Importantly, self-reflection is never attained in isolation. Becoming self-conscious is a process that human beings only ever achieve when they grow up among other human beings, in linguistic or language-speaking communities.[2] Consciousness, as the word itself indicates, is a "knowing with" (con- sciousness). We come to know things *with* others, by way of sharing in speech. Self-consciousness arises out of the human capacity to partake communicatively in the experiences of others.

Language typifies and preserves experience in words. It allows us to understand what others think of the world and of us. It also allows us to look back on our lives and ourselves. Through language we can view ourselves from a more detached, rational point of view, in terms of abstract categories, such as individuality and community membership. Thus the human capacity for sophisticated language and reason culminates in a political sensibility that makes humans truly unique. To summarize: political life depends on the ability of people to conceive themselves as individuals within a community of individuals. Thinking of oneself as an individual within a community of individuals, in turn, depends on self-reflective, abstract thought. Self-reflective, abstract thought depends on the development of language and reason.

Yet the development of language and reason depends on the existence of community. Which, then, came first, political life or language and reason? This quandary will likely never be solved. It is much like the puzzle of whether the chicken or the egg came first. There is no satisfying answer. Most likely, a rudimentary form of self-reflective language and reason developed simultaneously with a rudimentary form of political life in prehistoric human communities. The *zoon politikon* and the *zoon logon echon* always were, and remain today, one and the same animal.

Political life is a historical achievement. It was unavailable to the evolutionary ancestors of human beings who had less sophisticated capacities of language and reason. The tensioned balance that exists between the self-conscious individual and the community constitutes the core of politics. Our experiencing and organizing ourselves in the light of this balance defines our lives as political animals.

Aristotle rightly defined human being as a rational, speaking animal and a political animal. We must not forget the last word of each phrase. Human beings remain animals. We are biological creatures. By many measures, our similarities to other animals far outweigh our differences from them. Nature (the impact of biology) is often contrasted with nurture (the impact of culture). Both nature and nurture continue to play important roles in our political lives. Not only our culture but also our biology shapes and constrains our political institutions. To understand the link between human nature and politics, we must take this biological shaping and constraining seriously.

The Political Significance of Human Nature

What is the relationship between biology and politics, nature and nurture, and which is the more powerful force in our lives? These questions are as old as political thinking itself. What we do and should do in politics rests on the question of human nature. The tradition of political theory may be understood as a long struggle to understand this connection.

Plato's politics, for instance, follows directly from his understanding of human nature. Plato argues that the human soul is composed of three parts: an animal-like appetitive or desiring part, a humanlike emotional or spirited part, and a godlike intellectual or reasoning part. He structures the political realm to accommodate this innate, psychic composition. Three classes or castes of individuals come to represent the three facets of human nature. Merchants and tradespeople, who are mostly actuated by their appetites and base desires, form the lowest caste. Soldiers, who are mostly actuated by their spirited emotions and love of honor, form the middle caste. Philosophers and rulers known as guardians or philosopher kings, who are mostly actuated by their reason or intellect, form the top caste. Through intensive education, children of lower castes may occasionally gain access to the upper castes. By and large, however, Plato rigidly organizes the political community on the basis of individuals' natural propensities. Indeed he suggests, perhaps fancifully, that maintaining the best regime would entail a sophisticated program of eugenics or selective breeding. Human reproduction would have to be controlled so as to ensure the best stock for the ruling caste.

Integrating Plato's (and the neo-Platonists') distinction between the ideal and the real with Christian theology, St. Augustine (354–430), a North African bishop and philosopher, distinguished between the "City of God" and the "city of man." Augustine writes that "everyone, since he takes his origin from a condemned stock, is inevitably evil and carnal to begin with, by derivation from Adam."[3] Based on this understanding of humankind's fallen nature, Augustine concludes that secular government, the "city of man," is inherently unstable and doomed to disruption. His prescriptions for politics are grounded in these beliefs about the inherited features of human nature.

St. Thomas Aquinas (1225–74), the Italian scholastic and philosopher, brought medieval theory to its height by integrating Aristotelian philosophy with Christian theology. Aquinas argues that the government of a king is best because it follows the dictates of (human) nature. He writes:

> Whatever is in accord with nature is best, for in all things nature does what is best. In the multitude of bodily members there is one which is the principal mover, namely, the heart; and among the powers of the soul one power presides as chief, namely, the reason.... Wherefore, if artificial

things are an imitation of natural things and a work of art is better according as it attains a closer likeness to what is in nature, it follows that it is best for a human multitude to be ruled by one person.[4]

Aquinas also argues that humankind's natural reason leaves it relatively well equipped to lead peaceful, political lives. His politics follow directly from his understanding of human nature.

In modern times, Thomas Paine (1737–1809), the American patriot, theorist, and pamphleteer, argued for limited government based on his notion of the inherently social nature of humankind. He writes:

> To understand the nature and quantity of government proper for man, it is necessary to attend to his character. As Nature created him for social life ... she made his natural wants greater than his individual powers.... She has not only forced man into society, by a diversity of wants, which the reciprocal aid of each other can supply, but she has implanted in him a system of social affections, which, though not necessary to his existence, are essential to his happiness.... If we examine, with attention, into the composition and constitution of man ... we shall easily discover that a great part of what is called government is mere imposition. Government is no farther necessary than to supply the few cases to which society and civilization are not conveniently competent.[5]

In an original twist to an Aristotelian theme, Paine invokes the social nature of human beings as an argument against overbearing government.

James Madison (1751–1836), a contemporary of Paine, contributed his famous essay on factions to *The Federalist Papers,* which is considered by many to be the most important work of political theory written in the United States. Here Madison explicitly attributes political strife to the fallibility of human reason and the indelible effects of human passion and self-love. He writes that the "latent causes of faction are thus sown in the nature of man."[6] With this in mind, Madison sets out to construct a form of government that will compensate for humanity's inherent shortcomings.

Human nature provides the timber with which every politics must be constructed. Many political theorists, like Madison, argue that such crooked timber requires sophisticated architectural engineering, that is to say, the construction of a good constitution and government, to achieve adequate results. Other theorists forgo tinkering with political institutions and set out instead to straighten the timber of humanity itself through revolutionary practice. In either case, a theory of human nature becomes the prerequisite for a theory of politics.

Consider in greater detail how one political theorist famously carried on the tradition of structuring politics on a model of human nature. Thomas Hobbes (1588–1679) was much impressed by Euclidean geometry, a science that deduced firm conclusions from self-evident axioms. Like Plato, Hobbes strove to make his political theory mathematical. Making and maintaining a commonwealth, Hobbes writes, entails discovering and applying the same sort of rules as are found in arithmetic and geometry.[7] Hobbes's theory of human nature is vastly different from Plato's, however, and consequently so is the form of politics he proposes.

Hobbes was born in 1588 in an English coastal town then threatened by the Spanish Armada. He later wrote that fear and he were born twins. Indeed, Hobbes's political theory revolves around the notion that fear is the chief motivating force of politics. Human beings are subject to an endless pursuit of power, Hobbes insists. This pursuit is a product of their fear of death or deprivation at the hands of others more powerful than they are. One's power can always be undermined or destroyed by another's greater power or by one's lack of vigilance. Hobbes observes that even the strongest man can easily be struck dead in his sleep by the weakest man. Thus we naturally seek ever-increasing power to protect ourselves better from attack. Of course, everyone else feels the same way and acts accordingly. The result is the endless pursuit of power after power by all, which, in the absence of government, leads to violent anarchy. Without rules and rulers to enforce them, a war of all against all ensues. In this anarchic state of nature, Hobbes states in a famous passage, life is "solitary, poore, nasty, brutish, and short."[8]

Once we accept the premises of Hobbes's deductive theory, namely, that humans forever seek power after power "ending only in death," his conclusion inevitably follows. There is but one way to escape the constant fear of being killed or subdued. Everyone must agree to make one person (or a single governmental body) all powerful. This "Leviathan," as Hobbes calls the supreme governmental power, would become capable of forcibly maintaining peace and order among its subjects. The only alternative to anarchy, for Hobbes, is authoritarian government.

Why is submitting to despotism better than living in the state of nature? The submission to arbitrary rule may seem like jumping from the frying pan into the fire. Hobbes's response is that with the creation of a Leviathan at least one knows where the heat is coming from. The Leviathan has no reason to fear his subjects because he is already all-powerful. Accordingly, he has no reason to kill or deprive them unless they get out of line. For individuals primarily motivated by fear of death and deprivation, a peaceful life under despotic rule is better than freedom in a state of endless war.

Hobbes had translated the writings of the ancient Greek thinker Thucydides (c. 460–400 B.C.), considered by many to be the first political theorist. Thucydides participated in and wrote about the Peloponnesian War, a conflict between Athens and Sparta that lasted the better part of three decades. Hobbes appears to have well learned the lesson on power that Thucydides taught. As Thucydides recounts, the islanders of Melos requested that they be left out of the war and given liberty to pursue their own business rather than pay tribute to the city-state of Athens. The Athenians refused, responding that they could not, or would not, give up their imperial prerogatives. The Athenians justified their proposed destruction of the Melians by invoking a law of nature: "The strong do what they can and the weak suffer what they must."[9] The pursuit of power is natural and endless, Thucydides seemed to be saying.

Hobbes accepted Thucydides' pronouncement as a universal law. Nevertheless, Hobbes wrote his masterwork, the *Leviathan*, at the time of the Peace of Westphalia in 1648, when the European territorial state declared its sovereignty after centuries of dominance by kingdoms and empires recently ripped apart by bloody religious wars. Hobbes believed that within the sovereign nation-state, the interminable human struggle for power might be curtailed. The law of nature that dictated the endless pursuit of power could not be thwarted, but it could be brought under control by a supreme national ruler.

Human nature, for Hobbes, inevitably creates a world wherein the fear of violent death binds men and women together into groups ruled by a sovereign power. With reason playing only a minor role among human motivations and with the appetite for power running rampant, Hobbes did not think it prudent to await the arrival of a philosopher king. Hobbes deduces that the rational rule of philosophers is neither likely, necessary, nor even recommended. Peaceful despotism, in contrast, is achievable and quite acceptable. The despot need not be particularly intelligent, rational, or virtuous. In ending the anarchical war of all against all—the worst of all possible worlds—the Leviathan, whatever his faults and shortcomings, deservedly gains the allegiance of all. Though arriving at different conclusions, Hobbes, like most theorists before and after him, grounds his political theory on a theory of human nature.

As we approach the twenty-first century, many debates continue to rage about the relation between human nature and politics. Feminist political theorists question the biological basis of patriarchy or male domination and the cultural formation of gender distinctions. Environmental political theorists confront the "natural" human disposition for shortsighted, egoistic behavior, examine its ecological costs, and speculate on its possible remedies. Postmodern political theorists, in their concern with the "social construction" of identity, face the problem of determining the extent to which our biological nature constrains what we make of ourselves.

In these contemporary cases, just as for earlier theorists, the political processes and structures prescribed for human beings are grounded in particular beliefs about human nature. It should come as no surprise, then, that an examination of human biology provides access to the terrain of political theory.

Human biology does not determine human politics in any straightforward sense. Certainly biological knowledge will never settle our more pressing and enduring political concerns. But exploring the biological side of human nature may inform our understanding of its political side. This exploration also illuminates the role that theorists play in grappling with politics. Human biological reproduction serves as an apt analogy for the reproduction of concepts, norms, principles, and ideas that political theorists themselves undertake.

The Genetic Leash

Human beings, like all other animals, are largely products of their genes. Genes are the building blocks of life. They are composed of molecular coils, called DNA, that are capable of replicating themselves. Genes group together in large numbers to form chromosomes. Chromosomes are the biochemical codes, or "blueprints," that regulate the development of many of our features and characteristics. There are chromosomes, for instance, that determine one's sex, eye and hair color, general height, and many other physical attributes.

Human beings have most of their genes in common. Over 90 percent of any person's genes are identical to the genes of every other human being. This sharing of genetic structure is what makes us all members of the same species, *homo sapiens,* as opposed to cats or birds. Genetically, humans have much more in common than they have in contrast. The vast majority of the codes within our genetic blueprint ensure that we develop as human beings. A small minority of our genes ensure that we develop as different sorts of human beings. Most of this genetic variation makes human beings unique individuals. A much smaller amount makes human beings members of specific races or ethnic groups. Indeed, there is over six times the amount of genetic difference, for example, between two individual Swedes chosen at random than there is between the average of Swedes and the average of, say, Aboriginal Australians or African Bushmen.[10]

When investigating the extent to which our biology determines our politics, we must keep in mind that the genes that make us political animals are not solely the small proportion of our genes that make us unique individuals or members of particular races or ethnic groups. We are political animals because of the vastly larger proportion of our genes that make us human beings in the first place. As human beings, we are biologically enabled, one might even say that we are biologically determined, to live politically. Unlike other animals, humans are genetically designed to grow large, complex brains and organs of speech. Certain portions of our brains, specifically the neocortex and limbic systems, enable us to engage in sophisticated reasoning, abstract conceptualization and speech, self-reflection, and extended emotional attachment. These attributes make humans eminently political creatures.

Our genetic blueprints make us political animals, but to what extent do they determine the specific nature of our politics? The shaping and constraining of our political life by our biology is perhaps best illustrated by a metaphor. Consider the image of our biological nature holding our politics, and our culture as a whole, on a leash.[11] This leash is fairly long and quite elastic. Political life is free to develop in any number of directions, but it cannot totally free itself from its biological constraint. A people may decide to ground its collective life on democratic principles such that all adults receive a vote in deciding the management of common concerns. Biology has little to say about the nature of this democracy or even about the development of democratic government as opposed to despotic government. Yet biology does prompt political communities not to give equal political status to babies and small children. Since humans develop their emotional, intellectual, and physical capabilities at a very slow rate compared to other animals, humans remain incapable of effectively participating in political affairs for over a decade after their birth. As political beings, then, humans self-consciously shape their relationships and activities. Yet they carry out this shaping within certain limits set by their genetic constitution.

Although our genes constrain politics in certain respects, we must remember that these same genes make politics possible in the first place. In turn, politics—and culture in general—stretches the leash with which our genes shape and constrain our lives. Were we genetically incapable of developing a sophisticated political and cultural life, our genes would determine much more of our experiences than they do. As is the case with other animals, our genetic leashes would then be much shorter and much stiffer.

Among the erectly postured, apelike creatures that preceded the evolution of human beings some 12 million years ago, one may assume that culture and politics barely existed. Like the rest of the animal kingdom, the behavior of these early hominids was highly determined by their genes, by way of instinctive drives. Their genetic leashes were very short and very stiff. Over countless years of evolution, changes in genetic structure allowed rudimentary forms of culture and politics to emerge. As this culture and politics grew, the genetic leash became increasingly stretched, allowing further and faster cultural and political development.

Ethical discourse, for instance, was impossible before humans gained the capacities for speech and reason. These capacities, in turn, could not develop until humans underwent the physiological evolution that produced their uniquely structured larynx and brain. Once the capacities for speech and reason allowed early human beings to engage in moral thought and action, the boundaries of the activities that were circumscribed by our genetic blueprints were increasingly stretched. Moral precepts, for example, could effectively restrict the behavior that instinct and appetite would otherwise induce. That is to say, not only do our genes hold our politics and culture on a leash, but our politics and culture also hold our genes on a leash. Indeed, the entire history of human development is largely a product of the pulling and tugging between our genes and our culture.

Let us look at an example of this pulling and tugging between nature and nurture. It is likely that among the immediate precursors to *homo sapiens,* who lived over 300,000 years ago, the physiological growth of brains was not only the cause but also the effect of cultural development. Among these hominids, cultural development fostered and accelerated physiological evolution. The development of midwifery or aided childbearing allowed baby hominids with larger heads, and hence larger brains, to pass more successfully through the relatively small pelvic cavities of their mothers. (Being upright walkers, hominids, like modern humans, had narrow hips.) These larger-brained children would eventually reproduce, passing on their genes for larger brains to their own children.

Thus the development of social cooperation during childbirth contributed to the evolution of larger brains. "Whereas many accounts of the expansion of hominid evolution focus on male activities, such as hunting, group defense, or knowledge of the terrain," a political scientist observes, "an explanation based on social cooperation [of women during childbirth] emphasizes a factor that otherwise would have limited evolution toward larger brain size.... It is often argued that humans cooperate in society because they have big brains. Perhaps the truth is that we have big brains because we cooperate in society."[12] The complex structure of the human brain, not only its size, accounts for our capacities for sophisticated speech, reason, and cultural development. Neanderthals had larger heads and larger brains 40,000 years ago than we do today. Yet they were virtually without culture. Nonetheless, the general point remains: the growth of large, complex brains fostered the development of culture, yet some rudimentary culture was needed to foster the proliferation of humans with large, complex brains.

Human biological development and cultural development have gone hand in hand from time immemorial. Attempting to distinguish completely between biology and culture, nature and nurture, as competing causes of human development, a distinguished biologist observes, is like attempting to determine whether the area of a rectangle is caused more by its length or its width.[13] To understand human development, including human political development, one must know something about both the biological and the cultural foundations of life.

Genes and Mores

As single units or in complex combinations, genes provide the information directives that produce and sustain organic development in nature. The corresponding role in the realm of culture is taken on by mores. Mores are the building blocks of political life. The word *mores* comes from the Latin translation of the Greek word for custom, which was "ethics." For the ancient Greeks, ethics was a broader concept than what we understand by the term today. It pertained not only to individual conscience and explicitly moral duties but to all standards or norms grounded in social tradition. Likewise, mores pertain not only to the moral rules that regulate individual behavior but to all the concepts, conventions, principles, rules, and understandings that maintain a social order.

Like all rules, mores restrict behavior. But they also serve as resources and stimulants of behavior. The rules of grammar, by way of comparison, restrict the manner in which we speak. But these same rules allow us to speak intelligibly in the first place. Likewise, mores induce forms of behavior that are conducive to the formation and main-

tenance of a particular social order while they impede other sorts of behavior that would prove destructive of this order. Certain mores, like
the principles of justice, may prove antagonistic to (some features of)
an existing social order if that order is grounded in exploitation and
domination. There are revolutionary mores just as there are conservative ones. There are mores designed for ideal worlds just as there are
mores developed for the real world.

What genes are to nature, mores are to culture in general and to
politics in particular. Just as genes order the biological construction and
maintenance of organisms, mores order the cultural construction and
maintenance of societies. Yet mores are not immune to the effects of
our genes. To retrieve our metaphor, we might say that our genes hold
our mores on a leash. This simply reiterates the point that our biology
influences our political and social life without determining it in every
instance. The genes that cause us to grow hair on various parts of our
bodies, for example, do not determine what we will do with that hair.
Different cultures have an almost unrestricted latitude to prescribe vari-
ations in its cutting, shaving, extirpating, tending, coloring, and adorn-
ing. Likewise, some of our genes determine us to be sexual reproducers
(as opposed to asexual reproducers, like flatworms). These genes ensure
that sex between men and women will occur in all cultures and that the
sexual drive will not easily be ignored. Consequently, these genes effectively determine that all societies will develop mores to regulate and rit-
ualize sexual relations and sexuality. Yet the expression of human sexuality is extremely varied and plastic. The kind of sexual mores that
develop are highly dependent on their historical and cultural contexts.
What is invariable, however, is that sexual mores of some sort develop.

Likewise, our genes determine that children remain dependent during the first few years of their lives. Human babies and young children
are incapable of fending for themselves and reproducing during this
rather extended period. (Mice, by way of contrast, not only nourish,
shelter, and protect themselves, but start to reproduce by two months
of age.) Many different aspects of human culture have developed in response to this biological constraint. The institution of marriage, the celebration of family life, and the development of educational institutions
name only a few of the more obvious cultural artifacts that compensate
for or take advantage of our lengthy period of childhood immaturity
and dependence. Indeed, Aristotle already observed that the springs of
politics and justice are to be found in the extended bonding of parent
and child.[14]

The nature of the rules, principles, customs, conventions, and understandings surrounding marriage, family life, and education differs

markedly from culture to culture and even within the same culture. Yet the extent to which humans can wholly abandon these mores is severely circumscribed by the biological facts of human propagation and development. Until we can produce more viable infants by way of genetic engineering—a frightening thought—culture will always be forced to compensate for the extended helplessness of children. Thus while it is inevitable that certain social arrangements and institutions develop to accommodate childhood dependency, the manner in which these arrangements and institutions develop is open to tremendous variation.

Consider a more controversial issue. Only women bear children. That is genetically determined. Historically, women have also filled the role of their children's primary caretakers. That is not genetically determined, but it is likely that genes had something to do with the development of this behavioral pattern. A human being's genetic constitution largely determines the production of hormones and enzymes. Particular hormones and enzymes induce most boys from a very early age to be relatively more aggressive, while other hormones and enzymes induce most girls to be relatively more nurturing. Good evidence also suggests that in the aggregate women are genetically endowed with greater verbal ability, perceptual speed, and fine motor skills, while men have the edge in spatial perception and quantitative calculation. These differences are likely the product of hundreds of thousands of years of genetic adaptation among early hominids faced with the distinct demands of childrearing and hunting.[15] Yet even here, where genetic influences are ascertainable, the question of whether culture can and should attempt to augment, controvert, or ignore particular biological inheritances is left unanswered. While the existence of a genetic leash is evident, its specific length and level of elasticity is largely unknown. Moreover, the extent to which we should stretch it remains very much open to debate.

We are genetically constrained to grow legs and arms rather than fins, wheels, or wings. That explains why humans for most of their early existence have walked or run to get places. But that does not mean that we should never swim, ride bicycles, or fly in airplanes. Humans are also genetically induced, via the production of certain hormones and enzymes within their bodies, to respond aggressively to certain threatening situations. Nonetheless, culture and politics frequently curb, manipulate, and sublimate these aggressive tendencies, and rightly so. Likewise, the fact that genetics has produced a historical legacy of female childrearing does not mean that women should remain the sole or even primary caretakers of children today.

All cultural institutions, one might say, have genetic foundations.

But these foundations are broad enough to allow the construction of very large and diverse moral and political structures within which humans find themselves at great liberty to roam. Each one of us has some 100,000–200,000 genes, composed of 6 billion nucleotides that form the letters of the genetic code. The amount of information stored in our brains, however, assuming for the sake of argument that it corresponds to the number of neural connections, is many thousands times greater. (The brain is made up of 100 billion cells, each composed of many thousand connections.[16]) We may interpret these facts to mean that human beings are genetically destined to develop cultural mores and technical means that challenge and stretch their biological propensities and capacities. Indeed, the leash on which genes hold culture is so long and flexible that culture has become the greatest force structuring most human relationships and activities.

The development of a political life is impossible for centipedes and other animals for one simple reason: they do not have our genes. Our genes allow us, one might say they require us, to structure our lives by mores. That these mores at times appear to conflict with primitive, unmediated instincts speaks less to the antagonism between nature and nurture than to the complex interdependence of human nature and human nurture.

We are born genetically disposed to learn a great deal in this life and to alter our behavior according to this learning. Human culture develops not in opposition to human biology but as a consequence of it. To the extent that our genes determine our nature they determine us to be cultural beings whose cultural life is relatively autonomous. The leash with which genes hold on to us is sufficiently long to allow, or rather induce, self-consciousness. Making use of our self-consciousness is thus no rebellion against our genes. If anything, a creature biologically designed for self-consciousness that did *not* produce mores to regulate its life would be the true rebel against nature.

Humans are genetically programmed to grow large, complex brains. Hence one might say that humans are genetically designed to develop both moral understandings that challenge their instinctive impulses and technology that extends their biological capacities. It is no less "natural" for human beings to restrain or channel their behavior according to moral standards or technological possibilities than it is for them to abandon themselves to unmediated instinct and undeveloped propensities. The mere existence of particular drives or physiological characteristics does not tell us very much about what human beings should (attempt to) do in and with their lives. Heeding ethical dictates is as natural as following appetites, at least for adult human beings who speak and reason together. The fact that human genes constrain but do not determine the range and development of human activities and relationships makes for the dilemmas that we alone among the animal species face. These are the dilemmas of a political animal.

Biological and Cultural Reproduction

Human genes propagate themselves by way of the sexual reproduction of the individuals who possess them. Hence we carry on the genes of our parents, just as our children shall carry on our genes. Richard Dawkins, a zoologist, first suggested that genes had a cultural analog. He coined the word *meme*, from the Greek *mimeme*, which means "imitation," to define the unit of culture that replicates itself.[17] Memes, Dawkins suggests, serve as the units of cultural transmission. What Dawkins means by memes is simply a more general case of what we have called mores. Whereas *meme* refers to any cultural transmission (including, say, technical inventions, artistic manners, and fashion styles), *mores* refers specifically to those concepts, conventions, principles, rules, and understandings that structure social order and political life.

Genetic transmission first began billions of years ago in the primal soup of the earth's cooling seas. Here DNA molecules first appeared and started to reproduce themselves. Eventually, these molecules combined to form the genes of basic organisms that became capable of reproduction. The diversity and sophistication of these primitive forms of life slowly increased, with each particular species bearing and reproducing its own unique "pool" of genes.

The transmission of memes, in contrast, only began millions of years ago, when tribes of primitive hominids began to produce and pass along expressions, information, skills, rules, and rituals by way of gestures and speech. The conglomerations of memes that get passed along through cultural reproduction may be understood as "symbol pools" that correspond to the "gene pools" passed along through biological reproduction. Gene pools are effectively programs for transforming energy and matter into particular sorts of organic life. Likewise, symbol pools may be understood as programs for transforming energy and matter into specific sorts of cultural life.[18] Today we know a good deal about the chemistry that allows the genetic conversion of matter and energy into organic life. But what is the "chemistry" of cultural life? How, we might ask, do symbol pools maintain and transform themselves? In other words, how do memes and mores reproduce?

Memes and mores propagate themselves through social interaction. As Dawkins writes, they leap "from brain to brain via a process which, in the broad sense, can be called imitation.... When you plant a fertile meme in my mind you literally parasitize my brain, turning it into a vehicle for the meme's propagation in just the way that a virus may parasitize the genetic mechanism of a host cell."[19] In other words, when we speak or act in a way that influences others to speak or act in a similar way, we are effectively propagating a meme. A good example might be the coining of a new word that quickly becomes popular. Technological media (e.g., radio, television, newspapers, magazines, books, direct mail, and electronic print and images), dramatically increase the pace at which memes propagate. Indeed, a major advantage of memes over genes is the speed with which the former reproduce. This speed accounts for the growing comparative strength of the cultural over the biological structuring of human relationships and activities.

The propagation of memes and mores may prove more successful than the propagation of genes for other reasons as well. Only half of one's genes are passed on to one's children. The other half of a child's genes come from the other parent. In turn, grandchildren carry on only one-fourth of one's genes, and great grandchildren only one-eighth. This diminishing role of our genes continues indefinitely, to the point where distant descendants are little more related to us than complete strangers living on the other side of the globe.

Our memes and mores, in contrast, may survive relatively intact across countless generations. Dawkins explains that

> as each generation passes, the contribution of your genes [to your progeny] is halved. It does not take long to reach negligible proportions.... But if you contribute to the world's culture, if you have a good idea, compose a tune, invent a sparking plug, write a poem, it may live on, intact, long after your genes have dissolved in the common pool. Socrates may or may not have a gene or two alive in the world today ... but who cares? The meme-complexes of Socrates ... are still going strong.[20]

Both memes and genes achieve a sort of immortality through their self-replication. Unlike genes, however, certain memes and mores survive down through the generations in a form that remains very close to their original form. Socratic thought continues to be taught in thousands of university classrooms, and it continues to exert its effect on countless minds. One cannot claim the same sort of immortality for the genes that Socrates passed on to his children, which today are as scattered as dust in the wind.

Over time, the replication of particular mores is likely to produce many mutations and hybrids. Indeed, when it comes to political theory, one might consider most successful not those mores that faithfully duplicate themselves but those that stimulate the accelerated development of related yet altered versions of themselves over time. Here, as with genetic transmission, mutation remains at least as important as replication for the continuation and enrichment of life. If genes did not mutate over time, new species of animals would not develop that were better suited to their environments. Soon biological diversity would dwindle as new forms of life failed to develop while old forms continued to perish in the midst of changing circumstances. Likewise, mores that fail to adapt to a changing world may have quite limited life spans. Those that mutate successfully may exercise their influence over numerous generations.

Again, Socratic thought comes to mind. As recorded by Plato, many of Socrates' concepts and ideas remain with us today in a relatively intact form. Yet Socrates understood himself to be playing the role of the midwife, aiding in the birth not of particular thoughts but of particular ways of thinking. He produced a *macro*-meme known as the "Socratic method." This is a method of teaching by means of posing a probing series of questions. Though the Socratic method is still widely employed today, it may foster mores that are quite different from those Plato recorded in his dialogues. Socrates' own mores, in turn, have undergone countless mutations at the hands of his many interpreters. They have also experienced cross-fertilizations from other thinkers. Like political theories, mores often achieve their greatest influence not through faithful reproduction but through their capacity to stimulate adaptation and innovation. Indeed, a more is perhaps most "alive" not when it is permanently etched in stone but when it serves as a parent or partner to the birth of new mores.

We might observe one final parallel between our genes and our mores, the biological and the cultural building blocks of life. Genes, like mores, influence but do not dictate how we think and act. Genes do not determine every aspect of our physiological and behavioral development. Instead, genes determine the boundaries or limits within which our physiological and behavioral attributes are at liberty to adapt to the environment. The genes that give us opposable thumbs, for instance, do not determine whether we should plant potatoes or use sickles to harvest grain. They do make these and many other activities possible. Were we endowed with paws or hooves instead, our range of adaptation to the environment, and the types of food we consume, would be much more limited.

In describing the boundaries of adaptation with which each organism must contend, biologists use the term *reaction range*. A reaction range is the range within which an organism's physical traits or behaviors may develop given a particular environment and the limitations imposed by its genetic inheritance.[21] Genes that produce wings or fins do not determine what an animal will consume, but they do preclude its planting potatoes or using sickles to harvest grain. Genes that produce opposable thumbs allow a much larger reaction range. Nonetheless, the reaction range is still limited. Our having opposable thumbs on our hands precludes the great efficiency in swimming that is gained by having fins or the ability for unaided flight that is gained by having wings.

Like genes, mores do not determine the specific behavior of individuals in particular situations but delimit a range of adaptive behavior, inducing particular sorts of thought or action and dissuading others. Mores produce a certain cultural reaction range within which people who adopt these mores are predisposed to operate. We cannot say exactly how someone influenced by Platonic mores is likely to think or act in any particular situation. Yet we can foresee that someone who adopts a Platonic conception of human nature is unlikely to advocate a Hobbesian style of politics. For the Platonic valorization of philosophic reasoning is incompatible with the rule of a despot having no philosophic training or knowledge.

Plato's concept of the three-part human soul with reason ruling the emotions and appetites has produced cultural mores that have lasted more than 2,500 years. These mores continue to reproduce themselves today, effectively leaping from brain to brain through the media of books and lectures. Individuals who adopt these mores will tend to interact with their political environment within a particular reaction range of thought and behavior. Of course, even a dyed-in-the-wool Platonist may change his mind and become a Hobbesian thinker or actor. Alternatively, one might combine Plato and Hobbes to arrive at a hybridized set of mores that somehow integrates these two conceptual universes. In short, the human capacities for freedom of thought and freedom of will, barring cases of complete brainwashing or indoctrination, preclude the possibility of particular sets of mores exerting total control over the lives of those who adopt them.

The mores systematized in political theories may prescribe or proscribe quite specific beliefs and behavior. More often, they set out a bounded conceptual field within which collective human existence may be examined and evaluated. The mores of a political theory, developed through the use of various conceptual lenses, sketch out the features of an epistemological and ethical reaction range. These mores influence the types of thought and behavior that individuals acknowledge or ignore and accept or reject as laudable, tolerable, and sanctionable within political life.

Hobbes was certainly aware of the importance of the mores that political theorists develop and advance. These mores, grounded in language, channel our thinking and acting. Hobbes thus proposed an extensive streamlining of language along the lines suggested by his geometrically grounded thinking. The effort to settle the definitions of words and stabilize the meanings of concepts was no mere academic affair. It was, Hobbes held, the basis for a stable social and political life. It required an all-powerful Leviathan who could enforce the proper use of language.

Theorists do not have Leviathans at their disposal to settle the meanings and uses of words once and for all. Competing political mores —the concepts, conventions, principles, rules, and understandings that constitute the stuff of political theory—will always be found in abundance, at least wherever freedom of thought, freedom of speech, and freedom of the press exist. Platonic mores and their Hobbesian counterparts are only two of countless rivals doing battle on theory's field of hor or.

It is unlikely that any theoretical victories won in this realm will be complete or permanent. Theorists have no way of assuring that their mores will be faithfully reproduced and proliferate, or any way of assuring that their mores will not be used in quite unintended ways. There is, in short, no end in sight to the ongoing theoretical struggles waged for the hearts and minds of citizens. The competition is stiff —and that is a good thing. For any end to the epistemological and ethical struggles to understand, order, and transform political life would also be an end to human creativity and freedom.

Despite the intense competition, particular theories do come to exert considerable influence. Some even become hegemonic for a time. They replicate their mores, or stimulate their evolutionary development, across the land and down through the generations. Those among us who yearn for immortality might find the practice of political theory a more effective means of satisfying their ambitions than the standard genetic route. The stakes for political theorists, therefore, are quite high. In their attempt to understand, order, and transform collective human existence, theorists have the opportunity to bear many intellectual and moral offspring. Their epistemological and ethical legacies may endure long after these theorists, to employ Hamlet's brooding phrase, have shuffled off their mortal coils.

Suggested Readings

Thomas Aquinas. *The Political Ideas of St. Thomas Aquinas*
Aristotle. *Nichomachean Ethics* and *Politics*
St. Augustine. *The Political Writings*
Richard Dawkins. *The Selfish Gene*
Daniel Dennett. *Darwin's Dangerous Idea*
Thomas Hobbes. *Leviathan*
Melvin Konner. *The Tangled Wing*
Roger D. Masters. *The Nature of Politics*
Thomas Paine. *The Rights of Man*
Plato. *Republic*
Thucydides. *The Peloponnesian War*

3

Politics, Power, and the
Public Good

Politics is often defined as the art and science of government. Government refers to the institutions and processes through which binding decisions are made for a society. Politics, then, pertains to the means employed to organize and regulate collective human existence.

Politics is found everywhere that humans are found. There are no areas of human life completely beyond its reach or wholly untouched by its effects. To say that there are few if any areas of human life unaffected by politics, however, is not to say that everything is or should be political in the same way or to the same degree.

Politics pertains to the organization and regulation of communities of distinct individuals. As individuals, we maintain private lives. We hold that certain realms of our lives are not appropriately subject to political control. They are personal affairs, properly conducted between and evaluated among friends and family. Likewise, we hold that certain matters ought to remain subject only to individual conscience and personal choice and not be open to public scrutiny, debate, or interference. In countries whose governments are based on liberal principles and constitutional order, these areas of private concern are often protected by a Bill of Rights.

If there are matters that are and should remain private, how can we say that politics is pervasive? The answer is that politics largely determines what realms of human affairs can and will remain private. It is politics, moreover, that safeguards these realms, effectively guarding them from its own intrusions. The civil rights that protect the privacy of individuals and families from state interference, for example, are themselves created through political actions and maintained through political institutions. Individual rights to privacy, in this sense, are political rights. Like the constitution in which they are embedded, rights to privacy are politically decided, politically instituted, and politically preserved. Politics is pervasive because it is involved in creating and maintaining the separate yet interrelated spheres of human affairs. Politics is pervasive not only because it brings many concerns into the public realm but because it determines what things are to remain, as much as possible, shielded from the public realm.

Take the question of religious freedom. Freedom of religion, at least in modern, liberal states, is an important civil right. In states where religious freedom is maintained, if, how, what, or whom one chooses to worship remains a matter of individual conscience. The political community neither promotes religious dogma nor prescribes religious ritual. There remains, as it is commonly known, a separation of church and state. The separation of church and state means that an individual is allowed to practice any religion as long as this practice does not interfere unduly with the lives of others. A religion that called for forced conversion of infidels or the burning of heretics, for instance, would be politically intolerable. Here the church would be encroaching on a prerogative uniquely held by the state in modern times, namely, the use of physical force to protect its citizens or defend its interests.

Many political communities of the past were theocratic, that is, they were governed by rulers who claimed to be the vicars or representatives of a deity or deities. Typically, this meant that the head of state was also the high priest of an officially maintained religion. Even today, fundamentalist religious leaders and parties have gained political power in certain countries and maintain some form of theocratic rule. In the United States, as in many other countries, the separation of church and state is explicitly maintained by a constitution that sets out the structure and boundaries of political life. When the U.S. Constitution was written in 1787, however, only two states—New York and Virginia did *not* have religious qualifications for public office. Most of the other states required that one be a Protestant to hold office. The separation of church and state is itself a historical achievement of politics. Without politics, the safeguarding of realms of life such as religious worship from politics would be impossible.

Economic freedom is also an important right in modern societies. It allows us to hold private property and to engage in financial enterprises of our own choosing. Like religious freedom, economic freedom is a crucial aspect of individual freedom and autonomy. Like religious affairs, economic affairs in modern, liberal states remain privatized to a great extent. And, like religious freedom, economic freedom has its limits, limits that are politically established and maintained through laws, regulations, and customs.

Economic freedom allows us to earn and spend money in many different ways. Nonetheless, our economic transactions must not interfere unduly with the rights and freedoms of others. We may not spend money in any way we want. It is illegal, for instance, to buy a slave. Nor can one legally buy votes. In many countries, there are also strict limits on the amount of media coverage and advertising that one can buy to run a campaign for election to public office. Similarly, the ways one may earn money are restricted. Wealth must be gained in some legitimate fashion rather than by means of fraud of extortion. Likewise, one may manufacture goods to be sold for profit, but one cannot sell anything one wants or manufacture things in any way one wants. One cannot legally sell contaminated food, or dangerously pollute the land, air, or water during the processes of manufacturing. Goods manufactured and sold must truly be goods, that is, they must not obviously harm the consumer or the public domain.

These restrictions on economic affairs are necessary to ensure that economic rights and freedoms do not overstep their boundaries to inte fere unduly with the enjoyment of other rights and freedoms. Deciding on and maintaining these boundaries between potentially conflicting rights is itself a collective enterprise that entails the issuing of regulations, the making of laws, and the crafting and maintaining of constitutions. It is, in short, a matter of politics.

Just as politics structures our lives by supplying the scope and limits of our activities and relationships, so political theory structures politics by supplying its conceptual and normative scope and limits. Our effort to theorize politics, then, is no mere academic affair. Understanding the meaning of politics is crucial to understanding the way we lead our lives, including those aspects of our lives that we justifiably presume to be largely beyond the ambit of politics.

According to Aristotle, the study of politics does not allow for the level of certainty, exactitude, or generalization that might be gained through natural or mathematical sciences like physics or geometry. Despite this apparent shortcoming, Aristotle claims that the study of politics remains the master science. His reasoning is straightforward. Politics orders the social realm as a whole, allotting the diverse activities and relationships of human beings their proper places and prerogatives. Though politics does not determine how every human endeavor, such as religious worship, economic enterprise, artistic creation, or philosophical reflection, is to proceed within its legitimate borders, politics does demarcate the appropriate boundaries of these endeavors. Political theory is an intellectual and moral effort to identify and justify these boundaries.

What is the most recent political event that you have witnessed? In order to answer this question, you have to make some pretty fine discriminations. You have to distinguish between numerous recently witnessed events, throwing out of contention all those activities that fail to meet certain (yet unnamed) criteria, selecting out others, and finally choosing the one that best fits the bill. Even if you have never thought about the definition of politics before today, your ability to respond to the question demonstrates a tacit knowledge of its meaning.

Perhaps you responded to the question by saying that you recently witnessed an electoral rally or a congressional session in person or on television. That seems a safe bet. But what if someone responded by saying that the most recent political event she had witnessed was not some action engaged in by legislators, candidates, or voters, but an extended discussion by students in a classroom, or a varsity basketball game? You may disagree with this person's understanding of politics. But how would you argue that the words and actions that occur in the classroom or on the basketball court are less political than those that occur in Congress or at an electoral rally? When one thinks about politics explicitly, tacit understandings may begin to unravel. Clear and concise definitions of politics are neither easy to come by nor easy to maintain when confronted with sustained interrogation.

If you picked a congressional session as the best example of a political event, then you chose something commonly assumed to evidence the essence of politics, namely, the use of public power. More precisely, politics might be defined as an exercise of power that influences people to pursue particular objectives or adopt particular norms that direct or order their collective lives. But does not the power of persuasion exercised in the classroom also bear this potential? And do not the basketball players agree to follow rules and procedures that regulate their common endeavor? It seems that we must theorize some more about the meaning of politics.

Power and Force

The history of politics is the history of the efforts of individuals or groups of individuals to accumulate, exercise, and distribute power. Hence questions of power figure largely into the discussion of most, if not all, other political concepts. The question, Who should wield power? is the question of leadership or rule. The question, How should power be (institutionally) distributed? investigates the best form of polity or government. The question, How can power be exercised fairly? describes the problem of justice. The question, What should the limits of power be? introduces the issue of liberty. Politics is first and foremost about power. Political theory, it follows, is the study of the nature of power—of the uses, effects, and limits of power.

Reflecting on the importance of power to the study of politics and society, the British philosopher Bertrand Russell (1872–1970) wrote that

> the fundamental concept of social science is Power, in the same sense in which Energy is the fundamental concept in physics. Like energy, power has many forms, such as wealth, armaments, civil authority, influence or opinion. No one of these can be regarded as subordinate to any other, and there is no one form from which the others are derivative.... To revert to the analogy of physics: power, like energy, must be regarded as continually passing from any one of its forms into any other, and it should be the business of social science to seek the laws of such transformations.[1]

Power, for Russell, is defined as the capacity to produce intended effects. It is, in short, the ability to get what one wants. Figuring out how people get what they want is the job he assigns to political scientists.

In like fashion, Thomas Hobbes wrote that "the power *of a Man* (to take it Universally) is his present means to obtain some future apparent good."[2] Hobbes speaks of different sorts of power, including bodily power or strength, which is the physical means one has to move heavy objects and obtain some apparent good by so doing. Our present concerns, however, are not with strength or other sorts of physical power. We are concerned with power as it is manifest in political life. Like Russell, we are interested in power as the fundamental concept pertaining to the study of political society. This sort of social and political power may take many forms, which, while conceptually distinct, often go hand in hand or become transformed, one into the other.

Power is generally thought of as "power over," as a kind of control over the decisions people make and the choices they have. One exercises power by influencing people to do, say, believe, or value particular things. This may happen in many different ways. One may pay them (the power of wealth); win them over in speech (the power of eloquence); appeal to their sense of duty or rightful obedience (the power of authority); rely on one's reputation (the power of prestige); exercise the prerogative to carry on a legacy (the power of tradition); or simply intimidate them (the power of coercion). Each of these forms of power

—wealth, eloquence, authority, prestige, tradition, and coercion—has its own limitations.

The power of rational debate and persuasion typically displays its limits once battle lines have been drawn and active hostilities have begun. Wealth, in turn, may get you much of what you want in this world. As the saying goes, however, you can't buy love. Love must be won in other ways. Most often, the limits of one form of power are established in confrontation with another form of power. Hence a popular musician may influence thousands of people to drink a particular brand of soda. Yet her fame or prestige may be quite ineffective when marshaled to promote certain ethical views. In ethical debate, rational persuasion, the power of tradition, or the influence of moral authority may prove more effective.

Many political theorists hold that force is one form of power. Some suggest that violent force, as evidenced in military action, for example, is the ultimate form of power. There are good reasons for accepting this definition. It enjoys a wide currency and a long tradition of usage. One commonly speaks, for instance, of the power of might. Here, however, we explore a different understanding of power, one that is also well established among political theorists. Power influences, but does not force. We thus define power to include any means of intentionally influencing people short of physically forcing them to comply with one's wishes.[3]

The matter is confusing because nonviolent forms of influence may be so compelling that they seem to constitute a kind of force. The power of wealth, for instance, when used to influence the actions of the desperately poor, may prove virtually irresistible. The power of authority, when unquestioned, may be overwhelming. Of course, intimidation, in the form of a coercive threat, explicitly flirts with force. If these forms of power can be so compelling, one might ask, then why should the compulsion of actual force not also be considered a form of power? The answer is straightforward. Adopting the understanding that power is distinct from force allows one to define politics in terms of power while discriminating between regimes that are more or less political in nature.

Power, rather than force, is wielded if the object of influence retains the potential for resistance or refusal, effectively exercising an opposing form of power. Power does not destroy or deny the freedom of the individual over whom it is exercised, though power may and often does make the exercise of freedom more difficult or dangerous. If I shackle someone to a wall to keep her from voting in an election, then I am not exerting a form of power. I am simply exerting force. The individual's potential for effective resistance has been destroyed and her freedom has been wholly denied. In contrast, if I persuade this person not to vote, arguing that her vote will not make any difference to the outcome of the election, then I have exercised power. Likewise, if I am a rich landowner to whom a peasant family is heavily indebted and I announce that it will greatly displease me were anyone to vote or otherwise participate in an upcoming election, then I am exercising the power of coercion. In this case, the peasants, unlike the person shackled to the wall, retain the option of ignoring my intimidating threat, casting their ballots in spite of it, and awaiting my hinted-at reprisals.

Admittedly, the line drawn between force and the power of coercion in this case is very thin and of little consolation to the intimidated individuals. If I persuade you to hand over your wallet by pointing a loaded gun at your head, you remain at liberty to retain your wallet (for the moment) and pay the consequences. But this seems to be splitting hairs. For all practical purposes, when the threat of violence is clear, immediate, and imminent, that is, when direct violence is almost certain to follow a threat, then we are justified in interpreting such a threat not as a form of coercive power but as an exercise of force. Once power gains enough coercive strength to deny all effective forms of resistance, as it may through the cultivation of intense fear, it effectively ceases to be power and becomes force. To be a form of power, influence must meet with some resistance. Power that effectively destroys all resistance, that is, power that denies freedom altogether, becomes sheer force

The task of distinguishing power from force is compounded because political rulers not only wield power but also exercise force. Thomas Hobbes, adopting the tough-minded orientation of political realism, insists that violence is the natural and ultimate expression of political power. His reason is that promulgation of the rules, regulations, and laws needed to order collective life does little in itself to secure the peace unless these rules, regulations, and laws are backed by the threat of force. Some form of punishment for lawbreakers and transgressors is necessary. Covenants without swords, Hobbes tersely remarks, are but words. In like fashion, the Florentine political theorist Niccolò Machiavelli (1469–1527), who along with Hobbes largely defines the modern realist tradition, maintains that good politics ensue from good laws. Yet he insists that "there cannot be good laws where there are not good arms." Machiavelli advises a ruler or prince to become feared by his subjects. Fear alone, however, does not adequately sustain political rule. Hence Machiavelli counsels the prince not only to cultivate respect by instilling fear but also to seek the love and avoid the hatred of his subjects whenever possible. This latter task is best achieved when the prince abides by his own laws.[4]

For better or worse, political rulers often employ force to back up their power. They also generally deny that option to others. Max Weber proposed that the modern state is best defined as that political entity having a monopoly on the legitimate use of violence or force. All modern states, and most other forms of national or imperial government throughout history, have claimed the exclusive prerogative to exercise force within their borders. This prerogative is justified as the means to secure internal peace. Most states also claim the prerogative to exercise force beyond their borders in order to defend against aggressors or to secure national interests.

Today, as in the past, most political power remains backed up by the force of arms. With the exception of pacifists, people generally consider the use of force by political rulers legitimate in principle, as a means to secure internal peace and defend against foreign threats. In practice, however, the use of force by government is usually subject to criticism or condemnation from some quarter, and often for good reason. Governmental abuse of the prerogative of force is an all too common affair. This is true not only in the waging of war or the commission of other acts of aggression against foreign governments and people. Deadly force and violence is often wielded by states within their own borders, against their own citizens. In fact, governments in the past century have killed over three times the number of their own citizens (for political reasons, that is, excluding nonpolitical, criminal executions) than they have killed foreigners in war.[5] Violence and political power are certainly no strangers.

Force, Hobbes and Machiavelli declared, was necessary to back up the rule of law. The power to legislate rests on the power to coerce. While we might deplore its abuses, the threat of force remains an intrinsic part of political life. It has even been suggested that political theories that do not take into account the need for force are not *political* theories at all. Political scientist Robert Dahl, for instance, criticizes anarchists for this reason. In their effort to safeguard the independence and autonomy of individuals, anarchists argue that all coercion within the political realm is illegitimate. They consequently advocate the abolition of government. Dahl understands this as an abolition of politics as well, and an abolition of the need for political theory.

The word *anarchism* first appeared during the French Revolution. It was employed to characterize those who opposed the heavy-handed rule of the Jacobins and advocated the formation of communes. The French social theorist Pierre Proudhon (1809–65) revived the term in

1840, though most of his followers preferred to describe themselves as "mutualists." By the early 1870s, while struggling with the followers of Karl Marx for the heart and soul of the First International Working-man's Association, the Russian thinker and activist Mikhail Bakunin (1814–76) and his followers proudly embraced the term anarchism and developed its principles.

Much in keeping with the ideas of Proudhon and Bakunin, the well-known American anarchist Emma Goldman (1869–1940) defined anarchism as "the philosophy of a new social order based on liberty unrestricted by man-made law; the theory that all forms of government rest on violence and are therefore wrong and harmful, as well as unnecessary."[6] Anarchy literally means the absence of rule. It is based on the utopian hope that in the absence of rulers, people will still lead peaceable social lives. These lives would be blessed with greater freedom and happiness than could be got through the institution of a coercive government.

According to Dahl, the denial of the legitimacy of law and force makes "anarchism ... not so much a *political* philosophy as a *moral* doctrine."[7] Dahl is effectively accepting Weber's famous distinction between the "ethic of responsibility" that is appropriate for political affairs and the "ethic of ultimate ends" that pertains to matters of conscience. The ethic of ultimate ends holds that good intentions are of paramount concern in judging the rightness of actions and that the unintended ramifications of good actions may be ignored. The ethic of responsibility, in contrast, gives an account of and takes responsibility for the "foreseeable results of one's action." The ethic of responsibility also regretfully accepts the fact that, to achieve good ends, "one must be willing to pay the price of using morally dubious means or at least dangerous ones."[8] The use of force is considered by Dahl and Weber the dangerous but necessary means to protect civil rights and social order. The option of employing force is part of an ethic of responsibility, and such an ethic is intrinsic to political life.

To insist that a theory of politics cannot ignore the need for force to back up the rule of law is not to say that politics amounts to the rule of the strong and the law of the jungle. Force and violence should not be equated with politics. Nonetheless, force and violence effectively mark out the boundaries of the political realm. In other words, politics (and power) ends where force and violence begin. Yet most forms of political life—certainly all national forms—would never arise and could not persist unless the threat of force was at hand. We arrive at a complex but consistent principle. A theory that wholly denies the legitimacy of the threat or use of force ceases to be a political theory. At the same time, a practice wholly defined by the threat or use of force ceases to be a political practice.

Hobbes considered the use of violence by rulers legitimate because everybody had an interest in internal peace and external security. This peace and security could not be assured without a Leviathan threatening the use of force and occasionally employing it. For Hobbes, the ruler can be said to rule in the public interest simply by meeting the minimum requirement of preventing a war of all against all. Consequently, Hobbes argues that the sovereign can never be justly punished in any way for any acts he commits. He cannot commit injustice or unjustly injure his subjects. In becoming sovereign ruler he gains the right and authority to do whatever he wills.

In creating the Leviathan, Hobbes maintains, each subject explicitly states: "*I Authorise and give up my Right of Governing my selfe to this Man.*" This act of submission, carried out simultaneously by all, unites the multitude of actors milling about the state of nature into a single commonwealth. The Leviathan is considered a *"Mortall God"* to whom its subjects owe their lives and allegiance.[9] King James I of England (1566-1625) took this sort of claim quite seriously, though he had a religious, as opposed to pragmatic, Hobbesian justification for his own despotic reign. If confronted by unjust and tyrannical rule, James states, "the people may do no other than flee unresistingly from the anger of its king; its tears and sighs are the only answer to him allowed it, and it may summon none but God to its aid."[10] A king has a divine right to rule, James was saying. This rule is absolute and should meet with no resistance whatsoever.

Few people today accept James's legitimation of absolute monarchy on religious grounds. Most would also argue that Hobbes's legitimation of sovereign power and violence goes too far and that his understanding of common interests or the public good is too narrow. Ruling for the public good requires more than the mere prevention of anarchy or war. Establishing basic order is a necessary condition for good government, but it is not a sufficient condition.

Tyrannies may be very orderly states, but they are not very political ones. That is because tyranny is a form of rule grounded in violence rather than power.[11] Tyrants rule by force. They deny their subjects any sort of meaningful resistance short of armed revolt. The difference between tyranny and more political forms of rule is that tyranny denies people the opportunity to influence the organization and regulation of collective life. In short, tyrants do not acknowledge their subjects as individuals capable of exercising power for the public good. The tension between the individual and the community that is the essence of politics is absent in tyrannies because the basic freedom of the individual is denied.

Just as force is seldom if ever wholly absent from political rule, so politics is seldom if ever wholly absent from rule by force. Politics is diminished whenever force is routinely substituted for power as the means of regulating collective life. Yet even in the most despotic regime, power is generally still exercised through the influence of wealth, eloquence, authority, prestige, tradition, or intimidation. Tyrannies remain political regimes to a certain degree. Even in the case of an absolute tyranny, where force and violence, rather than power and compliance, best characterize the relation of the ruler to the public, the relation of the ruler to his small coterie of advisers, bodyguards, and elite backers generally remains political in large degree. Power, not force, for example, typically holds violent oppressors together as a group, whether this group is a street gang or an authoritarian government. Thus politics percolates through even the most violent forms of rule. Perhaps only in such places of pure violence as concentration camps is the opportunity for politics completely extinguished.

While order might be established and maintained through force alone, other aspects of the public good, such as individual freedom, can be established and maintained only through the exercise of power. Too much freedom leads to anarchy. Too much order leads to tyranny. What the correct balance between order and freedom should be is the topic of ongoing political debate. Different forms of political rule offer more order or more freedom, depending on their nature. Baron de Montesquieu (1689–1755), a French political philosopher, argued that monarchical states place more value on order, while republican states place more value on freedom. Similarly, Plato argued that democracy raises the pursuit of freedom to its greatest level and enshrines it as its first principle. By Plato's reckoning, however, democracy's infatuation with freedom leads to intolerable breakdowns in social order. Plato prefers the monarchical rule of philosopher kings.

The Nature of Political Power

To exercise power is not necessarily to secure one's interests at the expense of others. Nor does one's exercise of power always constitute a threat or diminution of another's power. Many theorists, including Hobbes and Weber, assume that the exercise of power is a "zero-sum game." They believe that any increase in the power held by one person means a decrease in power held by another, with the net sum always being zero. Other political theorists, such as Hannah Arendt, insist that cooperative activity—acting in concert—constitutes an exercise of power wherein influence is reciprocally exercised and interests are mutually served. As social order is established, mutual influence grows, and so does power. While this growth of power is seldom shared in an wholly egalitarian manner, it certainly need not be zero-sum. Cooperation begets a positive-sum game of power.

If cooperation ceases to be a form of mutual accommodation and becomes instead a complete convergence of interests and ideas, then the exercise of power stops. That is to say, power that encounters no resistance whatsoever ceases to remain power. In the complete absence of resistance, where all intentions and desires literally converge, influence becomes unnecessary, and in the absence of influence, power disappears. A state of harmony exists instead.

Such harmony between individuals seldom arises and never endures. In the political realm, which is defined by its plurality of unique individuals, the full convergence of interests never arises. Even within particular social classes, political parties, or special-interest groups, ideas, opinions, and concerns vary. Collective harmony may well be impossible for humans. Perhaps it is occasionally achieved between musicians playing in concert, or between lovers engulfed in mutual desire. It is never fully achieved between citizens. Indeed, even musicians achieve their harmonic interaction only by following the authoritative lead of a conductor who interprets the music in particular ways and shapes their playing to accommodate this interpretation. And romantically entwined couples face the inevitability of "lovers' quarrels," which painfully demonstrate that interests, understandings, and ideas can only be temporarily unified.

Whenever we adjust our attitudes, beliefs, or actions owing to the intentional influence of others, even when this adjustment may serve our own interests or purposes, the exercise of power has occurred. The exercise of power is seldom if ever wholly mutual, and interests are seldom equally served. Most people provide for their own interests—or the interests of their kith and kin—first and foremost. In a world of scarce resources, this primary concern for self-interest breeds competition and conflict.

Conflict is inherent to politics. But so is cooperation. Indeed, politics might be defined as the task of mustering cooperation and mitigating conflict in collective life. For this reason, politics has been called the art of compromise. The political animal accepts limitations to conflict in order to avert violence. Likewise, the political animal makes concessions and adjustments in order to achieve cooperation in the absence of

harmony. The means employed by political animals to muster cooperation and mitigate conflict is the exercise of power.

Power is the capacity to influence people to pursue particular objectives or adopt particular norms. It follows that power is not just any
form of influence. I have not exercised power if I get hit by a truck
while running across a busy street and my (bad) example influences a
fellow pedestrian to wait for the green light before crossing. My affect-
ing the actions and redirecting the intentions of another person is evident. But my influence was unintentional. Yet a parent who demands of
her child never to run across a busy street, and in so doing influences
her child's behavior, is indeed exercising a form of power. We might
say, then, that power is the capacity to influence people according to
some design.

To influence someone means to get someone to do something that
she would not otherwise do. I am not exercising power, for instance, if
I stand in front of the gymnasium and suggest to people entering that
they engage in some form of physical activity. That was already their
intent. I have not affected their behavior. Then again, I might persuade
my colleagues to join me in a game of basketball by extolling the virtues of the sport. Regardless of whether they enjoy the game or
not—even if they enjoy it and benefit from it more than I do—I have
exerted some form of power over them. Without my asking, they
would not have played at all.

Politics is about power and power is about influence. Whenever
you have people in contact with each other, the exchange of influence
arises. Hence politics is pervasive to the extent that we share a collective existence. In our collective lives we inevitably adjust and react to
each other's needs, requests, and demands. Not all forms of influence,
however, constitute exercises of power—unintentional influences do not
count. Likewise, not all exercises of power are political—power that
does not affect our public life is not political. Indeed, a good portion of
political power is devoted to the effort to ensure that other forms of
power, such as that exercised by religious leaders, do not exceed the appropriate boundaries of private life. Only power can limit power, and
political power is constantly involved in determining and reestablishing
the appropriate limits of nonpolitical forms of power. Nonpolitical
power, in turn, is constantly testing these limits and frequently trans-
gressing them. This means that almost any intentional exercise of influence can be considered political to some degree whenever it establishes,
affirms, tests, or transgresses the boundaries of public life.

In the end, the difference between power that is political and power
that is not political is less a difference in kind than a difference in

degree. Even such private affairs as parent-child relationships are marginally political. They are political, first, because the privacy of the relationship itself is politically maintained. They are political, second, because the effects of private power are almost always of some public concern. To return to our example: the parent demanding caution from the child crossing the street is instilling values of respect both for (parental) authority and the (traffic) law. This fostering of respect for authority and law impinges on the larger realm of politics. One might also suggest that public safety is inherently political. The collision of a child with an automobile may cause other accidents, involving other motorists. It would also bring into service the police and certain medical professionals or institutions that are maintained at public expense.

Indeed, if the costs of health care are even partially born by the state, then on this ground alone anything we do to endanger our health becomes a political issue. In the United States, one-third of the medical costs of tending to motor vehicle injuries is paid by taxpayers.[12] This fact has been used to justify the promulgation of seat-belt and motorcycle helmet laws, which restrict one's freedom to act in a way that seemingly endangers only oneself. Likewise, our use of public highways or schools or any other part of the infrastructure provided by the modern state, just as our having a job and hence contributing to the state's coffers through taxation, is a political affair.

The process of expanding the realm of politics to include almost any action that involves or has the potential to involve public institutions, public services, or other citizens underlines the complex interplay of our social relations. At the same time, this conceptual expansion of the realm of politics has a cost. If everything we do may be considered equally political, the word "politics" ceases to do any useful work. There is nothing to distinguish political phenomena from any other activities or events. Politics ceases to mean more than something of human concern. It is of utmost importance, therefore, to discriminate between things that are more and less political. Hence we must discriminate between different forms of power.

The Public Realm and the Private Realm

Politics is about how the power employed to order collective life is accumulated, exercised, and distributed. Most generally put, we may say that politics is about power that is primarily public rather than private in its exercise and in its ends.

The word "private" does not refer only to personal or familial affairs. Many interactions and transactions that take place outside the walls of our homes and involve large numbers of strangers are in fact predominantly private affairs. Most business transactions and religious ceremonies, for instance, are private in the same sense that most family discussions are private: none primarily involves or concerns the public as a whole. Less political than the building of a city hall or a mass transit system, then, is a business transaction to form a private club or construct a private dwelling. Here again, the distinction between ends that are private and ends that are public, while evident in theory, may prove ambiguous in practice. The public, for instance, has legitimate concerns about the zoning permits, building codes, and tax assessments for private dwellings.

The same argument holds for all other business engagements and even for household management. The energy consumed, the air or water pollution created, and the trash generated by the very act of living our lives or doing business in the modern world have become legitimate issues of public concern. Only the inhabiting of a cave by a hermit in an unpopulated hinterland might remain wholly beyond political concern, assuming that the hermit left no dependents at home to become wards of the state and did not disturb the wildlife of the region that other humans valued. In an increasingly populated and ecologically precarious world, few activities or affairs do not in some way affect the lives of others. The general rule of thumb is the more an activity or affair reflects, addresses, or impinges on the collective existence of the citizenry as a whole, the more political it is. The more public the exercise or ends of power, the more that power is political.

An example of power that is wholly public in its exercise is an open debate. Here anyone may participate in the processes of influencing and persuading people to adopt a certain agenda, proposal, or point of view. This form of power—rational persuasion in open discussion—is eminently public in its form. An example of power that is eminently public in its ends would be the effort of citizens to establish a law, build a city hall, create a mass transit system, or gather a volunteer fire brigade. This form of power, oriented to the use or creation of civic institutions or law, is wholly public in its content. Its substantive product—the newly established law, city hall, mass transit system, or volunteer fire brigade—will serve the needs not of particular individuals but of the community as a whole.

In the example of open debate, the public nature of power is most evident in the form of influence. In the example of the creation of laws or civic institutions, the public nature of power is most evident in the content of influence. The most political event of all, one might then suggest, is one that evidences the public use of power in its form as well as its content. An example might be an open, public debate designed to institute a law or decide whether and how to create an institution to serve the public good.

Less political, by this definition, would be any effort to have some sort of institution created without public means of influence. Public influence need not take the form of open debate. Decisions may be made by elected representatives. Public influence may not even entail debate by elected representatives. A very attenuated form of public influence is evident simply through the public's compliance (or noncompliance) with laws. To act in accordance with the laws or the constitution of a state is, in some minimal sense, to participate in politics. In effect, one is influencing the lawmakers and upholders of the constitution to carry on business as usual. When laws or constitutions are too frequently ignored, disobeyed, or subverted, rulers must respond in some way, either by changing the laws or constitution, engaging in greater public education, or enforcing the laws or constitution more strictly or repressively.

Compliance or submission to laws, then, remains a mitigated form of the public exercise of power. It is, of course, not a particularly democratic form of political participation, but it is not, for that reason, insignificant. The English philosopher and political theorist John Locke (1632–1704) suggested that citizens "consent" to their rulers and become obligated to their governments simply by inhabiting the territory they do, by using its roads, and observing its laws. Passive public compliance is not to be equated with subjection to violence. At the point where compliance with laws or submission to rule is achieved through brute force alone or the cultivation of intense fear with little or no potential for public resistance or refusal, we are justified in saying that public power and hence politics has ebbed to the point of nonexistence.

The more public the exercise and ends of power, the more political the form of rule. Tyranny, the violent and arbitrary rule of a single individual, is therefore a less political form of rule than is monarchy (the rule of a king or queen), aristocracy, or oligarchy (the rule of a select few), and democracy (the rule of the people as a whole). This statement is true for two reasons. First, as Aristotle observed, what distinguishes the king from the tyrant or despot is that the tyrant rules only in his own interest, while the king has the public good in mind. The king's serving the public good makes monarchical rule at least minimally political in its ends. Second, as ancient Greek thinkers also maintained, the king, unlike the tyrant, is expected to consult with his subjects, or at least their representative leaders and elite members. He is not meant to rule arbitrarily. The king's solicitation and heeding of public opinion makes monarchical rule at least minimally political in its exercise.

What differentiates the monarch from the tyrant, then, is that the latter's rule is based solely on his subjects' surrender to force, while the former's rule, though also absolute, is based on his subjects' compliance with power. Of course, a king or autocrat, like any other political ruler, may only deceive the public into believing that he rules in their interest, all the while filling his own coffers. Yet even such deception constitutes a mitigated form of politics. By succeeding in his deception, the political ruler escapes the need to rule by violence alone. Political power is by no means always benign or good. Nonetheless, political power is always distinguishable from sheer force and hence is susceptible to public influence and solicitous of public compliance or approval.

The aim of tyrannical rule, political theorist Bernard Crick writes, is "to prevent the formation of a 'public.' For palace politics is private politics, almost a contradiction in terms. The unique character of political activity lies, quite literally, in its publicity."[13] Indeed, the word *politics* derives from the Greek *politica,* which means that pertaining to the *polis,* or city-state. To be political is to be of concern to the public citizen, or *polites.* When the Romans translated the works of Greek political theorists, they settled on the words *res publica,* or republic, to denote the political realm. The *res publica* literally means the "public thing" or "public affair." Likewise, the word *commonwealth,* often considered synonymous with republic, refers to that which pertains to the public good or, in Old English, the *common weal.*

There is a great irony in today's pejorative use of the word politics. Presidents and legislators often speak of the need to end "politics as usual." Likewise, citizens derisively characterize the actions of politicians as serving "political interests," by which they mean either the private interests of a few colluding individuals or narrow partisan interests. These deprecatory uses of "politics" and "political" represent a complete reversal of the etymological meaning of the terms. Rather than suggest a concern for the public good as a whole, "politics" and "political" are employed to suggest a complete lack of such concern. This reversal of meanings has a long history. Abraham Lincoln already observed in 1837 that politicians were thought of as "a set of men who have interests aside from the interests of the people, and who, to say the most of them, are, taken as a mass, at least one long step removed from honest men."[14] At the turn of this century politics was wittily defined as "a strife of interests masquerading as a contest of principles. The conduct of public affairs for private advantage."[15] This pejorative connotation has gained the upper hand in common parlance today and will likely persist as long as the pursuit of individual power, narrow partisan interests, and wealth dominate the political process.

Karl von Clausewitz (1780–1831), a Prussian military strategist and historian, once defined war as politics carried out by other means. In today's market-oriented society, politics is too often understood, and too often practiced, as private business carried out by other means. Thus politics is understood to pertain to the clash of private interests, rather than the development of public interests. Despite common usage, we may nonetheless maintain that politics is diminished whenever action, even if engaged by a group of individuals after much public debate, is oriented not to public concerns but to private ones.

The definition of politics as the public pursuit of the public good is grounded in the assumption that the individuality of those who speak and act in pursuit of the public good has not be quashed. That is to say, political speech and action is always the speech and action of *individuals*. While these individuals speak and act (or pretend to do so) with the public interest in mind, they do so from distinct perspectives. A public that ceases to be a community of individuals ceases to be a public. It becomes instead a mass or mob. Political life is not herd life —that is what makes humans different from other social animals. Political life is the public life of distinct individuals. Collective action that wholly eclipses the expressions or concerns of unique individuals is no longer truly political action.

Now, let us get back to the problem posed earlier. How do we decide whether a legislative session is more political than a classroom debate or a basketball game? By the criteria discussed above, we would have to say that the more political event is that which proved more open to the influence of the public (either directly, through elected representatives, or through compliance) and was more concerned with matters pertaining to the public at large. In most cases, legislative sessions would come out on top. Yet politics does not happen only in state capitals, and we should not restrict our understanding of political life to the selection of government officials or the influencing of governmental decisions. Campaigning, lobbying, voting, passing bills, and making laws predominate in our common understanding of politics, and many political scientists limit their understanding of politics to such activities.[16] Nevertheless, politics is about a great deal more.

The politics of classroom debate, for example, is real enough, and need not be insignificant. A classroom debate in political theory that affects the way its participants carry out their lives outside the classroom is certainly of political import. The debates that Socrates carried out with his students were considered of such political significance by his fellow Athenians as to warrant a criminal prosecution. Even the study of evolutionary biology or genetics might be considered political if it alters the mores that structure collective existence. In short, anything that affects the way people think about and order their' public lives is political in some degree.

Bernard Crick writes that "the attempt to politicize everything is the destruction of politics. When everything is seen as relevant to politics, then politics has in fact become totalitarian.... To ensure that there be politics at all, there must be some things at least which are irrelevant to politics."[17] Yet Crick goes on to admit that while politics cannot and should not embrace everything, nonetheless "nothing can be exempted from politics entirely" and that what can be considered political "is wider than is sometimes supposed."[18] The Italian political theorist Antonio Gramsci (1891–1937) had an even more expansive understanding of politics in mind when he asked: "Is not science itself 'political activity' and political thought, in as much as it transforms men, and makes them different from what they were before?" At the same time, Gramsci also cautions that if politics can be found everywhere, it becomes all the more necessary to make distinctions between different levels or degrees of political activity. In the absence of such distinctions, Gramsci observes, our discussions would lapse "into a wearisome and tautological catalogue of platitudes."[19]

Hard-and-fast definitions of politics have their place. Yet it is in the finer distinctions that political theory makes its mark. Navigating the extensive yet uneven terrain of political life entails the exercise of discerning theoretical judgment.

Suggested Readings

Hannah Arendt. *The Human Condition*
Aristotle. *Politics*
Michael Bakunin. *Bakunin on Anarchism*
Bernard Crick. *In Defense of Politics*
Robert Dahl. *Democracy and Its Critics*
Antonio Gramsci. *Selections from the Prison Notebooks*
Alexander Hamilton, James Madison, and John Jay. *The Federalist Papers*
Friedrich Hayek. *The Road to Serfdom*
G.W.F. Hegel. *Hegel's Philosophy of Right*
Thomas Hobbes. *Leviathan*
John Locke. *Two Treatises of Government* and *A Letter Concerning Toleration*
Steven Lukes. *Power: A Radical View*
Niccolò Machiavelli. *The Prince* and *Discourses*
Alexis de Tocqueville. *Democracy in America*

4

Modernity and Postmodernity

olitical theory is anything but predictable today: its objects of study are multiple, its methods are varied, and its orientations are manifold. Within the tradition of political theory, many distinct and opposing conceptual, methodological and ideological "camps" vie for position. These divisions are inevitable among creative thinkers. They often prove fertile grounds for theorizing, though frequently they stifle original thought by means of false dichotomies and rigid barriers. One of the most fertile and troubling divisions today is that between *modern* and *postmodern* theory. In this chapter we investigate the division between the modern and the postmodern and explore the benefits of crossing borders.

Modernity arose out of the Renaissance, the Protestant Reformation, and the Scientific Revolution, events of the fourteenth to seventeenth centuries that marked a radical transformation of the artistic and literary world, the religious world, and the world of inquiry and knowledge respectively. These three events intermingled to produce a widespread and thorough challenge to tradition and authority. They marked a vibrant assertion of the growing power of the human mind.

The word *modern* refers to that which is at present or recently in existence. A *modernist,* by this definition, is someone who prefers the new-fashioned to the old-fashioned. The term modernist was first used with this connotation in the sixteenth century. It referred, often pejoratively, to someone who spurned tradition and advocated either new techniques of scientific inquiry or the study and use of vernacular or contemporary languages rather than classical Greek or Latin. Modernism stood in contrast to traditionalism, which signaled a tendency to adhere to methods of inquiry, orientations, and languages that had been handed down from ancient and medieval times.

The term modernist may never actually have been used in his own day to describe the Italian astronomer, mathematician, and physicist Galileo Galilei (1564–1642). Nonetheless, we may view this key figure of the Scientific Revolution as embodying the central features of modernism. Galileo abandoned traditional standards of inquiry and authority. He took exception to Aristotle, who until that time had stood as the chief authority in matters of science no less than in matters of philosophy. Against Aristotle, for instance, Galileo insisted that bodies do not fall with velocities proportional to their weights. He dropped different weights from the tower of Pisa to prove it. Galileo also accepted the theory of the Polish astronomer Nicolaus Copernicus (1473–1543) that the earth was not the center of the solar system but revolved around the sun. In 1633, Galileo was brought to Rome and forced to renounce this belief, which contradicted the accepted Ptolemaic (earth-centric) view as well as the teachings of Catholicism. The church's effort to force Galileo to recant his belief might be seen as the first attempt by the forces of tradition to stifle the nascent forces of modernism. While the traditionalists won the battle—Galileo regretfully recanted—they would lose the war. The tide of modernism proved unstoppable.

Copernicus developed his heliocentric theory, which held that the earth revolved around the sun, on the basis of an extensive reexamination of ancient astronomical charts. Though eventually banned, Copernicus's thesis was initially unopposed by the Catholic church, perhaps because it was a highly theoretical piece of work that did not seem likely to gain widespread support. Galileo, however, made the "Copernican revolution" come to life. In 1632, he published a defense of the heliocentric theory based on hard empirical evidence, namely, the numerous observations he had made through a device of his own construction, the astronomical telescope.

Modernism largely developed in the Western world owing to the growing power of science. This was a new, empirical science, no longer grounded in the metaphysical musings of ancient authorities or in the authority of religious creed. "I think in the discussion of natural problems," Galileo wrote, "we ought to begin not with the Scriptures, but with experiments, and demonstrations." From this point on, nothing was to be taken for granted or accepted on the basis of faith or authority. Everything was to be validated through reason and grounded in repeated observations of experimental investigations of the concrete, physical world. As Albert Einstein wrote, the leitmotif of Galileo's work was "the passionate fight against any kind of dogma based on authority."[1] In the midst of this fight, modern science was born.

Francis Bacon (1561–1626), an English philosopher contemporary

with Galileo, stated that "ancient times were the youth of the world."
He believed that there was much growing up to be done. Bacon wrote
the *Novum Organum,* or New Logic. This work was meant to supersede the old logic developed by Aristotle, who had composed a work
called the *Organum.* Bacon's new logic was also meant to supersede the
metaphysical speculation that developed within the medieval theologi-
cal philosophy of scholasticism. Scholasticism aimed to complement
and strengthen faith in the Christian God with a good dose of Aristotelian logic. In proposing a new form of logic to guide inquiry, Bacon
challenged both the authority of Aristotle as well as the relevance of religious faith. Bacon's new logic was based on induction, the process of
reasoning from the particular to the general, from particular observations of the natural world, for instance, to the general laws to which
nature conforms. It stood in contrast to the ancient logical methods
mostly based on deduction, which argue from the general to the particular, from cosmological principles, for example, to particular moral im-
peratives.

Voltaire (1694–1778), the French philosopher and man of letters,
spoke for many in calling Francis Bacon the "father of experimental
philosophy."[2] Indeed, Bacon's work on induction was particularly well
suited to the emerging empirical sciences. Rather than start from a general principle, which was often theologically grounded and based on
the idealistic, metaphysical speculations of ancient authorities, Bacon
suggested starting with numerous concrete observations of the real
world. These observations would allow the scientist to discern patterns
or regularities in the workings of nature. On the basis of these observed
regularities, the scientist could then form hypotheses and theories that
described the general laws of nature. These natural laws were held to
function in strict accord with logic and remain wholly independent of
deities. The scientists' theories were objectively verifiable. They could
be tested and refined by repeated observation and experimentation. Nature can be commanded, Bacon wrote, only by obeying her laws.
Learning nature's laws was the first step to mastering her. Mastering
nature became a central goal for the modernists.

The movements of heavenly bodies were discovered by Copernicus,
empirically validated by Galileo, theoretically refined by Johannes Kep-
ler (1571–1630), who calculated the mathematics of planetary motion,
and effectively explained by Isaac Newton (1642–1727), who outlined
the role of the universal force of gravity. The Scientific Revolution inaugurated by these men not only yielded insight into astronomy. It also
demonstrated that the laws of physics applied to objects on the earth.
Building on the work of the French philosopher René Descartes

(1596–1650), scientists described the world in language that would have been foreign to medieval thinkers. It was proposed to operate solely by means of mechanical forces that acted causally on material objects. These forces could be rationally deduced, empirically measured, and expressed in mathematical terms. God, theologists, and the metaphysical philosophers had little to say or do in this modern world. The book of nature was written in the language of mathematics, Galileo said, and scientists had usurped the task of reading it.

Modernism was grounded in the assumption that the order of the universe is natural, accessible to reason and observation, and describable in impersonal, materialistic, mechanical, and mathematical terms. Francis Bacon famously maintained that "knowledge itself is power," meaning that he who understands nature can control her. For the last four centuries, modernism has flourished in the wake of the power accumulated through scientific knowledge and technical engineering. With this in mind, we might say that the first characteristic of modernity is *scientism*, that is, a belief in the preeminent power and prerogatives of science.

The modern celebration of science actually had scholastic roots. The scholastics relied on Aristotle, who, unlike. Plato, attempted to combine rational inquiry with empirical investigation of the natural world. Modernists were receptive to the empirical orientation of Aristotle. Scholasticism took Aristotle as an authority, however, and was preoccupied with logical, deductive argument and its relationship to religious faith. Modernists rejected ancient authority. Moreover, modernists advocated a humanistic orientation that was opposed to the theocentric or God-centered orientation of the scholastics.

This "secular" humanism was a legacy of the Renaissance, a period that broadly marks the transition from the Middle Ages to modernity. The Renaissance, which literally means "rebirth," began in the fourteenth century as a rediscovery of the humanistic orientation of the Greeks and Romans. These ancient people were greatly admired for their celebration of human beauty, intelligence, and individual greatness. In its modern form, humanism became increasingly individualistic and voluntaristic, valuing the power of the human mind and will and the autonomy of the individual above all. These values stood in marked contrast to the traditionalism and humility advocated by the medieval church, which roundly condemned the sinfulness of human pride and was suspicious of human ingenuity.

The Renaissance reached its peak in Galileo's and Bacon's time. By then the privileged throne of humankind at the center of God's creation, like the privileged position of the earth at the center of the solar system, was crumbling. Yet humanism could maintain its celebration of human values and the human spirit because it aimed to unlock the secrets of the universe through human ingenuity, that is to say, through science and reason. Humankind was also gaining the power to control more and more of its world through the development of technology. At this time America had recently been "discovered" by Europeans, the globe was being circumnavigated, and the human mind, it was assumed, was just beginning to exercise its full potential. This age was unique, the famous French historian Jules Michelet (1798-1874) reflected, in achieving both the "discovery of the world" and the "discovery of man." The second central characteristic of modernity, then, is its humanism. Modernists celebrate humanity as the master of its world.

This brings us to the final key characteristic of modernity. In addition to its scientism and humanism, modernity is inherently progressivist. To be progressivist is to believe that the world is constantly changing for the better. Modernists assume that such steady improvement can be sustained owing to the continual advances made though the power of the human mind. Minimally, modernists believe that there will always be progress in the accumulation of knowledge and in the capacity to better our material conditions through technology. As Descartes writes, if humankind puts its "long chains of reasoning" to work in a methodical, empirical fashion then "there can be nothing so remote that we cannot reach to it, nor so recondite that we cannot discover it." In this way we can "render ourselves the masters and possessors of nature."[3] Particularly since the Enlightenment, which was at its heyday in the eighteenth century, the modernist celebration of reason took a new turn. Rational capacities were increasingly applied not only to the conquest of the natural world but also to the control of the social and political world, duplicating in culture the mastery achieved over nature. Modernists suggested that humanity's moral stature, not simply its material condition, was undergoing or could undergo constant improvement.

Such progressivism found one of its more extreme statements in the work of the Marquis de Condorcet (1743-94), a French philosopher who wrote a work entitled *Sketch for a Historical Picture of the Progress of the Human Mind*. Condorcet traced the development of humanity through nine epochs and predicted a tenth in which the "indefinite" perfectibility of the human race would become irreversible. Most modernists do not share Condorcet's utopian hopes for humanity's moral and intellectual perfection. Still, modernists share in the belief that humanity can steadily progress in its overall development. Like Condorcet, they attribute this potential for progress to the character of the human mind and will. Modernity effectively exchanged scholasticism's faith in God for a faith in humanity. Its progressivism is grounded in the belief that rational and scientific inquiry, the ever-growing power of technology, and moral evolution will steadily improve the lot of humankind.

Individualist Theories of Politics

Our definitions and conceptualizations of politics and power in the previous chapter proved quite useful, allowing us not only to speak about the nature of politics but also about the different degrees to which particular activities or affairs can be considered political. The working definition of politics that we employed—an exercise of power that influences people to pursue particular objectives or adopt particular norms that direct or order their collective lives—is held by many contemporary political theorists and political scientists. Its key characteristics are its individualist and voluntarist orientations. These orientations are legacies of modernism's overarching concern with the power of human agency.

The standard understanding of power is individualistic because it takes the individual to be the key unit of analysis. The individual both exercises power and is the object of power's exercise. The standard understanding is also voluntarist because it assumes that the person exercising power is always engaged in a voluntary or willful act. As either the wielder or object of power, the individual is assumed to be an independent actor and autonomous moral agent with self-evident interests. The manner in which this relatively sovereign and atomic individual interacts or should interact with individuals around him, and how the political community comes to form and transform as a result of these interactions, become the foci of study for modern political theorists and scientists.

The individualist and voluntarist understanding of power is generally directed to three central concerns: (1) the nature and degree of power held by particular individuals (e.g., studies of presidents, prime ministers, other political leaders, or elites); (2) the nature of the political processes and institutions that distribute and manage the power held by individuals (e.g., studies of elections or of various branches of government); and (3) the moral and rational standards that the individual ought to apply to the exercise of power or to the resistance of power exercised by others (e.g., studies of civil rights and duties, the nature of justice and liberty, and other concerns of normative political theory). The common feature of these otherwise distinct fields of investigation is that each focuses on individual actors as the autonomous wielders or resisters of power. Collective political existence, in turn, is viewed as the aggregated sum of the numerous relations of power in which individuals are engaged.

This individualist and voluntarist orientation is clearly evident in Hobbes. Hobbesian individuals willfully exercise power on each other to serve their interests in the state of nature. Owing to a common interest in security, they decide to give up their weapons and rights to a Leviathan, who then rules absolutely. Whether in an anarchical state of nature or in a society ruled by a despot, Hobbesian individuals intentionally wield power (in lesser or greater degree) as wholly autonomous agents.

Of course, the result of individualist and voluntarist theorizing need not be a Hobbesian form of politics. Indeed, the liberal tradition—from John Locke through contemporary champions of individual rights and freedoms—has taken a strong stand against the political absolutism promoted by Hobbes. As the work of many contemporary liberal theorists demonstrate, the perspective of the autonomous individual may be used to promote a democratic politics grounded in constitutionalism, limited government, and inalienable civil rights.

One of the more widely accepted individualist and voluntarist definitions of politics forms the title of Harold Lasswell's classic book, *Politics: Who Gets What, When, and How*.[4] Politics is about the power to decide who gets his interests served, according to what processes, and on whose timetable. It is about the struggle of particular individuals to secure their particular needs or wants. Lasswell is primarily concerned with the allocation of scarce resources because conflict over their pursuit is understood to be inevitable. Hence the governmental regulation of social interaction is also inevitable, lest violence and injustice rule the day. For Lasswell, politics is about the use of governmental power to regulate social interaction and allocate scarce resources. This understanding of politics is common among those who view power primarily in individualist and voluntarist terms.

This modern definition of politics has proven very useful for political theorists and scientists, allowing them to chart the exercise of power and argue for its appropriate limits. It often fosters elegant theorizing. Yet, like all theoretical perspectives, it is a limited view. Politics is not only about how individual needs become satisfied in a world of scarce resources. Politics also plays a role in determining how these needs are created in the first place, how they become articulated, and what sort of relationships form around them. Politics comes into play in the way we are influenced to perceive our particular needs as needs and in the way we are influenced to perceive our particular rights (to see these needs fulfilled) as rights. Politics precedes and exceeds the distribution of scarce resources and the pursuit of individual interests because it concerns the ways we define and understand our resources, our interests, our relationships, and ultimately ourselves as individuals.

Politics, in this sense, is not simply a process that concerns the decision of how to divvy up the pie. Politics also entails an ongoing debate and struggle over the way we become identified and identify ourselves as pie makers, pie cutters, and pie eaters. Political philosopher Alasdair MacIntyre argues that to answer the question "What ought I to do?" one must first answer the question "Who am I?"[5] What one wants and what one does is largely a product of who one understands oneself to be. Politics, it follows, is not only a question of doing what you do to get what you want but also a question of being and becoming who you are. Politics is not only a question of actions that serve particular interests but also a question of identities. Indeed, the key political question for *postmodern* theorists concerns the formation and contestation of identities.

To speak of identity in the abstract is problematic. People do not have abstract identities. They have particular identities that bear particular features. They are sons or daughters, mothers or fathers, students or teachers, artists, singers, or football players. Identities, moreover, are not one-dimensional, monolithic, or unchanging. They are multilayered, complex, and subject to development over time. Finally, identities necessarily coexist with difference, in the sense that one can "identify" oneself only by way of differentiating oneself from something or someone else. If one's identity is extremely unified, closed, and rigid, it is likely that this one-dimensional understanding of the self is achieved by maintaining an equally one-dimensional understanding of others. From a political perspective, then, the interesting point is not simply that we all have identities but that we are all constantly involved in negotiating which parts of our identities will be privileged and accentuated, which parts will be suppressed or ignored, and what sort of relationship our identities will form with difference.

Politics always pertains to two (related) questions. The first question is: What power does the individual (or group of individuals) exercise on others in its social environment in order to achieve its interests? This is the modernist concern. The second question is: What power does the social environment exercise on the individual (or group of individuals) to construct its identity? This is the postmodernist concern. Both sorts of questions are worth asking. Indeed, they are probably most fruitful when asked together.

The modern (individualist and voluntarist) orientation to politics assumes that the individual willfully exercises power as an independent agent with an unchanging nature and relatively stable, enduring, and freely chosen interests. The postmodern orientation assumes that individual and collective identities are formed over time within a social context and that individual and collective interests are largely derived from these identities. In this latter case, power is exercised not wholly or even primarily by individuals on their social environment, but by the social environment as a whole, or by some subsection of it, on individuals.

Structuralist Theories of Politics

One might think of the power of the social environment as related to, but broader than, the power of custom or tradition. The concern here is not simply the power of an individual who utilizes tradition or customary practices to achieve his particular goals. Instead, the concern is with the power exerted by the social environment itself, by the panoply of its traditions, customs, practices, and institutions as a whole. These traditions, customs, practices, and institutions are collectively known as *social structures*. Social structures influence the way we understand ourselves and our world, but they remain without specific authors and agents. Those who adopt a concern with the power of social structures—in distinction to those individualist and voluntarist theorists who emphasize the power of human agency—are known as *structuralists*. Structuralists paved the way for postmodern theorists.

Those who reject structuralism and adopt the modern individualist and voluntarist orientation are often known as *methodological individualists*. For methodological individualists, the whole is defined by adding up its parts. Their methodology for analyzing political life is based on the assumption that society may be explained by aggregating the actions and relationships of individuals. A key characteristic of structuralism, in contrast, is the belief that the whole is greater than the sum of its parts. A central tenet of structuralism is that society is more than an aggregate of individuals. Social structures have qualities or features that are not reducible to the sum of similar qualities or features held singly by its constituents or participants. But how can a collectivity gain a quality or feature that is absent in the individuals who make it up? How can society have a life of its own, so to speak, apart from the various comings and goings of the individuals that compose it? Émile Durkheim (1858–1917), the French sociologist, believed that society did indeed have a life of its own. His work inaugurated the structuralist perspective.

Durkheim explained the nature of society by way of a biological metaphor. He writes:

> The living cell contains nothing but mineral particles, as society contains nothing but individuals; and yet it is patently impossible for the phenomena characteristic of life to reside in the atoms of hydrogen, oxygen, carbon and nitrogen.... Let us apply this principle to sociology. If, as we may say, this synthesis *sui generis* which every society constitutes, yields new phenomena, differing from those which take place in individual minds, we must, indeed, admit that these facts reside in the very society itself which produces them, and not in its parts, i.e., its members.[6]

In one bowl, we have a fish swimming in water. In another bowl, we have a small pile of minerals and other elements as well as gases suspended in water, the same types and amounts of minerals, elements and gases as are contained in the live fish in the other bowl. It is obvious in this case that the whole (live fish) is indeed greater—not only more complex but qualitatively different—than the sum of its parts (bits of minerals, other elements and gases). Gathering together an assortment of molecules, even if they are combined in precisely the right quantities, will not produce a living creature. The living creature has behaviors and capacities, like reproduction, that exceed what its constituent molecules are capable of on their own or in aggregate form. Yet, from the methodological individualist perspective, a living organism is simply a particular arrangement of individual molecules.

Applying this understanding to the study of society, Durkheim argues that social structures far exceed in power and scope the aggregated activities of the individual members that compose them. Social structures largely determine how individual members of a society behave and interact. They do so just as the physical constitution of a fish or any other living organism largely determines how the molecules that compose it will interact.

Durkheim's point is that we can say that society is made up of individuals only because the individual is first made by society. "Society does not find the bases on which it rests fully laid out in consciences; it puts them there itself," Durkheim insists. He goes on to state that "although society may be nothing without individuals, each of them is much more a product of society than he is its maker."[7] Social structures produce the observable regularities of the social world. These regularities are rigid in the sense that most individuals cannot alter them even though they are affected by them. As individuals, we cannot appreciably alter the rate of employment, income curves, matrimonial laws, levels of access to education, class, race and gender hierarchies, and hierarchies organized around age, power, wealth, and prestige. Yet as individuals we are affected by these structures. They influence our behavior and contribute to our identities.

Durkheim suggested that the way people think in primitive societies mimics the social order of their society. Individual cognitive systems and mental schemata are patterned upon the existing social structure of the group. This understanding has been extended to contemporary societies by Pierre Bourdieu, a renowned French sociologist. Bourdieu argues that individuals internalize as "mental dispositions" and "schemes of perception and thought" the organization of their external reality. The word Bourdieu uses for these dispositions and schemes is *habitus*. He uses the word *field* to describe a network of social arrangements that embody and distribute positions and relations of power. The mental structures composing one's habitus, then, are reflections of the social structures composing the fields in which one participates.

Habitus is an internalization of social fields much like the soccer player's repertoire of behavior reflects the constraints (rules and boundary markers) of the soccer field. Unlike the rules for the game of soccer, however, the rules of social fields are seldom explicit or codified. They are learned, mostly without effort or intent, simply by living in a complex network of social relations. In this sense, social fields or social structures are analogous to the human unconscious. There is only indirect evidence for their existence. They are known primarily by their effects, that is to say, by the way that they pattern behavior.

Social structures may be thought of as particular arrangements of social relations that elicit certain other relations or actions from social members. Following Durkheim, Bourdieu insists that these structural configurations are *sui generis,* that is to say, they are unique entities unto themselves. They are not simply the aggregate sum of individual actions and thus "cannot be reduced to the interactions and practices through which they express themselves."[8] Despite their influence, social structures often remain undetected by those they affect. They constrain the relations of individuals without those individuals necessarily becoming aware of them. Like those who cannot see the forest for the trees, individuals in society do not generally notice the structures that affect their behavior. They fail to perceive these structures because they are focused on the behavior of other individuals like themselves.

Claude Lévi-Strauss, a French structural anthropologist, held that the myths that ground social life do not find their ultimate origins in the creative efforts of individual authors. Myths reflect the structure of the collective human mind. Human beings necessarily think and communicate in certain ways, according to set mental patterns, such as binary oppositions or dichotomies. Totemic and kinship systems also evidence these structured patterns, which reproduce themselves and their effects in all cultures at all times.[9] For Lévi-Strauss, cultural institutions are the external projections and manifestations of universal structures, just as sentences are external manifestations of general grammatical rules. While individuals may create innumerable "original" sentences, they can do so intelligibly only by following rather strict grammatical rules about the way certain kinds of words and phrases can be combined. Likewise, while individuals may create various cultural arrangements, they can do so, Lévi-Strauss suggests, only by following strict yet unwritten rules that dictate how the phenomena of cultural life are structured.

This line of thinking might be traced back to the German philosopher Immanuel Kant (1724–1804), who argued that the human mind has innate faculties that organize its perceptions of the world according to certain "rational" constraints and categories. Without these faculties, which determine the "mode of our knowledge of objects" and maintain the stable categories of space and time, experience would be reduced to haphazard and largely incommunicable sensations.[10]

Structural Marxists, such as Louis Althusser,[11] likewise hold that individuals are epistemologically and behaviorally molded according to deep patterns that transcend culture and time. For structural Marxists, these patterns are neither set in the collective mind, as Lévi-Strauss proposed, nor in innate mental categories, as Kant proposed. Instead, they are found in concrete economic relations that undergo logical and predictable patterns of transformation. These patterns depend on the level of a society's technological development. For structural Marxists, individual agents are like puppets on strings. The strings are being pulled by historical economic forces, forces largely beyond any individual's control. For the most part, these strings remain invisible to the individual agents themselves. It takes the demystifying work of theorists to make these strings apparent.

Structural Marxists tend to deny the importance of human individuality, volition, and freedom. Other structuralists, such as Durkheim, Bourdieu, Lévi-Strauss, and the sociologist Anthony Giddens, do not take such a hard line. They propose a more balanced tension between the social structures that constrain us and the freedom we demonstrate as individuals.

Individuality, for Durkheim, is a valued product of modern times. Greater individuality and greater freedom, Durkheim argues, arise with the division of labor and the development of larger, more complex societies that allow individuals to escape the constraints of both instinct and convention. Lévi-Strauss similarly points out that the true value of liberty only arises once we understand that liberty itself is a cultural creation.[12] Giddens insists that structures are involved in the generation of our daily practices but that these practices, taken together, also generate and maintain social structures. His theory of "structuration" suggests that social structures are both the "medium and result" of human practices.[13] Human agency continues to play an important role. Bourdieu similarly argues that habitus, though a reflection of social structures, is also creative and subject to change. Though "durable," it is "not eternal."[14] Individuals may transgress, redefine, invent, and improvise within the boundaries of their fields. Indeed, this is all part of the game. As a structuralist, however, Bourdieu maintains that these redefinitions, transgressions, inventions, and improvisations are neither limitless nor completely free-floating. They are themselves conditioned by the rewards and sanctions typically meted out in social fields. Durkheim, Bourdieu, Lévi-Strauss, and Giddens insist that individuality and freedom arise only through human interaction, and human interaction only ever occurs within social structures that constrain, channel, and enable behavior. The greatest freedom arises when we become aware of the structures that both constrain us and make our actions possible and intelligible. Only by understanding the power of our social environment do we become better equipped to navigate or reform it.

From the 1940s until well into the 1970s, the social sciences were animated by debates between social structuralists and methodological individualists. For the most part, and particularly in the United States, the methodological individualists held the day. Liberal political theory, the most common political theory studied today, remains largely aligned with methodological individualism. Debates about the relative importance of social structures and human agency persist, however, though in a somewhat abated form. In all likelihood the debate will never be resolved in favor of one side or the other. The question as to how social and political life is best understood and explained—by way of the social structures that mold individual behavior or by way of the aggregated individual behavior that constitutes social life—has never been satisfactorily answered. Perhaps the only adequate answer is that social and political life is a largely mysterious combination of both processes.

Poststructural and Postmodern Theories of Politics

Beginning in the late 1960s, structuralism itself underwent a challenge from an upstart movement that came to be known as *poststructural-*

ism. Poststructuralists reject the idea that social structures are invariant or evolve according to fixed cultural or historical patterns. Unlike methodological individualists and like structuralists, poststructuralists maintain that power is not always or even primarily a tool willfully employed by the individual actor in pursuit of freely chosen interests. The social environment is assumed to play a larger role. Unlike structuralists, however, poststructuralists do not view power as emanating solely from stable institutions such as kinship systems, mental faculties, or economic classes. They see power as widely dispersed within the social whole and constantly in flux.

Poststructuralists have been reluctant to construct grand theories. Unlike structuralists, they have shunned the temptation to speculate how powerful institutions or traditions transform social life across time and space according to a singular, identifiable logic. Instead, they engage in specific analyses of how particular forms of power achieve particular effects within particular historical periods, cultures or texts. Poststructuralists reject the notion that there are ahistorical, cross-cultural categories of experience or structures of social existence. Spurning the (structuralist) task of discovering and scientifically defining these categories and structures, poststructuralists set out to undermine our belief in them.

Certain poststructuralists, such as the French philosopher Jacques Derrida, engage in something called *deconstruction*. Like much of modern philosophy, deconstruction exhibits what philosopher Richard Rorty refers to as "the linguistic turn." It focuses on language. The roots of deconstruction may be traced back to the Swiss structuralist linguist Ferdinand de Saussure (1857–1913). Saussure's theory of language held that meaning is not determined by the stable relation of words (signifiers) to concrete things or even to conceptual representations of these things (the signified). Meaning is determined by the relation of words to other words. It is a structured play of signs. Deconstruction focuses on this unstable relativity of language.

Deconstruction utilizes the rhetorical features of a text to undermine or cast suspicion on its manifest content or argument, particularly if the text asserts or legitimates stable categories of experience or structures of social existence. Deconstruction demonstrates the self-contradictory linguistic tendencies within any attempt to conceptualize neatly these categories or structures. It also demonstrates that certain rhetorical forms, such as binary oppositions between subject and object, appearance and reality, mind and body, male and female, self and other, speech and writing insidiously establish hierarchies of values.[15]

Deconstruction is concerned not only or even primarily with the capacity of language to represent reality. It is concerned with the capacity of language to construct reality. Likewise, poststructuralist theory is not only or even primarily concerned with the capacity of power to constrain action and desire. It is concerned with the capacity of power to construct identity, and by so doing, induce action and desire. Poststructuralists investigate the generative effects of power. Hence many poststructuralists, such as the French philosopher Michel Foucault (1926–84), focus less on the linguistic forms and rhetorical contradictions found in texts than on concrete institutions and other historical legacies of power. By focusing on the contextual relativity of these institutions and legacies, poststructuralists seek to undermine the grip various forms of power have on us today.

The poststructural concern for dispersed forms of social power also grounds the orientation of postmodern theorists. Postmodernism is the direct heir to poststructuralism. Indeed, for our purposes we need not distinguish between the two terms, although postmodernism is more encompassing in its scope. Postmodernism generally refers to a widespread cultural sensibility, tendency, or mood that is loosely grounded in or serves as a grounding for poststructuralist theory.

Postmodern theorists are far from a unified bunch. They have been usefully described as constituting a "constellation" of thinkers, that is to say, a juxtaposed cluster of elements that resists reduction to a common core.[16] The thinkers and writers commonly considered postmodernists—such as Jean Baudrillard, William Connolly, Gilles Deleuze, Jacques Derrida, Michel Foucault, Frederic Jameson, Jean-François Lyotard, and Richard Rorty—have all criticized certain tendencies of postmodernism and have denied that the term neatly applies to their own work.[17] They approach the practical and theoretical world from varied perspectives and seldom see eye to eye among themselves. Nonetheless, like structuralists and unlike methodological individualists, postmodern theorists are primarily concerned with the social construction and contestation of identities. In turn, like structuralists and unlike methodological individualists, postmodern theorists do not so much celebrate the power of human agency as worry about its fragility.

While acknowledging the power of government and economic classes, postmodernists caution us not to conclude that these are the only institutions that shape our lives. Unlike structuralists, postmodern theorists insist that our identities are the products of a panoply of protean social forces. In particular, postmodernists focus on the discourses, which may be understood as systematized groups of mores, that permeate society and channel its activities. Unlike structuralists, postmodernists insist that discourses and other social forces can only be investigated piecemeal, from the ground up. One must begin with individual practices, particular institutions and singular events that are themselves the products of the sorts of power being investigated. In turn, one's investigation must originate from one's own particular standpoint, a standpoint that is also largely a product of social power.

This leads postmodernists to adopt a *perspectivist* position. The philosophy of perspectivism was originally proposed by Friedrich Nietzsche (1844–1900), the German philosopher commonly credited with blazing the trail for postmodernism. Nietzsche maintained that "objectivity" as traditionally conceived was a "nonsensical absurdity." He denied that there was "knowledge in itself" that did not bear the marks of the situated individuals who created it. Only interpretation from particular points of view exists. Nietzsche insists that "there is *only* a perspective seeing, *only* a perspective 'knowing.'"[18] With this in mind, postmodernists do not attempt to uncover universal structures or patterns that operate according to a stable logic or scientific laws. They assume that their own identities, desires, and predilections are the products of social power and therefore acknowledge that their investigations will only reveal the effects of particular relations of power as they are theorized from a particular vantage point. Like many modern individualists, structuralists had hoped to develop a social *science* that would yield objective truth along the lines of the natural sciences. Postmodernists suggest that we can never achieve an objective, scientific overview of the social forces that shape us. The most we can hope for is a wide variety of limited accounts obtained from multiple perspectives.

Perspectivism undermines any claim to absolute knowledge about the political world. It therefore leads to an ironic stance, that is to say, an engaged yet playful interaction with the world grounded in a skeptical disposition. The irony of postmodernists stands opposed to the self-assured, scientific aspirations of modernists. The three major features of postmodernism, then, are its focus on the social construction of identity, its perspectivist denial of (epistemological or ethical) foundations, and its ironic demeanor. We further explore the meaning of irony in chapter 7, where it is contrasted to ideology.

Postmodernists challenge the very notion of a single, uniform human nature. What makes humans what they are, postmodernists claim, is not some metaphysical or even biological human essence, but a particular historical development, one that has been and remains grounded in social processes. As Richard Rorty states, the postmodern assumption is that "socialization, and thus historical circumstance, goes all the way down—that there is nothing 'beneath' socialization or prior to history which is definatory of the human."[19] Thus postmodernists do not assume the unchanging nature of the individual who willfully wields power in pursuit of chosen interests, as modern individualists do. Neither do postmodernists take for granted the unchanging nature of the social structures that shape individual human behavior, as structuralists do. Instead, postmodern theorists insist that human identities are continually being constructed and contested within particular social environments owing to the interactions of specific forms of power.

In rejecting the notion that there is a stable essence that defines humanity, postmodernists are not saying (though sometimes their rhetoric belies them) that people can simply choose who or what they want to be according to whim. Identities are not just roles people choose to play, roles that can be exchanged or given up at will from one day to the next. Identities are complex patterns of norms and desires, modes of thinking and behaving, that are formed over time owing to the integration of individuals within dense social networks. The postmodern orientation to politics assumes that individual and collective identities are intricately constructed and not easily transformed. Certain postmodernists, such as Jean Baudrillard, meld postmodernism with an extreme form of structuralist determinism, maintaining that individuality and agency have been completely destroyed in the contemporary world. Humans, Baudrillard suggests, are now wholly enslaved to commodities and images.[20] Other postmodernists, however, argue that our identities remain the object of fairly constant contestation. Power and resistance, Foucault insists, always go hand in hand.

Identities are formed in a social environment, or better said, in multiple social environments. We are members, participants, and subjects of various groups, associations, relationships, and organizations that shape our opinions, values, behavior, and self- understandings. Family and friends; places of study, work, and worship; clubs and teams; professional, philanthropic, political, religious and ethnic affiliations; business associations and interest groups; film, television, print and electronic media; municipal, state, national and international movements, organizations and institutions—these are some of the networks of relationships that define our social environment. Each of these networks is itself historically and culturally circumscribed. Our embeddedness in this diverse environment largely defines who we are by both constricting and enabling our experiences, influencing what we feel, believe, know and do. For the postmodernist, even basic individual desire and will are less the trademarks of individual autonomy than the constructs of a social environment.

Many political scientists who do not consider themselves postmodernists are also concerned with how attitudes are created and how particular forms of behavior are stimulated by the speeches and actions that make up the "drama of the state." A common concern is how political leaders "with access to mass media ... shape and even create 'public opinion' by naming the issues and crises about which people come to have opinions."[21] Arguing against the individualist and voluntarist view that people are independent agents that always act in accordance with their preexisting beliefs and values, one student of political behavior writes:

> The common assumption that what democratic government does is somehow always a response to the moral codes, desires and knowledge embedded inside people is as inverted as it is reassuring. This model, avidly taught and ritualistically repeated, cannot explain what happens; but it may persist in our folklore because it so effectively sanctifies prevailing policies and permits us to avoid worrying about them.[22]

Here the concern is how economic and political elites shape specific political agendas and public opinion through government lobbying and the media. In like fashion, many political scientists concern themselves with the "continued, insistent, and ubiquitous process" of communication and intimidation through which elites "win minds" and establish in them a predilection for "order, obedience, the status quo, deference, political docility, and inequalities of income and wealth."[23] Notwithstanding the economic concessions made over the last centuries, which have resulted in the improved welfare of the masses, many students of political behavior are concerned with the way in which elites manipulate political agendas and the media to amass a preponderant amount of power. This power is systematically employed to form and shape the opinions, attitudes, and values of the public.

These investigations of elite power follow the lead of the Italian neo-Marxist Antonio Gramsci, who was concerned with the "hegemony" enjoyed by the dominant political class that controlled the state apparatus.[24] Gramsci formulated his theory to account for specific historical developments, namely, the longevity and increasing strength of capitalism in the twentieth century. Its unabated growth contradicted orthodox Marxist theory (particularly as elaborated by the Second International), which predicted proletarian revolution and the quick demise of capitalism. Gramsci attempted to explain the anomaly. He focused on the how the dominant class used the political and cultural tools at hand to manipulate the other strata of society into accepting, and often endorsing, unjust and exploitative social relations. While orthodox Marxism often spoke with the voice of economic determinism, Gramsci pointed to the power of elites and elite institutions to postpone social revolution indefinitely.

Postmodernists have many of the same concerns as Gramsci and certain contemporary theorists of political behavior. But postmodernists are not concerned solely, or even primarily, with how powerful elites shape people's opinions, attitudes, and values. Postmodernists are concerned with how entire identities are constructed, and how certain opinions, attitudes, and values follow therefrom. As a specialist on the media writes: "The best way to control and manipulate an individual is not to tell them what to do; that always generates resistance, hostility and defiance. Instead, tell a person *who* and *what* they are. They will end up eating out of your hand."[25] Postmodernists investigate how people become who and what they are. Importantly, they investigate this shaping of identities not only as it occurs at the hands of particular elites. Though not denying the power of elites to manipulate the public, postmodernists tend to focus on more ambiguous forces—modes of discourse and other systems of mores—that shape identities within the social environment. Modernist theorists of political culture maintain that people process their experiences into opinions, attitudes, values, and action through predispositions that are products of socialization.[26] Postmodernists share this concern. At the same time, postmodernists believe that the process of socialization goes deeper than most modernist theorists of political culture and behavior would be willing to admit. Reality itself, postmodernists suggest, is a social construct.

Certain theorists of political behavior, for example, observe that people tend to ignore hard facts, data, and knowledge until it is conveniently and perhaps misleadingly packaged for them by elites.[27] Postmodernists suggest that there are no independent "facts" or "data" about the world at all. Knowledge always comes prepackaged within its particular social context. For the postmodern theorist, the world itself is the product of the symbols, gestures, discourses, and dramas of social life.

Identity and the Exercise of Power

The power to shape and create identities is unevenly exercised in society simply because some people are more powerful than others. Take the question of political power. Inequality in the exercise of political power has until quite recently been institutionally entrenched. In ancient times, political power was mostly held by monarchs or aristocrats, who passed on the right to rule to their sons. With the rise of democracy, the opportunity to compete for political office was made available to more people. In turn, the right to vote allowed citizens a say, albeit an indirect one, in the way laws and policies were crafted and hence in the way mores and identities came to be formed.

While the United States is often celebrated as the contemporary exemplar of democratic politics, Americans' participation in politics always has been and still is severely limited. Only about 160,000 people out of the nearly 4 million inhabitants of the American colonies voted for the delegates who ratified the 1790 constitution. That amounts to about 4 percent of the population. At this time, a large number of people—women, Indians, and blacks—were explicitly excluded from political participation, while others (white men without property) were restricted in their manner of participation. Most restrictions on white male suffrage were lifted in the early 1800s. African Americans were not constitutionally enfranchised until 1870, women in 1920, and aboriginal peoples in 1924. (Likewise, Britain has been considered a democracy since the end of the eighteenth century, though at that time only one adult in twenty had the right to vote.)

Inequality in the exercise of political power also occurs when no or few legislative restrictions apply to curtail participation. "Water, water every where/Nor any drop to drink," wrote Coleridge of the sea. One might say something similar about democracy in America. It ostensibly surrounds us. Yet for many there is very little of it to be tasted. In the United States today, only 3 percent of the population is politically active above and beyond the practice of voting. By way of comparison, something like 10 percent of the population of ancient Athens was politically active.

Certainly something like democracy is enjoyed in the United States every few years, at election time. Even here, however, whether at municipal, state, or national levels, those participating often number less than half the eligible voters. Perhaps the reason is that the limited choices available at the electoral table make for sparse pickings. In any case, with the partial exception of referendums that institute particular policies or laws, American citizens do not immediately engage in democratic self-government. They do not directly make decisions about how their collective lives will be governed. Instead, they periodically decide who shall make these decisions for them.

The exercise of other forms of power follows a similar pattern. Only a small percentage of the population, for instance, has access to the media. Few people can afford it. It has been observed that freedom of the press belongs to those who own it. One might add that freedom of the press (and other media) also belongs to those who supply it with the advertising revenues on which it depends. Despite our common use of the term, speech is seldom free.

Economic power, in turn, is very unevenly distributed in the United States. The richest 1 percent of the population earns a greater proportion of the nation's income than the bottom 40 percent. It also owns almost two-fifths of the nation's wealth. The richest 10 percent of the population own close to nine-tenths of the nation's wealth. And increasingly since the 1980s, the rich have gotten richer while the poor have become poorer. Income inequality in America is growing.

Throughout history, elites—whether politicians, the media, intellectuals, bureaucrats, business leaders, clergy, or officers of the armed forces—have played a preponderant role in wielding power. Recognizing this fact, certain social and political theorists have focused on the role of elites in politics and society. Some theorists, such as Gaetano Mosca (1858–1941) and Vilfredo Pareto (1848–1923), accepted elite power as an unavoidable fact of life and defended it. Others, like C. Wright Mills, have sharply opposed elitism despite its acknowledged tenacity.[28]

Evaluating the specific effects of the power of elites in the social construction of interests and identities as well as evaluating the means of resistance to it are demanding tasks. Postmodern theorists have often been criticized for inadequately taking on these tasks. Their preoccupation with ambiguous forms of social power, critics suggest, leaves them blind to the concrete forms of power exercised—ruthlessly at times—by specific elites. In turn, critics charge that the postmodern interrogation of power further undermines moral and political engagement owing to its perspectivist and ironic stance. While postmodernists may be good at exposing the contingencies of our current social and political practices, perspectivism undermines their capacity to suggest improvements (since the criteria for better and worse depends on one's point of view). Irony, in turn, keeps them from taking seriously the need for improvements. As one philosopher suggests, for many theorists postmodernism has become "an excuse not to believe in anything, to avoid both personal and political involvement and take refuge in apathy, despair, or mere ambition."[29] Certain environmental thinkers, in turn, worry that the postmodern notion that reality is socially constructed may undermine needed efforts to protect the natural world. "If nature is only a social and discursive construction," one critic of postmodernism rhetorically queries, "why fight hard to preserve it?"[30]

Postmodernists have not been able to provide wholly reassuring answers to these questions. At the same time, their work displays insights that should not be dismissed out of hand. Michel Foucault has frequently been subject to the sorts of criticisms mentioned above. A brief look at Foucault's efforts to theorize power allows us to investigate these charges while further illustrating the difference between postmodern theory and modern political science.

In describing the nature of contemporary power, Foucault offers the image of a spider's web without a spider. Because everyone is embedded in the social whole, everyone is caught in the web of power. Everyone becomes not only the object of power but its vehicle. Foucault writes that power is not so much "possessed" by elites as it is exercised in "capillary" form throughout society.[31] Power is everywhere in play, creating the interests and identities of those among whom it circulates.

This is not our intuitive understanding of power. It is difficult to imagine power as a spider's web that does not have an actual spider that made it and sits in control over it. We are accustomed to think of power as exercised by specific agents. Foucault suggests that the difficulty arises because our current understanding of power remains under the "spell of monarchy." In our political thinking and theorizing, Foucault graphically states, "we still have not cut off the head of the king."[32] In other words, Foucault recognizes the persistence of the ancient and modern conventions of viewing power as either held by a specific individual ruler (monarchical power) or embodied in the rule of law (juridical power). These monarchical and juridical views of power, he maintains, are now outdated. Power is not solely or even primarily exercised by identifiable agents of authority. Power extends beyond the influence of law and governmental rule. The strands of power entangle us from all sides within an inescapable social web.

Foucault's postmodern understanding of power bears a striking resemblance to the sort of power that Alexis de Tocqueville (1805–59), the French political theorist, observed in America in the early nineteenth century. Tocqueville was concerned with the "tyranny of the majority" that arose in the United States owing to the pressure its citizens felt to conform to custom and majority opinion. This pressure, in Tocqueville's judgment, was more powerful than the rule of kings or the rule of law in shaping the lives of the citizenry. In his famous analysis of American democracy, Tocqueville wrote: "The authority of a king is physical and controls the actions of men without subduing their will. But the majority possesses a power that is physical and moral at the same time, which acts upon the will as much as upon the actions and represses not only all contest, but all controversy.... Under the absolute sway of one man the body was attacked in order to subdue the soul; but the soul escaped the blows which were directed against it and rose proudly superior. Such is not the course adopted by tyranny in democratic republics; there the body is left free, and the soul is en-slaved." Tocqueville goes on to contradict popular belief about the type of liberty enjoyed in the absence of monarchical power by stating: "I know of no country in which there is so little independence of mind and real freedom of discussion as in America."[33] Likewise, Foucault suggests that power today mostly impinges on us not through the overt political rule of elites or legal sanctions but by way of our enmeshment in an ubiquitous social network of relations. Like Tocqueville, Foucault maintains that power often exercises its greatest influence when it re-mains largely hidden from view. It enchains the soul, not the body.

When postmodernists insist that power permeates the social envi-ronment, they are not suggesting that there are no elites who exercise a preponderant amount of influence. Foucault agrees that from an indi-vidualist perspective, power remains the product of a "calculation" made by particular individuals or groups of individuals. It is always ex-ercised as an "intentional" act with definite "aims and objectives" in mind.[34] Nevertheless, Foucault goes on to insist that relations of power between individuals and groups of individuals eventually amalgamate into larger, more complex relationships, which remain "anonymous and almost unspoken." By the time these complex networks further co-alesce into the major "apparatuses" of power that structure society at large (or the "discourses" on which apparatuses ground themselves), they are no longer directed by particular individuals. While invested with power, and while serving the interests of certain individuals more than others, these networks of power—such as scientific, medical, pe-nal, military, academic or political institutions, class or caste structures, and their respective discursive disciplines—escape individual control. They take on a life of their own and form a relatively anonymous web that envelopes everyone.

Nonetheless, the point remains that seldom if ever is political power equally exercised by all. And seldom if ever is political power exercised in the equal interests of all. One must always ask the emi-nently political question, "Cui bono?"—"Who benefits?" Particular be-liefs and values benefit some individuals more than others even if those who benefit the most are not solely responsible for the formation and propagation of these beliefs and values.

Consider respect for the law. The French novelist Anatole France (1844–1924) once ridiculed that "the law, in its majestic equality, for-bids the rich as well as the poor to sleep under bridges, to beg in the streets, and to steal bread." Reverence for the law, which is cultivated throughout society by parents, schoolteachers, the clergy, employers, policemen, judges, jailers, and politicians, benefits the rich and comfortable a good deal more than the poor, cold, and hungry. The rich have their own well-prepared food and posh accommodations in any event, whereas the poor who abide by the law are left wanting. The law that forbids sleeping under bridges, begging in the streets, and stealing bread saves the rich the annoyance of petty theft and the discomforting sight of tattered beggars. The poor, for their part, have no obvious gains. Such laws, and the beliefs and values that buttress them, do not equally serve the interests of all. Yet they are held in place by a vast and relatively anonymous web of social relations.

As with respect for the law, many other opinions and beliefs, norms and desires, modes of thinking and behaving, interests and identities are created and shaped not only by particular elites with particular interests in mind but by countless ambiguous social forces. Theorists interested not only in the distribution of resources but also in the construction and contestation of identity have to face the fact that a person's identity is formed and transformed by multiple sources of power. Perhaps in very small, isolated communities, one might still observe the relatively straightforward construction of identity by particular elite individuals. Within isolated religious sects or cults, for instance, leaders might successfully invade and control the hearts and minds of followers. Yet in contemporary, complex societies, the formation of identity is anything but a straightforward affair. Today, our sense of self is molded by the subtle interplay of innumerable social, political, cultural, economic, and technological relations and forces.

For this reason, postmodernists insist that the effects of power in human affairs goes well beyond the relatively easily observable influence exercised by elite individuals or groups of elite individuals. Their concern is with the power of the social environment, taken as a whole, to form and transform the identities of its members. Because the social environment does not have intentions per se, however, its power is not exercised according to specific designs that overtly serve specific individual interests. It is a more anonymous form of power that serves multiple and changing interests. This sort of power is woven into the very fabric of social life. Indeed, this power binds the social fabric together.

Consider one of Foucault's examples. Foucault doubts that one can account for the power and growth of science by examining intellectual biographies alone. The formation of scientific knowledge is not adequately explained by the accomplishments of individual scientists understood as autonomous agents. Focusing on individuals or classes of individuals, Foucault insists, does not "do justice" to the dense development of scientific understanding and power in the modern world. Instead, Foucault asks "whether the subjects responsible for scientific discourse [that is, the scientists] are not determined in their situation, their function, their perceptive capacity, and their practical possibilities by conditions that dominate and even overwhelm them."[35] Foucault is alluding to the methodological standards for creating or transmitting scientific knowledge that silently structure the social environment in which scientists operate. How scientists come to view the world, their role in it, and themselves, Foucault suggests, is largely a product of the dominant mores within their social and professional environment.

Much of postmodern theory investigates the ways we come to understand and treat ourselves, our fellow human beings, and our world as a result of our socialization. In this sense, Foucault's postmodern project might be seen as the reversal of Hobbes's modern project. Hobbes hoped to escape the anarchical war of all against all that erupts among fearful, isolated individuals in a state of nature. A despotic Leviathan is chosen who establishes and enforces the rules and norms by which all abide. Foucault, in contrast, attempts to demonstrate that our identities are already largely formed, our thought and behavior largely circumscribed, by a social Leviathan. The rules and norms structuring social life—including its political apparatuses, its technological developments, its cultural traditions, its intellectual discourses, and its economic relations—contribute to making us who we are, determining the interests we have and how these interests are pursued.

Hobbes assumed that individuals were independent, autonomous agents on whom power needed to be exercised by a despot to avoid anarchy. For Foucault, the problem is not anarchy but what might be called social despotism. In the contemporary world, he suggests, we need to worry not only or even chiefly about the need to constrain the autonomy of individuals, even though some may become dominant rulers or elites. Instead, we need to encourage and equip all individuals to struggle for their autonomy in the midst of a potentially despotic yet diffuse social power.

Unlike Hobbes, and going well beyond Tocqueville, Foucault rejects the notion that power is limited to something wielded *against* individuals. In contemporary society, Foucault insists, power largely creates and shapes individuals as well. Foucault writes:

> The individual is not to be conceived as a sort of elementary nucleus, a primitive atom, a multiple and inert material on which power comes to fasten or against which it happens to strike, and in so doing subdues or crushes individuals.... The individual, that is, is not the *vis-à-vis* of power; it is, I believe, one of its prime effects. The individual is an effect of power, and at the same time, or precisely to the extent to which it is

that effect, it is the element of its articulation. The individual which power has constituted is at the same time its vehicle.[36]

In the postmodern world, power is not only or even primarily a repressive force that constrains us. It is a creative force that makes us who we are. Power produces us as much as we produce power.

Following Foucault, postmodernists argue that social power does not limit itself to prohibiting the fulfillment of desire. Social power engages in the stimulation and production of desire itself. Power is no longer solely a repressive force, symbolized by a king or the law, restricting the movements of its subjects. Increasingly, power manifests itself as a creative force, evidenced in the social, political and technological networks that shape identities. The postmodern concern is that we have become the vehicles and chief effects of power, not simply the objects of its repression and constraint.

Social Power and Individual Freedom

The postmodern concern with the social construction of identity is effectively a concern with the mores or norms that maintain social order by structuring thought and behavior. These mores or norms are necessary to order and regulate social life. At the same time, they also restrict the freedom and autonomy we desire and cherish as individuals. Thus Foucault, like many other postmodern theorists, encourages us to struggle against the ubiquitous forces of "normalization" that impinge on our lives. We are encouraged to resist the power that envelopes us. But why should we resist? The German philosopher Jürgen Habermas sums up his objection to postmodern theory by asking what the point is of struggling against injustices such as domination if one never escapes social power anyway. If power is truly inescapable, why fight?[37]

Foucault understands resistance waged against normalization as the essence of freedom itself. Power, we recall, is not violence. It is a form of influence that induces and constrains but does not force. Those exercising power may employ force as an ultimate sanction. Yet power itself is grounded on the relative freedom of the individual to respond in any number of ways, even though the exercise of power makes certain responses more likely—more or less profitable, more or less pleasurable, more or less prudent—than others. For Foucault, it remains indispensable to every power relationship "that 'the other' (the one over whom power is exercised) be thoroughly recognized and maintained to the very end as a person who acts; and that, faced with a relationship of power, a whole field of responses, reactions, results, and possible inventions may open up."[38] Attitudes, values, behavior, and the formation of identity, in other words, may be largely but never exhaustively determined by the exercise of particular forms of power. In the absence of outright violence, the opportunity for resistance born of freedom remains.

While postmodern theorists advocate resistance to normalization, they also remind us that complete individual autonomy remains impossible. Indeed, they suggest that complete individual autonomy is a nonsensical concept. Our identity as free, independent, and autonomous agents is already a product of the power exercised within the social environment. To be human means, first and foremost, to develop within a web of social relations permeated by power. We never escape relations of power, we simply shift our position within them. There is no once-and-for-all revolution that might deliver us into a land of liberty. Yet our shifting of positions within the social web of power, our resistance to a singular, unchanging placement, demonstrates our capacity for freedom.

Being free and being subjected to power necessarily go together. Freedom is a precondition of power. This is why power degenerates into sheer force in the absence of freedom. At the same time, participating in a social web of power is a precondition of freedom, otherwise we would never come to develop the human capacities that characterize us as free individuals. For postmodernists, then, the political problem to be confronted is not the impossible task of wholly doing away with relations of power so that we might finally be free. Neither is it the Hobbesian project of wholly sacrificing freedom and centralizing power so that we might escape violent death. The political problem is that of balancing the exercise of power with the exercise of freedom, as evidenced in resistance to specific forms of power.

Postmodernists acknowledge the pervasiveness of politics. Power, they claim, is ubiquitous. Therefore, politics permeates all human relations. This situation is to be neither celebrated nor deprecated. It is simply an inescapable feature of collective human life. Power is not always bad, but it is always dangerous. We could not live, at least could not live socially, without power. At the same time, we must be wary about the ways we live with power. We could not live without power because power allows us to create mores or norms, to act in concert, and to develop as individuals. Yet we should be wary of power because these enabling mores or norms may become overly constraining, compelling, or unjust, because action in concert is seldom equitable in the interests it serves, and because we may, as individuals, develop identities for good or ill. The mores and identities that power is in the business of constructing require ongoing contestation, just as the action it sponsors requires vigilant criticism.

In charting the social construction of identity, the efforts of postmodernists are related to yet also diverge from the efforts of certain modern social scientists known as *behaviorists*. Behaviorists also investigate the power of the social environment to shape individual values and behavior. The roots of modern behaviorism go back to John Locke's theory that human beings are born as "blank slates" whose worldly experiences subsequently imprint them with knowledge and dispositions. The manner in which particular individuals think and act is thus a function of the way in which these individuals were introduced to and interacted with their environment. Based on this understanding of human beings as reservoirs of sensory experience and reactors to environmental stimuli, modern behaviorists aim to create a science of human behavior. Their goal is to predict the way individuals will respond when they receive various stimuli.

Postmodernists reject the attempt to create a science of human behavior. Their rejection is largely based on the belief that there is no singular human essence to serve as a base point for scientific study and no independent scientific facts, data, or systems of knowledge to be collected or generated about it. Human nature, they suggest, is as malleable as human identity. They are both social constructs. Postmodernists also suspect that the attempt to create a behavioral science is dangerous in itself. They believe that it will increase the power of social forces or elites to control people while weakening the individual's capacity for effective resistance. Any attempt to understand human behavior scientifically, postmodernists worry, will lead to efforts to control human behavior scientifically. To achieve such control, much that is spontaneous, unpredictable, and variable in human beings will become suppressed. Behaviorism, they maintain, will lead to intensified and more successful efforts to suppress diversity, which, for the most part, postmodern theorists are interested in fostering. Consequently, postmodernists challenge the social power that consolidates who we are, homogenizes our experiences, restricts our efforts at transformation, or otherwise impinges on how we think and act. They also argue against the imposition of any single, uniform, or "natural" identity on others. To the extent that postmodern theorists foster a normative perspective, then, it is frequently oriented to the celebration of difference and the cultivation of a "responsibility to otherness."[39]

The postmodern effort to stimulate resistance to the power of the social environment sharply contrasts with the heightening of that power advocated by certain behaviorists. The modern science of behaviorism found one of its foremost advocates in B.F. Skinner, an experimental psychologist. In order to outline the hoped-for benefits of applying behavioral science to the organization of society, Skinner wrote a utopian novel called *Walden Two*.[40] This book portrays an isolated community that secures an idyllic life through the extensive application of behavioral techniques. Its inhabitants achieve their utopia by manipulating and reconstructing both the natural and social worlds. They engage in the "conquest of nature" as well as the "conquest of man."

The "tyranny" of bad weather, for example, is overcome at Walden Two through mechanical engineering that makes most everything accessible indoors. In turn, the tyranny of antisocial drives and habits and dysfunctional social conventions is overcome through behavioral conditioning that reinforces useful behavior and discourages noxious conduct. In this way, benign drives, habits, and beliefs are scientifically inculcated through a technique of psychological reinforcement called "operant conditioning." Walden Two, as its chief engineer quips, is really a "Walden for Two." That is to say, it is an idyllic existence that, unlike Henry David Thoreau's original retreat to Walden Pond, does not merely escape the vexing problems of collective life but actually resolves them.

We learn from the protagonist of *Walden Two* that "religious faith becomes irrelevant when the fears which nourish it are allayed and the hopes fulfilled—here on earth." To this end, priests have been replaced by psychologists to guide the flourishing community. In turn, Walden Two is considered a "world without heroes," and for much the same reasons that it is a world without gods. We find that "a society which functions for the good of all cannot tolerate the emergence of individual figures" that might disrupt the equilibrium. More important, the inhabitants of this utopia have forsaken their belief in the freedom and dignity that heroic individuals are supposed to incarnate. At Walden Two everyone knows that there is no such thing as free, uncontrolled, or undetermined, and therefore heroic or dignified human behavior. Everything one does is a direct product of behavior modification.

The denizens of Walden Two do not pine for freedom because they believe that those who live outside their technological utopia are no freer than they are. It is simply a matter of *who* is doing the controlling or conditioning. At Walden Two, conditioning is carried out by scientists, psychologists, and social engineers. In the outside world, it is carried out by deluded priests, ill-informed parents, hucksters, and demagogues. According to its residents, Walden Two is actually the "freest place on earth." It deserves this distinction not because its behavioral technicians have actually made human beings free from control. They simply offer a more functional and benign form of control. By success-fully modifying behavior through techniques of positive reinforcement, physical coercion is no longer needed to achieve social harmony. Power does all the necessary work by creating and maintaining the right mores or norms. Violence is completely absent. At Walden Two, people do the things that benefit society, not because they are forced to do so, or punished if they fail to do so, but because they have been trained to *want* to do so. In this way one may simultaneously *"increase* the feeling of freedom" while providing all the comforts of civilized life.

The central conflict of the behavioral revolution, and its tentative resolution, is most straightforwardly described by Skinner in his subse-quent work, *Beyond Freedom and Dignity.* The book begins with a lit-any of environmental woes: the population explosion, the nuclear threat, world famine, pollution. These are the earth-threatening prob-lems that confront contemporary humanity. After explaining the theory and benefits of operant conditioning, Skinner concludes *Beyond Free-dom and Dignity* with a plea that we abandon the unnecessary and ul-timately fatal prejudices about freedom and autonomy that prevent the timely resolution of our worsening woes. Skinner proposes that we abolish

> autonomous man ... the man defended by the literatures of freedom and dignity. His abolition has been long overdue. Autonomous man is a device used to explain what we cannot explain in any other way. He has been constructed from our ignorance, and as our understanding increases, the very stuff of which he is composed vanishes. Science does not dehumanize man, it de-homunculizes him, and it must do so if it is to prevent the abo-lition of the human species.... Man himself may be controlled by his en-vironment, but it is an environment which is almost wholly of his own making. The physical environment of most people is largely man-made ... the social environment is obviously man-made.... An experimental analy-sis shifts the determination of behavior from autonomous man to the en-vironment—an environment responsible both for the evolution of the spe-cies and for the repertoire acquired by each member.... We have not yet seen what man can make of man.[41]

The point is not that behaviorism assumes human life to be totally pre-dictable any more than meteorology assumes the weather to be totally predictable. There are simply too many variables, and measurements remain too imprecise. Still, much can be known, and, at least in the case of human behavior, much can be controlled. The object of the be-havioral revolution, here placed in its extreme form in the work of B.F.

Skinner, is the betterment of society and the conquest of nature through technological manipulation. The age-old conflict between the (autonomous) individual and its environment becomes a working relation between the scientist and the natural and social environments that are the crucibles of humankind. Although we shall have to abandon our beliefs in freedom and dignity once we understand how the environment ultimately controls us, behaviorists contend, we shall also increase our power to control the environment.

The contrast between postmodern theorists and behaviorists is particularly illuminating because of their many, seldom-noted similarities. Postmodernists, like behaviorists, assume that the individual is wholly malleable, a function of its social environment. For both postmodernists and behaviorists, the webs of social power are inescapable. We are all necessarily caught in the game of mutual manipulation and control. Power is the medium in which humans exist, a medium that forms as well as sustains us. We may resist power to be sure, but not because there are realms of absolute freedom we might discover or create. Resistance is the substitution, or offsetting, of one form of power by another. Freedom is not something we have or could ever gain once and for all. Freedom is simply the word we employ to denote the experience of getting a better grip on the reins of power.

The end of human freedom and dignity is applauded by Skinner. Indeed, he seeks to consummate their demise at the hands of a scientific elite. Foucault, in contrast, opposes the centralization of power required for Skinner's project. Foucault locates the chinks in the armor where power can be effectively challenged. He likens his writings to tool kits from which his readers may select conceptual devices for short-circuiting the system. The point, Foucault insists, is not that our entanglement in power is itself bad. It is simply, and constantly, dangerous. Hence Foucault advocates a "hyper- and pessimistic activism" on the part of all individuals who suffer the effects of power.[42]

Here Foucault truly parts ways with Skinner, who advocates a hyper- but *optimistic* activism on the part of social engineers involved in constructing ever stronger and stickier social webs. Foucault, like Skinner, argues that we create and perpetuate the social environment that inevitably creates, constrains, and enables us. But the goal for Foucault is to proliferate struggles against these dangerous networks of power. The object for Skinner is to structure these networks better so as to control human behavior ever more efficiently. The behavioral revolution was an effort to manage technical power over the human subject through the accumulation, centralization, and exploitation of scientific knowledge. Foucault, like most postmoderns, seeks to undermine and disperse this form of power by deconstructing the knowledge that generates it.

Theorizing at the Edge of Modernity

Postmodernists, as perspectivists, are skeptical of all grand theories that seek to explain everything. Hence they reject scientific theories of social construction, such as the behaviorist account, that present themselves as comprehensive. François Lyotard remarked that postmodernity is chiefly characterized by an "incredulity toward metanarratives."[43] A metanarrative is a story that subsumes all other perspectives to produce a singular, all-encompassing account of the world, an account that implicitly or explicitly legitimates certain social norms, political structures, or positions of power. Postmodernists, unlike behaviorists, shun metanarratives. They are reluctant to believe too strongly in any grand story, including the grand story they themselves tell about the social construction of identity. As we later see, this tendency to remain skeptical even of one's own historical or conceptual stories contributes to postmodernists' ironic demeanor.

One might say that modernism achieves its most extreme formulation, though many would argue not its most effective or ideal form, in behaviorist social science. Behavioral theorists such as Skinner chiefly celebrate the scientific aspects of modernism. But there are other kinds of modernists. Liberal theorists, for instance, emphasize the humanist side of modernism. Hence they valorize human freedom and individual autonomy. Both behaviorists and liberals believe in progress, even moral progress. But the former believes that progress will result from putting the laws of nature and human nature to work through science. The latter believes that progress will result from giving the greatest scope to individual freedom and autonomy.

Postmodernists generally reject the scientific, humanistic, and progressive pillars of modernism. The search for an objective, value-free science is abandoned. Were postmodernists to look to the sciences to inform their own investigations, their model would not be Newtonian mechanics but contemporary quantum physics or perhaps chaos theory. As Albert Einstein demonstrated, the laws of Newtonian physics fail to apply at speeds close to that of light. Here the notion of relativity becomes necessary. In much contemporary physics, informed by Werner Heisenberg's "Uncertainty Principle," such things as time, space, matter, and causality are no longer understood as the unchanging foundations of a singular reality that is available for objective examination. They are somewhat fickle categories that only ever measure facets of reality from particular points of view. As Heisenberg wrote, "what we observe is not nature itself, but nature exposed to our method of questioning."[44] Contemporary physicists are aware of the relativity and instability of categories of thought and aspects of reality previously assumed to be absolute. Postmodernists emphasize this relativity and instability.

In turn, postmodernists reject the modernist faith in the autonomy and freedom of the individual. In emphasizing the power of the social environment, however, their point is not to undermine individual freedom. They aim to demonstrate that freedom is a much more precarious achievement than liberal modernists assume. At the same time, most postmodernists claim that individual freedom is a much more resilient force than modern behavioralists assume.

Finally, postmodernists spurn the modern faith in progress, whether scientifically or humanistically grounded. They do not deny that advances occur in many fields of human endeavor. Nonetheless, they believe it important to highlight the costs of these advances. In industrialized countries, for example, more people live longer, are generally healthier, and have greater freedom of movement and profession than in centuries past. Whether they are happier is another question. Real costs have been paid for modern "progress," as evidenced in the degradation of the environment, the disintegration of the extended family, the hectic pace of life, and the loss of civic virtues. Perhaps most threatening, the growth of human power over the social environment returns to haunt us as we become increasingly subject to surveillance, conditioning, and control.

Foucault insists that "humanity does not gradually progress from combat to combat until it arrives at universal reciprocity, where the rule of law finally replaces warfare; humanity installs each of its violences in a system of rules and thus proceeds from domination to domination."[45] Such statements prompt modernists to criticize postmodernists for ignoring the fact that not all forms of domination are equally oppressive. Progress may occur, for instance, not because we have escaped all forms of social control but because we have developed less cruel or less harsh forms of social control. Most of us, for instance, would consider it a sign of progress that we no longer flay criminals or burn those accused of witchcraft at the stake. Yet we cannot deny that power is still exercised, often quite insidiously and for unjust purposes, through the media, the economy, and the rule of law.

One might summarize the distinction between modern and postmodern political theory by saying that modern political theorists are primarily interested in investigating the regulation of social interaction, while postmodern political theorists are primarily interested in studying the social construction of identity. Michael Walzer, a liberal political philosopher, argues the modernist cause, suggesting that "the central issue for political theory is not the constitution of the self but the connection of constituted selves, the pattern of social relations."[46] It is certainly important to inquire into the pattern of social relations, and Walzer is understandably reacting to a tendency among certain critics of liberalism to ignore this concern. Political theory, however, is ultimately about *both* the constitution of selves and the connections they establish. It is about the formation of identity and the regulation of interaction. Because these two phenomena occur simultaneously in political life, one cannot well be studied without the other. Taken together, they largely define the realm of politics.

Our theorizing most benefits by partaking of both the modern and postmodern perspectives. Indeed, the two orientations complement each other much more than is generally recognized. Just as modernism grew out of and remained nourished by scholasticism, so postmodernism grew out of and remains nourished by modernism. Although the difference between modernism and postmodernism is real enough, overlapping concerns persist. Many of the early polemics exchanged between modernists—those who carry on and critically reconstruct the unfinished Enlightenment project of humanistically transforming the world in the name of rational progress—and postmodernists—those who suggest that the Enlightenment project is historically exhausted, epistemologically bankrupt, and ethically censorable—are now giving way to more synthetic efforts of accommodation and dialogue.

Postmodernists acknowledge that identity is only formed through interaction. Hence the regulation of interaction according to rational processes, in deference to standards of justice, and mindful of the prerogatives of freedom remains, or should remain, a crucial component of their concerns. Modernists, in turn, build their theories of social interaction on shaky ground unless they inquire into the manner in which the identities of the interactors are constructed and sustained. At base, both modern and postmodern political theorists are concerned with that realm of public affairs wherein various forms of power meet resistance and wrestle with freedom. With this in mind, modern and postmodernist theorists have much to be gained from an open, mutual exchange.

Like most modernists, Bernard Crick focuses on the governmental regulation of interaction. He endorses the individualist and voluntarist effort to preserve realms of individual freedom and autonomy from the reach of politics and power. Yet Crick acknowledges that "anything *may* prove a proper subject of governmental intervention in a political system; but it is not a political system at all if there is a single authoritative source for the allocation of all values and for the determination of all policies."[47] In other words, politics occurs in the absence of an overarching system of values that would settle the questions of public life once and for all. Politics ceases and becomes a tyrannical exercise of force or a totalitarian effort to impose harmony once this settling of public affairs no longer allows for competing forms of power grounded in individual freedom, diverse values, and independent activity.

Postmodernists might say the same thing regarding the formation of identities. If some hegemonic force, be it a behavioral science, a governmental bureaucracy, or an educational institution, consolidated enough power to mold identities in their entirety, then politics would be destroyed. For politics is defined by power that does not destroy all forms of resistance. Fortunately, the social forces that shape our identities are sundry. In playing one off against the other, we exercise our basic freedom. Consider only a few of the major historical political events and documents that have done their share in molding the American identity. The Revolutionary War and the Declaration of Independence immediately come to mind. But the American identity has also been shaped by the Civil War and the Gettysburg Address, which deepened and redirected the commitment to equality and individualism. The experience of the war in Vietnam and Watergate again reshaped the American identity, reinforcing a distrust of government and perhaps instilling an abiding political cynicism. Countless other events, institutions, and discourses, not only national but also local and international, not only political but also economic, technological, social, and cultural, have played and will continue to play key roles in shaping who we are and how we behave individually and collectively.

It is said that nature abhors a vacuum. Power also abhors a vacuum. If a form of power is diminished or dies out, some other form of power quickly fills the void. What makes for freedom in politics, then, is not an absence of power but the multiplicity of its forms. Only amid the vast diversity of social life and the countless countervailing sources of power can the individual discover or create the "wiggle room" needed to express his freedom. The latitude for original thought and autonomous action may not at times be great. But where power has not been ousted by violence, human individuality will find room to grow. The pervasiveness of power does not in itself threaten individual liberty. The threat comes only when the various forms of power that pervade social life are reduced to a hegemonic force that proves irresistible.

To assert our freedom is not to escape power completely. It is actively to participate in the complex network of power that permeates collective life. To be free is to exercise and resist power. As Crick observes: "The price of liberty is more than eternal vigilance ... it is eternal commitment to political activity."[48] The preservation of freedom, modernists and postmodernists might agree, is not to be gained in the futile attempt to escape politics. Politics is pervasive. Freedom is found only by self-consciously entering the political fray.

Suggested Readings

Louis Althusser. For Marx
Robert Bellah et al. *Habits of the Heart*
Richard J. Bernstein. *The New Constellation*
Steven Best and Douglas Kellner. *Postmodern Theory*
James Burnham. *The Machiavellians*
William E. Connolly. *Identity/Difference*
Jacques Derrida. *Writing and Difference*
René Descartes. *A Discourse on Method*
Émile Durkheim. *The Division of Labor in Society*
Michel Foucault. *Discipline and Punish* and *Power/Knowledge*.
Anthony Giddens. *Central Problems in Social Theory*
Harold Lasswell. *Politics: Who Gets What, When, and How*
Jean-François Lyotard. *The Postmodern Condition*
Friedrich Nietzsche. *On the Genealogy of Morals* and *Beyond Good and
    Evil*.
B.F. Skinner. *Walden Two* and *Beyond Freedom and Dignity*.
Stephen K. White. *Political Theory and Postmodernism*

5

Identity and Difference

The belief that our sense of self or identity has a strong bearing on how we think and act is as old as political theory itself. Plato and Hobbes attempt to define politics (what we do or should do collectively) in terms of human nature (who we are). Like most political theorists, they try to convince us to pursue particular interests, to engage in particular activities, and to maintain particular beliefs and relationships, by explaining how we should understand ourselves. How we think and act and what interests we pursue largely depend on whether we follow Plato in construing ourselves as tripartite souls with reason reigning supreme, or whether we follow Hobbes in construing ourselves as conglomerations of independent drives dominated by fear and the insatiable quest for power.

Identities are not static and one-dimensional entities. Yet modernists often assume, to employ the language of social science, that identities are independent variables. They are understood as the stable cause rather than the changing effect of political actions and relationships. Given certain ethnic or class identities (the independent variable), for instance, the modern political theorist might seek to explain the existence or transformation of certain attitudes, interests, values, or behavior (the dependent variables). Postmodernists suggest that identities are not independent variables. They are products of a social environment infused with changing relationships of power. Identities are complex in their constitutions and susceptible to transformation. Thus postmodernists are critical of modern theorists who assume the polity to be an aggregate of stable, preformed, unchanging selves. They also spurn the use of such terms as "the American identity" or "the rational individual" that presume that the identities of people are unified constants.

In particular, postmodernists worry about the suppression of difference that occurs whenever theorists speak as if people's identities were homogeneous. They insist that identities are fluid, overlapping, and cross-cutting. Each individual's identity is multiply hyphenated, even though one or another facet of it typically gains prevalence. The postmodern concern is that the characteristics of the dominant players in the game often become generalized to describe all the participants, that the collective body—the nation, for example—becomes defined in terms of its dominant (social, political, ethnic, religious, or economic) group. Those who do not share in the salient features of the prevailing class will consequently have their interests and values excluded from consideration.

Take, for instance, these famous words, penned in 1776 by Thomas Jefferson (1743–1826):

> We hold these truths to be self-evident, that all men are created equal, that they are endowed by their Creator with certain unalienable Rights, that among these are Life, Liberty and the pursuit of Happiness. That to secure these rights, Governments are instituted among Men, deriving their just powers from the consent of the governed. That whenever any Form of Government becomes destructive of these ends, it is the Right of the People to alter or to abolish it, and to institute new Government, laying its foundation on such principles, and organizing its powers in such form, as to them shall seem most likely to effect their Safety and Happiness.

Commenting on this declaration, which inaugurated the American Revolution with as worthy a statement as has been written for a political founding, Jefferson wrote: "Neither aiming at originality of principle or sentiment, nor yet copied from any particular and previous writing, it was intended to be an expression of the American mind, and to give to that expression the proper tone and spirit called for by the occasion."[1] The Declaration of Independence, Jefferson suggests, is simply the rendering in words of a self-evident truth embodied in the American populace as a whole. The essence of an American way of thinking and acting, Jefferson held, came to be reflected in revolutionary words and subsequently in revolutionary deeds. As a result, an American system of government was formed. Jefferson, like most political theorists, believed that one's sense of self strongly influences how one acts in the world. He exemplifies this belief in a distinctly modern way.

Jefferson employs an individualist and voluntarist framework for politics. He assumes that independent, autonomous minds form specific beliefs and values based on preexisting interests. These interests are themselves products of stable identities or natures. Thus one's nature determines one's interests, and one's interests determine ones values and beliefs, and one's values and beliefs stimulate the speech and action that begets the formation of a particular social and political system. Such assumptions are intrinsic to the "social contract" theories of the state that are the hallmark of modern political individualism. Stemming from Hobbes, Locke, and the French political theorist Jean-Jacques Rousseau (1712–78), social contract theories suggest that free, autonomous, and independent individuals with distinct, preformed interests voluntarily join together to form a government so as to safeguard their interests.

There is, however, another side to this coin. Consider the legacy of Jefferson's own words. For over two centuries now, American school children have read and recited the Declaration of Independence. American youths and adults have discussed its meaning and reaffirmed its message. In turn, the system of government that this Declaration gave rise to has affected the development of American culture. In short, the social and political mores promulgated and stimulated by the Declaration have significantly contributed to the *political socialization* of Americans. Jefferson's suggestion that his words simply reflected the preexisting identity of the American colonists tells only half the story. For these same words have heavily contributed to the construction of the contemporary American identity.

Postmodernists would have us dig still deeper into Jeffersonian assumptions about unified (national) identities grounded in individualist and voluntarist beliefs. Though the Declaration ostensibly celebrated the freedom and autonomy of each and every individual, it obscured the patent lack of freedom and autonomy of well over half the population of America at the time. In championing the status of the autonomous individual, it was valorizing the experience of free white males and ignoring the status and experience of women, black slaves (in 1776, all thirteen colonies had slavery), and aboriginal people. Its "truths" were taken to be self-evident. They were supposed to be patent to all rational individuals. At the time, however, women, black slaves, and native Americans were not considered to be fully rational. Despite its rhetoric, Jefferson's Declaration does not reflect the status and experience of all or even most Americans, nor even of "all men." Instead, it reflects the status and experiences of free white male property owners, like Jefferson himself, in eighteenth-century America. Hence Jefferson's assumptions about the autonomy and independence of individuals were themselves products of a particular social, economic, and historical context.

A similar deconstruction of the Constitution displays how rhetoric belies reality. The American Constitution famously begins with the words "We the people of the United States." Yet it originally did not represent the interests of all the people of the United States. Constitutional guarantees applied only to "Free Persons." The Constitution expressly protected the institution of slavery and considered a slave to constitute only "three-fifths" of a person for representational purposes. It denied both native people and African Americans the rights of citizenship. Women at the time were not begrudged all civil rights, but they could not vote or carry out many business transactions. In turn, minor property regulations even restricted the political rights of white males.

The irony is that by celebrating the power and uniqueness of the individual, modern individualism and voluntarism effectively suppressed the power and uniqueness of a majority of individuals who did not share the privileged status of free white males in eighteenth-century America. As one social theorist generalizes,

> In social contract theory, the individuals empowered by the opportunity to participate in the implicit contract were so many members of a set of equivalent citizens.... The individuals joining in the social contract ... were prototypically educated, property-owning male speakers of the dominant language of the nation. Thus individualism ironically repressed difference.[2]

Jefferson said that all men were created equal and bore unalienable rights. Jefferson's famous celebration of individual equality, one might argue, perpetuated the repression of difference by ostensibly celebrating the equality of all people while obscuring the harsh truths of a much more exclusive social and political system.

Perhaps the words of the Declaration continue to serve this function today. By and large, and until quite recently, a dominant white male culture has largely defined what it has meant to be American. Yet words are fickle things. They may be put to many uses, including uses unintended or unrealizable by their authors. Particularly in this century, Jefferson's words have been employed by women, African Americans, native people, and other minorities to assert their political, civil, and economic rights. Many of the differences suppressed or obscured by the Founding Fathers have been reclaimed, defended, and celebrated using their own words.

The struggle over identity—over what it means to be an American, a man or woman, a member of a specific race, ethnic group, class, or religion—is ubiquitous and unending. It sits at the core of politics. This chapter examines the struggles over identity that animate political life.

It emphasizes the difficulty of recognizing, understanding, accepting, and respecting that which is different from oneself and that in oneself which is different. The chapter examines the politics of identity as it pertains to race, religion, gender, and class. It investigates the ways, means, and extent to which the identities of individuals are constructed by their social environments and pays particular attention to the inherent dangers of these constructions. It also pays attention to the suppression of difference that occurs whenever identities become overly unified and rigid.

As employed here, the term *politics of identity* is not meant to be equated with what is often called *identity politics*. The latter term generally refers to the formation of political movements that base their power on the assumed uniformity of the interests and character of certain groups of individuals (e.g., certain ethnically or racially based political organizations). Identity politics suggests that social groups have essential characteristics that extend equally and homogeneously to all their members, effectively determining their political interests. In contrast, the *politics of identity* is concerned with differences and how these differences are politically negotiated. Moreover, it is occupied not solely or even primarily with the features of individuals and social groups that define their political life. The primary focus is the manner in which political life itself defines the features of individuals. The politics of identity, then, is also the politics of difference. Postmodern political theory does its work under both these banners.[3]

Race, Religion, and Otherness

In the year 1492, the Spanish monarchs Ferdinand of Aragon and Isabella of Castille conquered Granada. In doing so, they put an end to the Moorish kingdom in Europe. That year, Ferdinand and Isabella also expelled all the Jews from Spain who would not convert to Christianity or who were suspected of retaining Jewish practices. Thus a dozen years after the Spanish Inquisition began, Spain was made homogeneously Christian. In this same year, when all non-Christians were forcefully driven from Spain, a separate effort was launched to lay the groundwork for the expulsion of Muslims from non-European cities and the conversion of Asians into Christians.

Eventually funded by Ferdinand and Isabella after eight years of supplication, Christopher Columbus (1451–1506), a forty-one-year-old Genoan, set sail to the West from Palos, Spain. Columbus was an avid explorer and brilliant navigator. Embarking on the flagship *Santa Maria* and accompanied by two other ships, Columbus aimed to find a western route to India. His intent was twofold. He wanted to facilitate the conversion of Indians to Christianity, and a more direct sea route to India would aid in this project. Columbus also hoped to amass enough profit from the increased sea trade with India to fund yet another religious crusade to wrest Jerusalem from the Muslims. "Gold is most excellent," Columbus wrote in his journal, "he who possesses it, can do as he wishes in the world. It can even drive souls into Paradise."[4] The concern for wealth repeatedly appears in Columbus's journals. Religious goals justify its pursuit.[5]

A little over two months after setting sail, Columbus and his crew stumbled on what are now called the Bahamian Islands. After exploring the Caribbean for some time, Columbus sailed back to Spain. He was made admiral and governor general of all newly discovered Western lands. Columbus made a number of return voyages in subsequent years that put him on the shores of South and Central America.

Upon his initial arrival, Columbus gave the name "Indians" to the inhabitants of the Caribbean. He called them Indians because the people of India were the people he set out to find. Columbus, it turns out, was pretty set in his ways. Indeed, he forced his entire crew to take oaths affirming that the island they had landed on one day—actually present-day Cuba—was the Indian subcontinent. In these and other matters, Columbus interpreted the world through European, Christian lenses that he could neither remove nor adjust. He saw what he expected to see. What did not fit neatly within his own intellectual, cultural, and religious conceptual scheme was either forced to fit in a Procrustean fashion or was ignored and devalued.

In his book *The Conquest of America,* Tzvetan Todorov examines the relations that Columbus established with the inhabitants of the Americas, as well as the relations subsequently established by the Spanish conquistadors and missionaries. Todorov wrote his book to investigate the "discovery *self* makes of the *other.*"[6] Despite being famous as an explorer, Todorov writes, Columbus never really explored the other. The reason is that the great discoverer of the new world never succeeded in escaping from himself. He remained too much a captive of his Christian, European identity to understand or appreciate the other in America. As Todorov observes, though Columbus discovered America, he failed to discover the Americans.

When Columbus was confronted with the unfamiliar languages, customs, systems of exchange, religions, and moralities of the aboriginal people, he failed to appreciate and acknowledge them for what they were. Because their creeds, languages, and cultural institutions were not what he was used to, Columbus assumed that they were meaningless.

Indeed, he maintained that the native people had no real language, religion, or cultural foundation at all. The natives he encountered were understood to be unmolded pieces of inferior metals awaiting the masterful hands of European sculptors. Despite being an excellent mariner adept at navigating unknown seas, Columbus proved quite inept at navigating unknown societies.

In 1519, years after Columbus had returned to Spain for good and had died in neglect, Hernán Cortés (1485–1547), a Spanish conquistador, left Cuba for Mexico with a few hundred soldiers. Within two years, Cortés managed to conquer and subdue the entire Aztec empire, which at the time spread out across most of Mexico and numbered over 10 million people. Cortés achieved this tremendous feat by making strategic alliances with the enemies of the Aztecs and with neighboring people who had been subjugated and forced to pay tribute to the Aztec empire. Cortés's amazing success was also due to the fact that Montezuma, the Aztec leader, mistook Cortés for Quetzalcoatl, the mythical god that the Aztecs believed would one day return to rule their land. Cortés cunningly exploited this mistake. Allowed entrance into the Aztec capital under this misrepresentation, Cortés quickly took Montezuma hostage. After gaining control of the palace, the conquistadors pillaged the capital and ruthlessly suppressed resistance.

Montezuma resembles Columbus. In mistaking Cortés for a god, he, like Columbus, failed to understand difference. Columbus and Montezuma could only perceive those unlike themselves as either a lower or a higher form of life. Where Columbus saw difference, he assumed inferiority. Where Montezuma saw difference, he assumed superiority. Neither could understand the other as different yet equal. Both men, mostly owing to strongly held religious and racial beliefs, proved incapable of escaping themselves. Consequently, neither could effectively communicate with those who were different.

Cortés, in contrast, was very skilled at understanding and communicating with the native people. For Cortés, however, communication was not an end in itself. It was a tool used to manipulate and extort. Cortés demonstrated great cunning. He realized that half the art of successful communication was being *mis*understood (e.g., as Quetzalcoatl) when misunderstanding served one's purpose. The other half of Cortés's art of communication consisted in understanding the other well enough to gain the upper hand. Thus Cortés quickly learned that only Aztec generals carried gold shields. He then instructed his men to kill first in battle all those warriors carrying gold shields. Once these easily identifiable leaders were killed, the Aztec army would quickly fall into disarray. For Cortés, communication and conquest went hand in hand. Unlike Columbus, Cortés got to know the native people quite well. Yet he sought to understand them only in order to master them. In reflecting on the exploits of Cortés, we learn that understanding, knowledge, and communication are not necessarily good in themselves. They may be and often are put to immoral and ruthless ends.

Columbus failed to understand the native Americans because he could not conceive of anything being markedly different yet somehow equal. Differences in language, culture, and race forever kept Columbus from recognizing a common humanity. He was blinded by the prejudice of superiority. In contrast, Bartolomé de Las Casas (1474–1566), a Catholic priest who accompanied the conquistadors, was blinded by the prejudice of equivalence. Las Casas could not conceive of anything that was essentially equal being somehow still different.

When Las Casas arrived in the New World in 1502, he also failed to understand or communicate well with the native people. Unlike Columbus, Las Casas recognized and acknowledged the full humanity of the natives. Yet he could do so only under the aegis of his religious beliefs. For Las Casas, the natives gained membership to humankind by way of their common potential for heavenly afterlife. The natives of America were simply Christians awaiting conversion under the eyes of a European God. This assumption kept the missionary from acknowledging the natives for who they were.

Columbus came to America, Las Casas wrote, to "open wide doors so that the divine doctrine and the Gospel of Christ might enter therein." By discovering the natives, Las Casas writes, Columbus ensured that "an infinite number of their souls ... was saved."[7] For Las Casas, the natives were essentially equal to Europeans because all were God's children. Las Casas offered the natives equality, but it came at a high price. It could be gained only at the cost of sacrificing much of their identity. They would have to abandon their religious beliefs and many of their cultural practices in order to convert to Christianity.

Eventually Las Casas, unlike Columbus, was able to exchange his Eurocentric lenses for less constraining ones. Observing the atrocities committed by the conquistadors firsthand and witnessing the humanity of the native people in their daily lives, Las Casas gained a new perspective. He learned to love and respect the aboriginals, not solely as potential Christians, but for themselves. No longer was love of the other limited to having the other serve as a mirror of the self. No longer was assimilation of the other into the self the only solution to the uncomfortable perception of difference.

The story of the Spanish conquest of America is illustrative of the power of religious and racial identities to affect, and undermine, the opportunity we have to understand those who are different from us. Columbus, and for a time Las Casas, were so enclosed within their own cultural identities that they could not adequately open themselves to others. Cortés was sufficiently enclosed in his identity as a conquistador that his skills in communication could be employed only to dominate and destroy otherness rather than respect or celebrate it. The opportunity for a truly political coexistence was lost.

The story of the Spanish conquest of America is also broadly illustrative of the ongoing struggle with power that each individual faces today. Once the Spanish landed in the Americas and established relations with the aboriginal people, the exercise of power was inevitable. The question is, how might this power have been exercised so as to demonstrate respect and appreciation for difference? This remains a crucial question for political life today. It pertains not only to the politics that occurs between different ethnic, racial, or religious groups but to the politics that occurs between all individuals. Today, no less than in the time of America's conquest, a central task of political life is the acknowledgment of the other.

Politics is about the exercise of power that does not slip over the line into the realm of force. Force erases difference by destroying the other or by eliminating the other's opportunity for meaningful self-assertion. But violent domination is not the only threat to politics. The attempt to impose harmony is also a danger. Politics pertains to the exercise of power that does not suppress difference in order to mimic a harmonic existence. True harmony never occurs in political life. In an effort to turn others into identical images of the self, as Las Casas's original efforts illustrate, the illusion of a loving harmony may be achieved. But the cost is high. What is unique in other individuals is necessarily suppressed.

The tragedy of the "discovery" of America is that the Europeans and the aboriginal people only rarely and briefly developed political relationships. In both the conquistadors' use of force and the missionaries' efforts to achieve harmony, the opportunity for politics—the recognition and sustaining of individuality within community—was sacrificed.

The Other in America

Given the human penchant for mastery, it may seem improbable that two distinct people could occupy the same land and yet share power in a manner that preserves difference. Unfortunately, a ruthless pursuit of mastery is well illustrated in the subjection of the native people of America to the European colonists. The former were overwhelmed by the power, and often the violence, of the latter. Aboriginal people had been living in the Americas for tens of thousands of years prior to the Europeans' arrival. In the 1500s it is estimated that more than 70 million native inhabitants were in the Americas. Within a few centuries, fewer than 5 million natives were still alive. Tens of millions of human lives were lost to disease, mistreatment, and outright slaughter.

We briefly examined some of the causes of this decline in what is now known as Central and South America. The genocide (destruction of a race or people) also took place in North America, though on a much smaller scale. At the time of the European incursion there were some 500 distinct nations of native people with a combined population north of the Rio Grande of 7 million. Five of those 7 million were in what is now the coterminus United States (i.e., not counting Canada and Alaska). Throughout the 1800s, these aboriginal people rapidly diminished in numbers, eventually dwindling to a few hundred thousand. Some speculated, and not without pleasure, that the natives might become exterminated altogether. Certain tribes, such as the Susquehanna, were indeed exterminated; others, such as the Pequot, came very close to extermination. On the burning of a Pequot village in 1637, one colonist wrote:

> Those that escaped the fire were slain with the sword, some hewed to pieces, others run through with their rapiers, so as they were quickly dispatched and very few escaped. It was conceived they destroyed about 400 at this time. It was a fearful sight to see them thus frying in the fire and the streams of blood quenching the same, and horrible was the stink and scent thereof; but the victory seemed a sweet sacrifice, and they gave the praise thereof to God, who had wrought so wonderfully for them, thus to enclose their enemies in their hands and give them so speedy a victory over so proud and insulting an enemy.[1]

Those Pequots of other villages who were not also killed or sold into slavery were, like many aboriginal people from other tribes, forbidden to speak their language or practice their customs. The few hundred Pequots that survive today have had to rely on anthropologists to recover fragments of their lost heritage.

Alexis de Tocqueville wrote in the 1840s that

> the [Indian] nations I have mentioned formerly covered the country to the seacoast; but a traveler at the present day must penetrate more than a hundred leagues into the interior of the continent to find an Indian. Not only have these wild tribes receded, but they are destroyed; and as they

give way or perish, an immense and increasing people fill their place. There is no instance upon record of so prodigious a growth or so rapid a destruction.[9]

The destruction was rapid indeed. At its nadir, between 1890 and 1900, the population of aboriginal people in the United States dwindled to between 4 and 5 percent of its former size. As one scholar writes, for native Americans,

> The arrival of the Europeans marked the beginning of a long holocaust, although it came not in ovens, as it did for the Jews. The fires that consumed North American Indians were the fevers brought on by newly encountered diseases, the flashes of settlers' and soldiers' guns, the ravages of "firewater," the flames of villages and fields burned by the scorched-earth policy of vengeful Euro-Americans. The effects of this holocaust of North American Indians, like that of the Jews, was millions of deaths. In fact, the holocaust of the North American tribes was, in a way, even more destructive than for the Jews, since many American Indian peoples became extinct.[10]

It is a sad fact that Adolf Hitler could claim that his concept of genocide was grounded in his study of the American extermination of its aboriginal people.[11] The comparison of the American settlers' destruction of the aboriginal people with the Nazis' destruction of European Jewry may seem harsh, particularly because many of the natives perished from disease. Nevertheless, early governments did pay scalp bounties to Indian killers, and it is known that U.S. General Jeffrey Amherst, among others, handed out blankets infected with smallpox to the Indians to facilitate their demise.

Many early European settlers celebrated the decline and extinction of the native people, finding them hindrances to the agricultural, residential, and commercial development of the land. Particularly from 1815 on, Indian lands were frequently stolen and broken up. These displacements decimated Indian populations through forced marches to small and distant reserves. At other times, they provoked war. Between 1600 and 1890, 200 major battles were fought between settlers and indigenous groups, and about three-quarters of the native population was destroyed. The infamous massacre of hundreds of Sioux Indians, mostly women and children, at Wounded Knee, South Dakota, in 1890, ended the so-called Indian Wars of the 1800s.

Even when outright violence was checked, the web of power in America was too tightly knit for native people effectively to resist.

Their autonomy, laws, and rights were denied; they were forbidden to practice many of their customs and rituals; and their ways of livelihood were whittled away as the land became increasingly settled. Plains Indians, for example, depended on the vast herds of bison, also known as buffalo, for food, clothing, shelter, pouches, paints, fuel, utensils, and religious worship. As many as 60 million bison roamed the Plains at the beginning of the nineteenth century. By 1895, less than 500 of these great beasts survived. Many were simply shot for sport and left to rot in the sun. Calvary troops were given explicit orders to shoot all bison on sight to make way for cattle ranching and as an explicit means of destroying native people. General George Crook's motto for his calvary was "Kill a buffalo, starve an Indian." With the destruction of the plains bison, a rich aboriginal culture and a way of life also died.

Many of our most esteemed statesmen had opinions or policies regarding the American Indian that are deplorable. President George Washington called for the "total destruction and devastation" of certain Indian settlements. Benjamin Franklin speculated that inducing alcoholism among Native Americans might be the means "to extirpate these savages in order to make room for cultivators of the earth." According to President Andrew Jackson, who oversaw the deadly forced march of Choctaw, Cherokee, and Creek Indians from the southeastern states to settlements west of the Mississippi, Native Americans had "neither the intelligence, the industry, the moral habits, nor the desire of improvement" to survive in competition with the "superior race" of white settlers. President Andrew Johnson told Congress in 1867 that "if the savage resists, civilization, with the Ten Commandments in one hand and the sword in the other, demands his immediate extermination." President Theodore Roosevelt believed that the settler and pioneer had "justice on their side" in their usurping and development of land that otherwise would have remained "but a game preserve for squalid savages." Congress, in turn, violated hundreds of treaties that Native Americans had signed in good faith.[12] In short, many of America's leading statesmen agreed with General Phil Sheridan's infamous remark that the only good Indian was a dead Indian.

Thomas Jefferson was one of the most compassionate and liberal of America's leaders regarding the native people (and regarding black slaves). Yet the only encouragement Jefferson could find for the Indians was to suggest that they abandon their way of life and join ranks with the European settlers in subduing the land. To survive, Jefferson argues, the American Indians must abandon their identities and cease to be what they always were: hunters and gatherers who lived off the bounty of the land with a rich cultural life but little in the way of formal legal and political institutions. In 1808, President Jefferson delivered these words to the Mohiccons, Delawares, and Munries:

> If you wish to increase your numbers you must give up the deer and buffalo, live in peace, and cultivate the earth.... Give every man a farm; let him enclose it, cultivate it, build a warm house on it.... When once you have property, you will want laws and magistrates to protect your property and persons, and to punish those among you who commit crimes. You will find that our laws are good for this purpose; you will wish to live under them, you will unite yourselves with us, join in our great councils and form one people with us, and we shall all be Americans.[13]

To survive, Jefferson insists, the native people would have to shed their differences from the white settlers and become like them, adopting their culture and trade. The power of the new, rising civilization would necessarily destroy age-old identities. When his efforts "to save and to civilize" American natives were met with resistance, Jefferson announced that their actions "justified extermination."[14]

There were, in short, too few spaces on the declining frontier and within the social fabric of American life for the traditional mores and practices of America's Indians to survive. Writing in the early 1880s, Black Elk summarized the unhappy fate of his people:

> Once we were happy in our own country and we were seldom hungry, for then the two-leggeds and the four-leggeds lived together like relatives, and there was plenty for them and for us. But the Wasichus [white men] came, and they have made little islands for us and other little islands for the four-leggeds, and always these islands are becoming smaller, for around them surges the gnawing flood of the Wasichu; and it is dirty with lies and greed.[15]

At about the same time, Washakie of the Shoshone tribe protested to the governor of the Wyoming territory, saying,

> What you proudly call America, not very long ago belonged to the red man.... [But] our fathers were steadily driven out, or killed, and we, their sons, but sorry remnants of tribes once mighty, are cornered in little spots of the earth all ours of right—cornered like guilty prisoners, and watched by men with guns, who are more than anxious to kill us off.... And so, after all we can get by cultivating the land, and by hunting and fishing, we are sometimes nearly starved, and go half naked, as you see us! Knowing

all this, do you wonder, sir, that we have fits of desperation and think to be avenged?[16]

Occasionally certain tribes or individuals would seek revenge and commit atrocities matched by those their people suffered. The resort to violence, however, only further ensured that the native people would fight a losing battle.

Beginning in the first half of the twentieth century, some of the demands of the native people for greater autonomy and economic improvement were met. Their population began to increase. While the number of native people has risen to over a million today, their cultures remain severely threatened and their general quality of life remains deplorable. Native Americans have the lowest life expectancy, the highest rate of alcoholism, the highest rate of unemployment, and the highest high school dropout rate of any group in the United States.[17]

In spite of these severe obstacles, many native people are bravely attempting to preserve their cultural identities or at least to have a say in how they will become transformed. Wub-e-ke-niew, a member of the Anishinabe-Ojibway tribe, claims that his people's identity remains intrinsically linked to the land. He writes:

> Our land and our forests are, and have always been, an integral part of our religion, our philosophy and our very identity. . . . I have spent my life hearing 'Hey Chief,' and 'Indian!' I am neither one of these; what the Lislakhs [nonaboriginal people of America] have created is not my identity. Making it rain, living in a teepee, tomahawks, tom-toms, woo-woo-war-whoops and smoke signals are all Hollywood stereotypes. . . . These stereotypes have nothing to do with the reality of Aboriginal Indigenous people. . . . When you have that deep gut feeling that you are a part of this land, then you will belong here and will know that the land is to be looked at with reverence and respect. You will understood what we mean when we say, 'Grandmother Earth is not to be sold, and all things are connected.'[18]

Wub-e-ke-niew warns that his people's intimate relationship to the land is difficult for nonaboriginals to understand, as it is grounded in the very structure of the language they speak. Nonaboriginal Americans may find it difficult if not impossible to cultivate this relationship without first transcending the "linguistic patterning of their mind[s]."[19] To respect difference we must first understand it. Understanding what is different requires a struggle that takes us to, and sometimes beyond, the deepest part of our selves.

What is said here of native people is in many respects true of other oppressed minorities. The slow progress in the acquisition of equal rights and opportunities for African Americans is a case in point. Hundreds of years of black slavery were ended with the Civil War. After the war, the Constitution provided that no state could deny any person equal protection under the law. But this proviso was largely unenforced. A period known as Jim Crow developed, initiating a semiformal acceptance of racial discrimination and segregation. Almost a century would elapse before Chief Justice Earl Warren led the Supreme Court to rule in the 1954 case of *Brown* v. *Board of Education* that segregation in schools should be outlawed. Although the Court repudiated the "separate but equal" doctrine, arguing that the educational separation of minority children "generates a feeling of inferiority as to their status in the community that may affect their hearts in minds in a way unlikely ever to be undone," it did not require that segregation be brought to an immediate end. It simply asked for "all deliberate speed" in ending segregation. This ambiguous formulation allowed for much inaction.

A decade later, the Civil Rights Act of 1964 prohibited racial discrimination (as well as discrimination based on religion, sex, or national origin) in employment practices, in places of public accommodation and commerce, and in any program or activity receiving federal financial assistance. The Voting Rights Act of 1965, in turn, forbade rules and arrangements whose purpose or effect was to deny or abridge the vote because of race, color, or membership in a minority-language group. As a result, the number of black elected officials rose fivefold between 1970 and 1992.[20] While the civil rights acts of the mid-1960s freed blacks from legalized segregation, the denial of voting rights, and blatant discrimination in the labor market, these acts did not prove themselves a remedy for the nation's racial divisions. Residential and educational segregation of African Americans has actually increased since 1965.[21]

Limiting Power and Respecting Difference

Throughout history and across the globe, racial and ethnic identities have been constructed and subsequently exploited as a means of oppressing and destroying people. Aboriginal Tasmanians were completely exterminated within less than two and a half centuries of Tasmania's discovery by Europeans. The population of aboriginal Australians declined from 300,000 to 60,000 after the first 130 years of Australia's colonization. Over a million Armenians were killed by Turks in 1915. Over 10 million Jews, Gypsies, and Slavs were killed by Nazi Germans between 1933 and 1945. This sordid chronicle of destruction could be extended manyfold were it to include genocidal practices grounded not only in racial and ethnic bigotries but in religious, cultural, and ideological beliefs.

In the face of countless brutalities committed against individuals because they belong to other groups, it is appropriate that we concern ourselves with the affirmation of difference. At the same time, the affirmation of difference should not create unnecessary divisions or become an apology for neglect, provincialism, or narrow partisanship. To affirm difference is not simply to take care of family and friends and let others fend for themselves. We all have an interest in "life, liberty, and the pursuit of happiness," and these rights need to be protected for everyone. As a contemporary liberal theorist remarks, the concern for difference ought not lead us to reject the ideal of "universal citizenship." Indeed, the concern for difference should underline our shortcomings in realizing such ideals. The problem is that "by failing to attend to the actual life situations and needs of certain groups, by glossing over and ignoring important and legitimate differences, we come to frame principles and norms that reflect partial, not generalizable interests."[22] The affirmation of difference, in short, is meant to broaden our beliefs, values, and interests, not to narrow them. Thus, while we seek to protect everyone's life and liberty and ensure justice for all, we should also recognize that these words may mean different things to different people.

In the same vein, the affirmation of difference should not turn into an apology for divisiveness. This divisiveness often results from a presumption that the members of particular races, economic classes, religions, ethnic or gender groups constitute a homogeneous body that is *essentially* different. To guard against a hostile pitting of "us" against "them," this essentialism must be challenged. In respecting "otherness," we want to avoid the mistake of assuming that all "others" are somehow the same. Human identity is too varied and too fluid to allow this homogeneity. The concern for difference is a recognition that each individual faces a struggle to maintain a unique identity within her community, and that includes the community of the social whole as well as the subsection(s) of it with which an individual primarily identifies or becomes identified. Those whom we identify as "Native Americans" or "African Americans" or "women" or "white males" are not collections of clones. They do not uniformly share the same traits. And the traits that they do share do not wholly isolate them from us. Culturally no less than biologically, what we have in common with other human beings is greater than what we have in contrast. Horizons may always be fused.

The exercise of power in collective life is unavoidable. We use power as a tool and we serve as its target and vehicle. We necessarily exercise power to navigate our social world, and simultaneously have power exercised over us. Thus we are all faced with the challenge of politics in our daily lives. How, then, do we determine which uses of power are good and ought to be cultivated and which uses of power are pernicious and ought to be avoided? That is, how do we determine when the exercise of power, by us and over us, is just? Postmodern theorists have at least as much difficulty answering these questions as their ancient and modern counterparts. Classical political theory, with its focus on the cultivation of civic virtue, and modern political theory, with its focus on the inalienable rights of individuals, have contributed greatly to the understanding of justice. In turn, the postmodern focus on the social construction of identity and the ubiquitous web of power that supports and constrains us offers fresh insight to the question of justice.

For postmodern theorists, one's sense of self or identity is largely a product of the relatively anonymous and ambiguous forms of power that embed one in a network of social relations. To acknowledge that we are products of power, however, is not to suggest that we should give up our individual opinions, beliefs, and values. The point is not simply to "go with the flow." Though we may be vehicles for power, we cannot abdicate the responsibility of being, at times and to a degree, in the driver's seat.

To live a political life, one must establish relatively firm epistemological and ethical positions. To hold such positions, one must make judgments about opportunities, events, institutions, and people. Refusal to make such judgments, as Todorov observes, produces a "flaccid sympathy with everything without embracing anything." Forming opinions and taking action are important. Even more important is having good reasons for one's opinions and actions. As Martin Luther King Jr. famously stated, living out the meaning of the self-evident truth that all men are created equal does not mean that we cease to make judgments about each other. It simply means that people "will not be judged by the color of their skin but by the content of their character." Likewise, in political life we ought not to yield thoughtlessly to power nor thoughtlessly to reject its use. We must exercise judgment and take action.

Political life is grounded in competing forms of power. Whenever power is not contested by power, political life ebbs away. Solicitous of our own interests and wary of the intentions of others, it is natural that we attempt to secure avenues of resistance whenever power is exercised over us. Yet if we are to establish and maintain truly political relationships, we must also allow others to resist our own exercise of power. This is a more troubling notion. Why should we care about the alternatives others have to avoid or contest our influence? Why should we restrain our exercise of power and keep it from becoming a compulsive force? If one is presented with the opportunity to dominate another, why not make good use of it?

To be sure, there are no easy answers to these questions. Certainly the pages of history are filled with examples of the unrestrained use of power and the seemingly futile attempts to curb its exercise in the name of justice. A traditional response is that only an appeal to ethics can restrain the exercise of power. One might, for instance, invoke the Golden Rule or some other ethical standard. But where do such norms come from? Postmodern theorists suggest that ethical standards are themselves social constructs, that is to say, norms are also products of power. In that case, ethical standards may have no more leverage than any other mores generated in society, including mores that stimulate the hegemonic exercise of power. This conundrum was already articulated by Plato in the *Republic,* where Socrates' philosophic appeals to justice are harshly derided by the character of Thrasymachus. Thrasymachus observes that justice is merely "the advantage of the stronger."[23] Justice is a concept developed in society by certain sorts of people to serve their particular interests. Those who practice injustice on a "sufficiently large scale," becoming the rulers of a country, for example, gain the power to redefine the world according to their interests. Faced with this possibility, is there any appeal to be made—excepting that to a Leviathan—that will keep the struggle for power from becoming a quest for ruthless domination or a deadly war of all against all?

Perhaps the beginning of an answer is found in the very notion that is causing us trouble, namely, the postmodern notion of a socially constructed identity. If our own identities—our most basic beliefs, values, and self-understandings, both epistemological and ethical—are generated within a complex social environment, then perhaps the varied influences of this environment should be defended. If one's own identity or sense of self was able to develop into its current form—presumably a form one appreciates well enough—only within an intricate web of power, then perhaps this network of competing forms of power ought to be sustained to allow one's further development. In other words, if we have become who we are by way of our interaction with difference, then perhaps one owes oneself the benefit of safeguarding this difference.

Political theorist Sheldon Wolin writes:

> A political being is not to be defined ... as an abstract, disconnected bearer of rights, privileges and immunities, but as a person whose existence ... draws its sustenance from circumscribed relationships: family, friends, church, neighborhood, workplace, community, town, city. These relationships are the sources from which political beings draw power—symbolic, material and psychological—and that enable them to act together. For true political power involves not only acting so as to effect decisive changes; it also means the capacity to receive power, to be acted upon, to change, and be changed."[24]

Politics entails mutual influence. Reflecting on the development of identity out of the confrontation with otherness may persuade one to remain open to otherness. The argument would be that one should not guard one's identity so tenaciously that one leaves no room for its further growth. To do so would be to abandon political life altogether.

Alternatively, one might ground an argument for the voluntary restraint of power on our (natural) desire for self-knowledge. Alasdair MacIntyre argues that answering the question "Who am I?" involves locating oneself in "a nexus of social relationships."[25] We understand who we are by way of the social relationships we form. We come to know the self by way of the other. One social theorist observes that "self-knowledge—always a construction no matter how much it feels like a discovery—is never altogether separable from claims to be known in specific ways by others."[26] To the extent we seek self-knowledge, therefore, we need to learn about those with whom we share our world. Truly understanding others means recognizing them as different yet equal. Only by recognizing others as representing a difference that should not be denied or dismissed does one remain most open to self-knowledge. To cultivate the conditions for this self-knowledge, the exercise of power must be mutual and the freedom of others to express their differences must not be suppressed.

As political animals, we are burdened and privileged with the construction and contestation of our identities. Learning how the power to construct and contest identity may be wielded, and determining how it should be constrained, is a central concern of political life and a central task of political theory.

Gender and Identity

Gender means sexual identity, that is, one's identity as a man or woman. Is gender a political category? Perhaps gender is politically relevant only to the extent that all private affairs have their boundaries established and safeguarded by political processes and institutions.

Most feminists would disagree with this statement. In her book *Sexual Politics,* Kate Millett suggests that "the personal is the political."[27] The phrase has become something of a watchword for feminists who wish to illustrate the political significance of gender. They argue that the public self that is the bearer of rights cannot truly exercise those rights if the private self is systematically dominated within the home and within the culture at large. The political significance of gender emerges in large part because the gender identities shaped in private impinge on the relationships men and women establish in public. A woman who is made to feel subservient by her husband, male acquaintances, or business colleagues is less likely to become assertive in public life or to pursue public office. This may explain why women remain severely underrepresented in government bodies despite the fact that women's and men's success rates in general elections at all levels of office are approximately the same. Comparatively few women choose to run in elections.[28]

The private self is politically significant because, ultimately, it is the same self who must fill both private and public shoes. As Millet argued, psychological and social relations of domination inevitably translate into political inferiority, despite constitutional or legal recognitions of equality. Indeed, feminists suggest that the problem begins with the way the public realm is envisioned in traditional political thought and culture. Generally, the public realm is projected as wholly separate from the private realm. Yet to posit an abstract, disembodied public self, feminists argue, is already to "buy into" a "masculinist" perspective that will likely jeopardize the political equality of women. By pretending that public and private selves may be easily separated, men have been able to keep the domestic and cultural domination of women out of political debate.

Gender has historically been a key factor in determining the political power one is likely to exercise. By being relegated to the personal and private realm of the home and the family, women throughout the ages and across the globe have been kept out of political life. By politicizing the personal, and challenging the distinction between public and private itself, feminist theorists have gained insight into how women have been politically disempowered and how women might gain a stronger public voice.

Feminists are not suggesting that privacy should be abolished. Neither do they argue that our lives ought to be wholly politicized, with political struggles consuming all of our time and energy and supplying us with the meaning of life. As one feminist warns, "To collapse the personal into the political is epistemologically simplistic, historically naive, and politically dangerous.... One does not demand of politics what it cannot give: wholeness, a complete self-identity, a uniform purpose."[29] The personal may be the political, but it is not *wholly* political. Politics pervades life, but for that reason it is not the whole of life. Feminists are concerned with maintaining certain distinctions between the public realm and the private realm. Nonetheless, they wish to contest the way the line separating these realms has traditionally been drawn. In turn, they wish to argue that the line is not so thick, so straight, or so impermeable as has traditionally been assumed.

Feminist proponents of abortion rights, for instance, generally argue that the government and the public should keep out of women's private lives. The "pro-choice" argument for abortion rights has mostly been based on a women's right to make personal decisions about her body and life, namely, whether to carry a pregnancy to term or to abort the fetus, without interference by the state. Indeed, it was on the fundamental right to privacy that the Supreme Court established a woman's right to abortion in its 1973 *Roe* v. *Wade* ruling. Invoking a similar argument about the right to privacy, a 1965 Supreme Court ruling, *Griswold* v. *Connecticut,* struck down laws in twenty-nine states that held the use of contraception to be illegal.

In contrast, feminists also argue that in certain respects the "private" household should be brought further into the public realm and made more legally, economically, and politically accountable. Some feminists advocate that household work, typically done by women, be officially remunerated just as is work performed outside the home. Minimally, this work should be recognized in the case of divorce, when household and assets are divided. Most all feminists maintain that husbands who physically abuse their wives behind closed doors ought to be subject to legal penalties and punishments and that measures of criminal justice need to be more assiduously administered. In these and related instances, feminists maintain, public law should be extended into the private home.

Feminists do not simplistically suggest that everything private should be made public, or that everything currently understood to be private should remain private. Instead, they insist that the line dividing the private realm from the public realms is itself a political demarcation. This line must be carefully analyzed and occasionally redrawn. Bernard Crick suggests that political theory and belief "inclines towards ideological thought," that is, it strays from the truth, whenever it "abolish[es] the distinction between private and public."[30] Many feminists acknowledge Crick's point. A private realm is necessary and worth fighting for. But feminists also insist that political theory and belief inclines toward ideological thought whenever it petrifies the distinction between the public and the private, closes it off from interrogation, and thus shields it from criticism and contestation.

Men throughout the ages have exercised power in relegating women to the private realm of domestic affairs. Is this power to exclude women best described as a form of *political* power? Politics pertains to speech and action that affects collective existence. In order for some to speak and be heard, others must remain silent. In order for some to lead, others must follow. In a democracy, however, this silence and compliance is understood to be temporary. Democratic politics, as Aristotle argued, is about ruling and being ruled in turn. In an ideal democracy, each citizen would take her turn at speaking and listening, leading and following. Oligarchic politics, in contrast, occurs whenever speech and action are systematically employed by certain groups to the exclusion of other groups. When men are doing most of the speaking and acting, and some of that speaking and acting is designed to keep women publicly silent and inactive, a form of oligarchic politics known as patriarchy develops. Patriarchy is the rule of men—in and out of turn.

The exercise of political power patently displays itself when different viewpoints come into open, public contestation. Political power is also exercised, though less obviously so, when certain issues are kept off the agenda so that certain points of view never gain an audience.[31] Setting the agenda for discussion is a central feature of political power. Politics occurs, therefore, not only when voices speak and vie for power in public. Politics also happens when voices are suppressed and kept powerless within a private realm. Silencing someone, or keeping her from attaining a full and equal voice, is a political (but not democratic) act. The power with which women have traditionally been relegated to the privacy of the home is certainly of political concern.

The Historical Development of Feminism

In ancient Greece, women could neither own property nor vote. They were mostly kept at home, where they would weave, direct any domestic slaves, and generally maintain the household. They were considered part of the domestic economy and were forbidden to participate in public affairs. Indeed the word *economy* comes from the Greek words meaning private household and management (*oikos* + *nemein*). In ancient Greece, the economy was explicitly distinguished from the political realm, the affairs of the home (*oikos*) were separated from the affairs of the city-state (*polis*).

Democracy in ancient Greece was a democracy of a very restricted type. The *demos* or people who held political power consisted only of free-born men. The time and leisure that free-born males found to engage in public affairs was largely gained through the privatized labor of women and slaves. The establishment of the Greek household as a private domain therefore served an explicitly political purpose and was maintained by explicitly political means. The line separating the public from the private in ancient Greece kept over half the population from engaging in politics and discovering their full potential as political animals.

The domestic realm remained at the center of economic life in ancient Greece and continued to play an important role throughout much of the West over the next two millennia. In being relegated to the domestic realm, women's exercise of political power was severely restricted. Although disabled from political participation, however, women remained important players in economic affairs. Though typically denied the right to own property, they often exercised economic power as the managers of the household.

The Industrial Revolution that began in Europe and America during the eighteenth century created job opportunities for women outside the home, freeing them from a singular domestic fate and increasing their economic power. In another respect, however, the Industrial Revolution diminished the economic power of women, at least the economic power of the vast majority of women who stayed at home. This was particularly acute for middle-class women. As the locus of the economy shifted from the home to the factory, women's status as key players in the home economy was eroded. When husbands and brothers left the farm and household to work in the city's factories, the wages they brought home secured their economic power and underscored the economic powerlessness of their wives and sisters. Denied political equality in the public realm, and increasingly denied economic equality in the private realm, women were left with fewer means to control their lives or affect the lives of others, except perhaps the lives of dependent children.

Modern feminism arose in the seventeenth and eighteenth centuries. It developed in response to the economic transformation of home and work as well as the political transformation of aristocratic and monarchical rule. At this time, women began to assert their rights to both economic and political equality. Mary Wollstonecraft (1759–97), one of the first modern feminists, responded to the popular appeal of Thomas

Paine's *The Rights of Man* by writing *Vindication of the Rights of Women* in 1792. Paine had attacked the privileges of the aristocracy in the wake of the French Revolution and gallantly defended the equality of all men. Wollstonecraft pointed out that despite all the grand talk of equality, Paine and the republican revolutionaries left women wholly out of the picture.

Despite Wollstonecraft's courageous effort, modern feminism had a slow and rocky start. It was close to a century later, in 1869, that the English liberal theorist John Stuart Mill would produce another important work in modern feminist theory. Strongly influenced by and often collaborating with his companion (and later wife) Harriet Taylor, Mill wrote *The Subjection of Women*. Here Mill straightforwardly argued for the equality of women, suggesting that such equality is the "surest test and most correct measure of the civilization of a people or an age."[32] Mill's effort, like Wollstonecraft's, was directed at ending women's oppression by gaining for women the rights already enjoyed by men.

Following English common law, the early legal system in the United States also assigned women an inferior status. Women were denied certain forms of education, barred from certain professions and occupations, excluded from juries and public offices, and restricted in their ability to own property, sign contracts, go into business, or write wills. Women had few if any political rights and subsequently had little say when they were denied economic rights by all-male legislatures, executives, and judiciaries. In an early attempt to challenge this injustice, Abigail Adams pleaded with and warned her husband, John Adams, who was in attendance at the Constitutional Convention in 1789. "In the new code of laws," she wrote in a letter, "I desire you would remember the ladies and be more generous and favorable to them than your ancestors. Do not put such unlimited power in the hands of the husbands.... If particular care and attention is not paid to the ladies, we are determined to foment a rebellion, and will not hold ourselves bound by any laws in which we have no voice or representation."[33] Despite the warning, John Adams imitated his ancestors and ignored his wife's wishes. The other attendees of the convention followed suit. Abigail Adams was slightly ahead of her time.

The women's movement in the United States did not germinate until the rise of the abolitionist movement against slavery in the 1830s. It was set fully in motion in 1848, at the Women's Rights Convention at Seneca Falls, New York. Here women gathered together for the first time to assert their rights in public. Paraphrasing the Declaration of Independence, the Seneca Falls attendees proclaimed: "We hold these truths to be self-evident: that all men and women are created equal...." But these truths were neither self-evident nor acknowledged by the male legislators of the day. Only in decades immediately prior to the Civil War did married women gain the right to hold property in their own names. Women would have to wait until the twentieth century to secure their full political rights.

Political equality for women was the goal of the women's suffrage movement, led by Elizabeth Cady Stanton and Susan B. Anthony. The suffrage movement simmered for half a century before becoming well organized in the last decade of the nineteenth century. By 1915, it had picked up the necessary steam. The first woman member of Congress was elected in 1917. The mobilization of women was spurred on owing to women's greater integration in the workforce. During World War I, many more women took on jobs outside the home. At the end of hostilities in 1918, they shifted back into a domestic realm as their industrial services were no longer needed with the return of the soldiers. Nevertheless, the ability of women to fill the nation's economic shoes had been demonstrated. When these efforts did not subsequently translate into political recognition, increasing numbers of women began to mobilize. After much popular protest and lobbying, legislators yielded to pressure in 1920. The Nineteenth Amendment was added to the Constitution, giving American women the right to vote. (In many other Western countries this right was yielded in subsequent decades. It was in place in most states by the 1950s; however, Switzerland enfranchised women only in 1971. In contrast, suffrage had already been extended to New Zealand women in 1893 and to Australian women in 1902).[34]

The percentage of women who vote has steadily climbed since female suffrage was instituted. By the 1980s, it equaled the percentage of men voting. Since then, the percentage of women voting has consistently surpassed that of men. Because women are slightly more than half the population, women already voted in larger numbers than men beginning in the mid-1960s. The equal right to vote and equal if not larger numbers of voters, however, has not translated into equal political power for women. Even today, women remain severely underrepresented in local, state, and federal political bodies. Women constitute about 10 percent of the members of Congress. Women's representation in state legislatures is double that figure, but they only hold about 2 percent of the governorships.[35] The United States has never had a woman president or vice president. (Worldwide, women also hold about 10 percent of the seats in national legislatures and occupy less than 4 percent of cabinet ministries. The proportion of the world's

200-plus countries whose national governments are headed by women is less than one in thirty.

Although certain forms of legal, civil, and political equality for women have been established, at least constitutionally, full economic equality still does not exist. The feminist struggle against economic discrimination did not truly begin until well after World War II. This pursuit of greater equality was spurred on by the 1952 publication of *The Second Sex* by French feminist Simone de Beauvoir. Betty Friedan's *The Feminine Mystique,* written in 1963, had an even greater impact, challenging the notion that women find fulfillment only in childrearing and homemaking. Friedan and others would go on to found the National Organization for Women (NOW) in 1966, which brought pressure on government and business to end discrimination against women and effectively initiated the "second wave" of contemporary feminism.

During this period, women's groups lobbied, petitioned, and marched in demonstrations to ensure that equal rights for women would be safeguarded by the Constitution in the form of an Equal Rights Amendment (ERA). The amendment stated that "equality of rights under the law shall not be denied or abridged by the United States or any state on account of sex." The ERA was not ratified by the required thirty-eight states within ten years of its passage by Congress in 1972; consequently, it failed to become law. The Equal Pay Act of 1963, the Civil Rights Act of 1964, the Equal Employment Opportunity Act of 1972, and the political and legal recognition of sexual harassment as a form of sexual discrimination in the 1980s formally put an end to overt sexual discrimination in employment. Nonetheless, in the early 1990s, women in commensurable positions in the American workforce continued to earn one-third less than their male counterparts. That figure marks a gain of only a few percentage points over what women already comparatively earned by the mid-1950s.[36] In turn, there has been a marked "feminization of poverty" in the United States. The number of impoverished households headed by single mothers more than doubled in the 1980s.[37]

The figures detailing the the economic inequality of women are similar across the globe. Women perform about 60 percent of the world's work, yet they own only 1 percent of the world's land and earn just 10 percent of the world's income.[38] In many countries, economic inequality produces an especially harsh reality for women. Female infanticide is not uncommon in certain poorer countries because impoverished families do not wish to invest their resources in raising a child who will not achieve economic viability. Less drastic, but no less problematic, are the lower levels of health care, nutrition, and education received by girls (and women). For example, worldwide over two-thirds of all illiterate people are women and over twice as many women as men live in poverty. These factors combine to lead to higher mortality rates for girls and much fewer opportunities for their economic and professional advancement. It also leads to overpopulation, as women with lower levels of education and diminished economic opportunities tend to have more children. A 1995 report by the UN Development Program summarized the problem by noting that no society treats its women as well as its men and "in no society do women enjoy the same opportunities as men."[39]

Gender Justice

Justice has been defined since ancient times as giving to each according to his or her due. But how do we determine what each of us is due, that is, what each of us deserves? This question has dogged political theorists for millennia. Certain laws set out what punishment one is due for the criminal actions one commits. This is called criminal justice. Constitutional law sets out what rights one is due as a civil and political being. In the modern, liberal world, for instance, it is constitutionally considered one's due to be treated as an equal. Discrimination against women, whether it is legal, political, economic, or social, constitutes the systematic denial of equal treatment. Feminists rightly decry it as a form of injustice.

The exercise of power or force that denies justice to a specific group of people is called *oppression*. Oppression does not simply mean suffering or deprivation. Suffering or deprivation may occur for all sorts of reasons, because of natural catastrophes or illness, for example. Oppression takes place only when suffering is systematically inflicted by those in power. When those who are unjustly treated are women (or men) as a group, the oppression is called sexism. Sexism is the exercise of legal, political, economic, or social power in a way that discriminates against individuals based on their gender.

Few would deny the fact that, historically, women have been oppressed. Yet many believe that such oppression is a thing of the past, particularly in a country such as the United States where everyone has formal equality, that is, equality under the law. Formal equality means that each individual, regardless of sex, race, religion, class, or other specified characteristics, stands before the law with the same rights and privileges as any other person. Formal equality is established through *procedural* (or formal) justice. Procedural justice exists when everyone is subject to the same rules and the same punishments if and when these rules are broken.

Procedural justice does not ensure that everyone is actually treated as an equal. The problem is that *equality under the law,* whether pertaining to legal, economic, or political affairs, does not necessarily translate into *equality of opportunity.* The reason, to recall Anatole France's observation, is that equal opportunity to sufficient nourishment and shelter is not guaranteed—indeed it may actually be undermined—by the equality under the law that forbids both rich and poor from stealing bread, begging in the streets, or sleeping under bridges.

Equality under the law may secure each citizen the equal right to dine in fancy restaurants, live in fashionable neighborhoods, and attend prestigious universities. For poorer citizens, however, such formal equality seldom translates into fine cuisine, posh suburban living, and Ivy League degrees. All other things being equal—which they seldom if ever are—not eating in fancy restaurants and not living in fashionable neighborhoods may not unduly restrict one's opportunities in the economic or political world, assuming one is sufficiently well nourished and one's own neighborhood is sufficiently safe and secure. Not getting a good high school and college education, in contrast, very well might diminish one's chances for economic or political success.[40] In turn, where one eats, sleeps, and works will largely determine whom one associates with, and one's associations certainly affect one's chances for economic and political success. Sorting out when equality of opportunity is crucial to the maintenance of political rights, or whether that equality can be adequately secured through formal, procedural means, is intrinsic to the pursuit of justice.

Equality of opportunity, most broadly understood, means that each individual receives the same chance to develop fully as a human being. To develop one's full potential as a human being, one must minimally receive some basic level of nourishment, health care, emotional support, and education. Equality of opportunity, for this reason, is often understood as a form of *substantive* justice. Unlike procedural justice, substantive justice requires that each person receive more than the due process of law. It requires that each person also receive the physical, emotional, and educational support required for self-development. In most cases, substantive justice entails a limited redistribution of resources such that the basic (economic, medical, and educational) needs of all are met by government programs financed through taxation.

Our political culture holds that each person deserves an equal opportunity to life, liberty, and the pursuit of happiness. Some argue that a simple equality of rights secured by formal or procedural means adequately fulfills this demand. Others argue that equal opportunity to life, liberty, and the pursuit of happiness entails the equal opportunity to make full use of these rights. Equal opportunity entails not simply the equal right to apply for a job, for example, but the equal opportunity to acquire the education and training that would make one's application for a job truly competitive. Substantive justice, understood as equality of opportunity, is a more demanding and more elusive achievement than procedural justice, understood as equality under the law.

Take the problem of rape. Laws in the United States categorically forbid rape, regardless of the gender (race, class, or creed) of the victim or perpetrator. This constitutes equality under the law. But over 99 percent of all rapists are men and an equally vast majority of their victims are women. Studies suggest that as many as one out of six women in the United States will become a victim of rape in her lifetime. (The United States has a rate of rape three to twenty-five times higher than other industrial nations.)[41] This means that the opportunity for American women to walk down the street safely, or even to live in their homes safely, is hardly equal to the opportunity for safety enjoyed by men. Regarding the problem of rape, equality under the law does not translate into equality of women's opportunity for physical security.

This is not to suggest that inequality under the law would lead to greater equality of opportunity for women. Harsher penalties for male rapists than female rapists, for instance, would hardly prove a better deterrent than harsher penalties for all rapists. Equal opportunity to safety and security may simply not be achievable through the law alone. The equal opportunity for women to live without rape or the fear of rape probably could be achieved only if broad social and cultural changes took place, changes in attitudes and values that incite male violence against women. It is unlikely that legal measures alone could bring about such change.

As in the case of safety and security, equality under the law also does not ensure equality of opportunity for women in the realm of economics. Regarding economic issues, however, some argue that inequality under the law would in fact lead to greater equality of opportunity. At least, that is how one might characterize the argument for affirmative action. Originally, affirmative action was aimed at the removal of "artificial barriers" to the employment of women (and minority-group members). Eventually it came to mean special efforts to recruit, hire, and promote members of disadvantaged groups so as to eliminate the present effects of past discrimination. Affirmative action thus aims to offset a tradition of discrimination against women (and minority-group members) by offering compensatory opportunities. Those opposed to affirmative action argue that it legislates favoritism and constitutes an unjustifiable "reverse discrimination." They argue that affirmative action is unnecessary because equality of opportunity merges with equality under the law in economic matters as long as the laws forbidding discrimination are both extensive and well enforced. Economic opportunities for men and women would theoretically be equal if laws forbidding discrimination in education, recruitment, hiring, promotion, wages, and benefits were strictly upheld.

Gender justice may still elude us even were these antidiscriminatory laws strictly and extensively enforced. Ending women's economic oppression may not simply be a matter of ending discrimination based on gender. The main problem is that men and women remain unequal in ways that can leave both equality under the law and equality of opportunity incapable of thoroughly rendering justice.

For instance, a law might require that all businesses allot a certain number of days a year to each employee to be taken as sick leave when needed. Businesses would also be allowed by law to lay off and replace employees who take more than their allotment. On first blush, this seems neither unfair nor discriminatory, as businesses need to replace employees who cannot or will not work if they are to stay in business. If, in turn, these businesses had to hire back all employees who had taken more than their allotment of sick days, then these businesses would have to fire replacement workers who over time had come to depend on their new jobs. Let us assume that these businesses also hire and promote employees in a "gender-blind" fashion, that is, in complete disregard of the gender of the applicants and employees. As nondiscriminatory as such practices and regulations may seem, they might not render justice, understood as giving to each according to his or her due. The reason is that the biological differences between men and women could make equal treatment less than fair under certain circumstances.

Unlike men, women get pregnant and deliver and nurse babies. This takes time and effort. Is it fair or just for women to lose their jobs more often than men because they exceed their sick-leave allotment when they get pregnant and deliver and nurse babies? One might suggest that women can choose not to get pregnant. Since nonpregnant women have the same opportunities for keeping a job as men, there would be no question of discrimination. But this simply shifts the problem of justice to adjacent terrain. Women who did not want to jeopardize their careers would have to deny themselves the opportunity of motherhood, while men who maintained their careers would not be denied the opportunity of fatherhood. Equal opportunity to motherhood or fatherhood appears to conflict with equal opportunity to job security and promotion.

The problem is that differences between men and women in some (biological) areas make their complete equality in other (economic) areas difficult if not impossible to achieve. Solving this dilemma might seem as easy as enacting a law that gives all women the right to maternity leave. This appears an appropriate and pragmatic remedy. Yet it does not create complete economic equality between men and women. Instead, it creates equality in one area by allowing inequality in another. Men, for instance, might object that maternity rights allow women to have it "both ways." Not only do women benefit from an experience—bearing and nursing children—that men, by nature, are denied, but women can also maintain their careers without any penalty for taking off time that men, by law, are denied.

Faced with *this* injustice, one might propose instituting maternity *and* paternity leave. The decision as to whether the mother or father stays home to take care of the newborn would then be left for the parents to work out among themselves. Have we now truly ensured equality? Probably not. While laws may allow fathers to take paternity leave, the majority of fathers will probably choose not to interrupt their careers. Moreover, such temporary leave policies would not address the more vexing problem of the different rates of promotion between men and women that arise because women's careers tend to be compromised by pregnancy, childbirth, and especially the demands of childcare. Here it is not simply a matter of retaining a job but of retaining a rate of promotion, which can only decline when the responsibility of being the primary caretaker of children restricts the uninterrupted hours and days that one can devote to one's job. To achieve true gender equality in economic affairs, many strongly held cultural beliefs about the role of women as caretakers and men as breadwinners would have to change so that more men would actually choose to take on the childcare roles predominantly assumed today by women.

Not all efforts to achieve greater economic equality between men and women would demand the same amount of government oversight, institutional support, social restructuring, and cultural transformation as the one we have just discussed. But the tension between the demands of the family and the demands of the workplace is illustrative of the general difficulty of translating equality under the law or equality of opportunity into full-fledged justice. The reason is that what one is due may depend as much on the ways in which one is different from others as on the ways in which one is the same. Gender justice demands the pursuit of equality grounded in the recognition of difference. Gender justice also demands that this recognition be translated into cultural mores no less than political policy and legislation.

A radical solution to the problem of gender justice is proposed by feminist Shulamith Firestone. Firestone argues that the physical differences between the sexes will always lead to a "fundamental inequality" in the economic, social, and political arenas. She suggests that the solution lies with the development of technological procedures that could overcome these physical differences. For Firestone, the only way for women to escape the "tyranny" of their biology is to do away with the "barbarism" of pregnancy. The answer to the problem of gender justice, it follows, is "artificial reproduction."[42] Only by becoming unburdened of biological demands can women finally achieve true equality with men. Equality under the law and equality of opportunity will never deliver justice, Firestone maintains. Only an equality of condition can do so. Men and women themselves, not simply the rules and opportunities they face, must be made the same.

Firestone's radical solution to the problem of gender justice has been widely criticized by feminists and nonfeminists alike. Firestone's egalitarian society, critics argue, is gained at much too high a price. Women's opportunities for greater social, economic, and political equality may indeed be increased in such a world, but only by denying their unique opportunities to give birth to children. Thus equality is achieved by destroying difference.

In the same vein, women could diminish their vulnerability to rape by taking steroids that would make them stronger and more capable of defending themselves or by surgically altering their (or men's) physiologies. Alternatively, as some "separatist" feminists suggest, women could simply be segregated so that contact between men and women could be strictly controlled. Separatist feminists argue that men "naturally" dominate women through rape and the threat of rape. They acknowledge, however, that technologically altering this biological programming is (practically) impossible. To end the "state of fear" women suffer through the threat of rape, separation of the sexes thus becomes necessary.[43] Were these proposals actually implemented, the problem of rape might be solved. But again the cost would be prohibitive. Certainly a situation in which men view women as pieces of property to be used and violated at will is intolerable. Still, the physiological differences between and coexistence of the sexes, despite the problems and injustices they give rise to, are worthy of preservation. Equality should not be achieved in one area by destroying or neutralizing cherished differences in another.

Most feminists argue that achieving equality under the law and equality of opportunity for women is best served by political rather than technological means and by greater integration and education rather than greater segregation. Political solutions, however, are usually grounded in compromise. Justice between the sexes, for this reason, always remains an ideal resolutely to be striven for rather than an achievement to be secured once and for all. The achievement of greater equality in one facet of collective life, moreover, often entails a loss, though not necessarily a prohibitive loss, in the realization of some other value. Greater equality may mean less freedom or perhaps greater instability of the mores that order individual relationships and the family. Wherever change is demanded and power is wielded to effect it, there will be resistance. Political life requires that this resistance be acknowledged even as it is overcome.

Achieving gender justice might not be such a difficult matter if disadvantages in one area of human endeavor were naturally offset by advantages in another. Most frequently, however, disadvantages beget further disadvantages. Economic disadvantages typically translate into political disadvantages, for example. Wealth allows for the greater leisure, education, and influence that make for political power. It is not simply a matter of having a large bank account. Active integration into an economic community promotes active integration into the political community. Most political leaders first hone their managerial and rhetorical skills and gain their respect and reputation in the marketplace. Hence any restriction of one's integration into the professional and business world will likely translate into disadvantages in the political world. If women predominantly stay at home (to care for children or maintain the household), their opportunities to translate economic activity into political power will be accordingly diminished.

Political equality is about more than an equal right to vote. It includes holding a fair share of the positions of leadership. In this respect, women in the United States and throughout the world remain political unequals. The economic disadvantages and discrimination that women experience contribute heavily to this political inequality. Yet the problem of political inequality cannot be reduced to the issue of economic disadvantage and discrimination. Both are part of a bigger picture. A long tradition of patriarchal mores contributes to the problem. Certain feminists suggest that religious inequality also tends to translate into political inequality for women. In *Beyond God the Father*, Mary Daly argues that women who worship a male deity are subject to a subtle form of psychological self-depreciation. They come to believe that they are inferior to men in spiritual affairs. This religious inequality supports and is supported by the economic, social, and political subservience of women within the broader community. The reverse, of course, holds for men, who may accept or seek to justify their worldly domination of women by calling to mind the masculinity of God or the patriarchy upheld in religious scripture.

To counteract sexism, Daly advocates that women assert their equality in religious matters. They are counseled to abandon patriarchal religion and adopt female deities. Effectively, a form of religious separatism is advocated. To combat patriarchy, which, Daly argues, is *"the prevailing religion of the entire planet,"* women must readjust not only their relationship to the world but their relationship to the heavens.[44]

There are good data to buttress the claim that economic inequality easily translates into political inequality. Historically and across the globe, wealth and political power have gone hand in hand. Daly does not supply us with an adequate historical or comparative analysis to validate her thesis that religious inequality, defined as the worship of a male deity, leads to political inequality. Her argument is more in the line of a suggestive psychological inquiry. Regardless, Daly's thesis deserves reflection. It confronts us with the important question of when and how cultural mores, such as religious belief, affect our political lives.

Equality and Difference

Many of the early suffragists of the late 1800s and early 1900s understood their struggle as having two distinct goals. First, they were fighting for the basic rights of women, who deserved equal status with men. Second, they were working to moralize politics. They hoped that women would improve political life by bringing higher moral standards into the public realm. The suffragists, perhaps naively, believed that the influence would run only one way. By making the private morality of women more public, the world of politics, they reasoned, would be made more moral. They did not assume or foresee that the private morality of woman might become contaminated by the vices of the public world, such as the lust for power.[45]

Certain conservative thinkers opposed to feminism and women's liberation have developed this line of argument. They suggest that a masculinization and moral degradation of women occurs through their participation in public life. This poses a threat to traditional sensibilities and values. They consequently argue that women can retain their distinctive virtues only by upholding their traditional roles. A women's place, they suggest, is in the home. Opposition to the passage of the ERA, for example, was based on this reasoning. It was feared that the amendment would subject women to the military draft and combat duty, thus masculinizing them. Feminism has also been blamed by conservatives for the "breakdown" of the family in contemporary times.

To be sure, in a culture such as America's that celebrates the principle (if not the practice) of equality for all, such socially conservative views are restricted to a minority. At the same time, many progressive feminists also remain wary of the struggle for simple equality. For these feminists, gaining equality at the cost of losing one's sexual identity misses the point.

It has been suggested that Westerners who "proclaim the equality of all mankind" are often the "staunchest upholders of the cultural superiority of the West." Upholding the principle of equality for these Westerners means conferring the "right and duty of all mankind ... to accept the ways of thinking of the Western societies."[46] Here egalitarianism amounts to a belief that others should be, and want to be, just like oneself. With similar concerns in mind, many feminists reject an equality that amounts to an implicit assumption that women should be more like men or that masculine ways of thinking and acting are inherently superior. Historically, they observe, it is men who have always defined the meaning of equality and the route to its achievement. Under such circumstances, women could gain equality with men only by becoming more like men—psychologically, spiritually, and ethically, if not physically. Equality could be achieved only at the cost of forfeiting distinctly feminine qualities.

Feminists do not want to let men play the role of Procrustes. They do not want to be made to "fit" into a man's world and argue that equality should not require the masculinization of women. As Carole Pateman writes, "women's equal standing must be accepted as an expression of the freedom of women *as women,* and not treated as an indication that women can be just like men."[47] Feminists aim to create a world where gender difference flourishes along with gender equality. To achieve this goal, the world itself—its mores, institutions, and practices—would have to become more feminine, or at least more balanced in its feminine and masculine features.

What would a more feminine world look like? To answer this question we must first ascertain whether, apart from rather obvious distinctions in physiology and physical capacities, differences between men and women have political or cultural ramifications. Are there distinctly feminine ways of thinking, feeling, or acting? Are there such things as a feminine epistemology and feminine ethics that are truly distinct from masculine epistemology and ethics?

Carol Gilligan, a well-known feminist theorist, has suggested that there are. Gilligan observes that girls do not easily fit within existing models of how children develop morally. Two possible explanations offer themselves: either there is something wrong with the moral development of women or there is something wrong with the standard models of moral development. Gilligan suspects the latter. It is probably not sheer coincidence, she observes, that these models were produced and employed by men. Viewing the world through masculine eyes, male theorists naturally produced models of moral development that reflected their own experiences. Women's experiences appear to be different.

Gilligan argues that women exhibit distinct social concerns and that these concerns lead them to employ different criteria to evaluate and arrive at moral decisions. In short, the mores that structure men's and women's ethical choices differ. Judging women in terms of masculine morality leads to misunderstandings and unfair evaluations. "It all goes back, of course, to Adam and Eve," Gilligan states, reminding her readers of the biblical tale where God fashioned the first woman out of a rib from the first man. Though left to prosper in the Garden of Eden, Adam and Eve were soon cast out of paradise for their misdeeds. The moral of the story, Gilligan writes, is that "if you make a woman out of a man, you are bound to get in trouble."[48] Gilligan is suspicious of any attempt to make unequals equal, particularly when doing so forces women to think and act more like men.

The differences Gilligan proposes between masculine and feminine moral orientations are relatively straightforward. Women tend to conceive the ethical realm as having to do with the requirements and responsibilities of relationships. Morality is about the duty to care for those within one's interpersonal network. We learn these duties and other moral responsibilities by carrying out our social roles. Moral dilemmas are approached as problems of correctly interpreting and repairing the contextual relations among individuals. Women arrive at solutions to moral dilemmas by increasing communication within their network of relations so that mutual responsibilities and caring might be reestablished and maintained.

Women, in short, develop what Gilligan calls a "morality of care." Within this morality, compassionate engagement, not adherence to abstract principles, fosters justice. Women strive to view others concretely, in the context of their actual relationships, and to interact with them based on this insight. They feel a duty to ensure that no one is excluded from the network of relations. Those who are hurt as a result of its inevitable fractures are to be quickly reintegrated. This puts a premium on the empathy required to discern the needs of others.

Men, in contrast, perceive the ethical realm as defined by the rules of fair play and the rights of autonomous individuals. One solves moral problems by consistently applying universally applicable rules in a neutral, objective manner. Moral problems are approached as logical puzzles. The task is deductively to sort out and prioritize conflicting rights, standards, duties, and laws. In this way, the appropriate boundaries between individuals may be reestablished and guarded against further transgression.

Men, in short, develop what Gilligan calls a "morality of rights." Impartiality and reasoning constitute the better part of justice. One strives to view others abstractly, as representative bearers of rights. In turn, one strives to pass judgment on them objectively, as if from a distance. Equality under the law, reciprocity, fair play, and individual liberty are the goals to be achieved and protected.

We might summarize Gilligan's thesis by saying that women's morality is primarily concerned with the maintenance of and mending of relationships, while men's morality is concerned with the problems that arise when relationships overly constrain or encroach on the freedom and autonomy of individuals. Gilligan does not suggest that men never evidence a (feminine) morality of care. Neither does she argue that women never evidence a (masculine) morality of rights. Gilligan is speaking of tendencies within the population as a whole. These tendencies do not necessarily reflect innate structures within the male and female psyche. They may also be artifacts of culture. Indeed, the morality of care may have developed as a means for women to cope with life in a (patriarchal) world that demanded constant sacrifice from them as sisters, wives, and mothers.

Gilligan warns that both feminine and masculine moral orientations have their shortcomings. The morality of care, particularly when exercised by women in relationships with men, may lead to dangerous self-sacrifice. The feminine penchant for such behavior is best tempered, Gilligan suggests, when women embrace aspects of a morality of rights. Incorporating this masculine morality produces a sense of integrity and independence and a willingness to stand up for one's due.

In turn, the equality of rights and hierarchy of rules promoted within a masculine morality is best tempered by a morality of care. The feminine orientation to the contextual nature of relationships may soften rigid rule-following and the insistence on a formal equality of right. A morality of care may help transform formal equality into a form of equity. Equity bespeaks a concern to uphold not only the letter of the law but also the spirit of the law. It ensures not only fair play but a fair share.

Neither masculine nor feminine moralities are sufficient on their own. Justice is best attained, Gilligan suggests, by balancing rights with care, law with equity, and independence with responsibility to others.

She maintains that within each of us, the potential for masculine and feminine morality exists. The goal is for men and women to let both voices speak together, achieving a greater inner harmony.[49]

Following the work of Gilligan, other feminist theorists have suggested that there are not only feminine and masculine ways of being moral but also feminine and masculine "ways of knowing."[50] That is to say, there is not only a feminine ethics but also a distinct feminine epistemology. Knowledge in general, not only moral knowledge, is gained and employed in particular ways by women. Whereas men tend to view knowledge as an objective representation of reality obtained through impartial observation, women view knowledge more contextually. For women, knowledge consists in the discovery of networks of relations. Knowledge is developed through mutual exchanges that reveal the nature of these networks. Again, the point is not that women and men cannot or do not ever "know" things in the same manner. But distinct tendencies exist for each sex.

If women's cultural mores, psychologies, and epistemologies are significantly different from men's, how and why does this arise? Nancy Chodorow, a feminist psychoanalyst, offers an explanation of these differences based on the early socialization of children. A girl's sexuality and sense of self, Chodorow theorizes, is "ascribed" to her through her relationship with her caretaker mother. It is experienced as given rather than earned. She naturally integrates herself into her world through an identification with her same-sex caretaker. Thus a girl comes to understand her identity as expressive of her own nature rather than dependent on specific achievements.

In most societies, a boy grows up largely in his father's absence, as work roles supersede caretaker roles for adult men. A boy's sexuality and sense of self are therefore much less the product of his identification with a same-sex, nurturing parent. Instead, a boy's identity must be "achieved" in distinction, and perhaps in opposition, to the caretaker mother. Achieving a stable male identity becomes a matter of asserting independence from the mother. It is a product of a defensive demarcation of ego boundaries. The independent, aggressive nature of the male identity is further accentuated by the cultural emphasis on the active rather than receptive character of the male sexual act.

Female identity is socialized as a relational *being,* Chodorow observes, whereas male identity, constantly in need of demonstration, is socialized as an assertive and often competitive *doing.* Feminine identity is a discovery of one's place in the world, while masculine identity is an assertion of one's prerogative to act in the world. This difference in the development of male and female identities in early childhood produces a disjunctive and hierarchical social structure, according to Chodorow. Male values of independence, competitive achievement, and aggressivity oppose, dominate, and are reinforced by female values of dependence, caretaking, and passivity. At the same time, a general antagonism to women and a fear of female authority arises owing to the predominant role of women in parenting.

The psychological development of children, in other words, has important, and potentially dangerous, consequences for public life. Chodorow concludes that "until masculine identity does not depend on men's proving themselves, their *doing* will be a reaction to insecurity rather than a creative exercise of their humanity, and woman's *being*, far from being an easy and positive acceptance of self, will be a resignation to inferiority."[51] Once again, the private and personal realm of gender, childhood, and the family asserts its political significance. The general recommendation made by Chodorow and many other feminists is that fathers should take a greater role in childrearing. Were this to occur, men and women would eventually develop more balanced moralities, epistemologies, and identities.

Surveying the different ways men and women are socialized, feminists suggest that what it means to be a man or woman is something that may change over time and space. Gender roles are largely a function of the historical period and cultural environment. Simone de Beauvoir put the point succinctly in *The Second Sex,* writing, "one is not born, but rather becomes, a woman."[52] Actually, one does not simply become a woman in some generic sense, one becomes a certain sort of woman. For this reason, those feminists who argue for an "essential" nature that defines all women have been sharply criticized.[53] They have been criticized mostly by other feminists, who insist that any attempt to define a female essence would privilege the characteristics of certain sorts of women (e.g., those belonging to a particular sexual or ideological orientation, class, race, or ethnic group) while depreciating others.

Carol Gilligan, for instance, has been criticized for speaking about a feminine morality in general when most of the women she interviewed were college students in the United States. Perhaps, then, Gilligan's observed feminine morality is really a privileged, white, middle-class morality. Gilligan's study may ignore the distinctive moralities of racial and ethnic minority women within the United States, who remain underrepresented in American colleges, as well as the distinct moralities of women of color living in developing societies. Thus feminist Hester Eisenstein deplores the "false universalism" within certain feminist writings.[54] When feminists, in their effort to champion the cause of women, speak on behalf of "all women" or claim to have discovered the essence of woman's nature, they may obscure more differences than they reveal.

John Stuart Mill anticipated Beauvoir's famous statement, writing that "what is now called the nature of women is an eminently artificial thing—the result of forced repression in some directions, unnatural stimulation in others." Mill recognized that to the extent his assessment was accurate, it applied not only to the construction of female identities but also to the construction of male identities. He goes on to state: "I deny that any one knows, or can know, the nature of the two sexes, as long as they have only been seen in their present relation to one another."[55] Mill's warnings bring home the point that sexual identity remains largely a product of historical and cultural context.

Feminism, Liberalism, and Patriarchy

John Stuart Mill was an early feminist, though the term was not current in his day. He was also a liberal. In the Western world today, many, perhaps even most, feminists consider themselves to be liberal feminists, as opposed to socialist feminists, conservative feminists, or radical feminists.[56] Yet most feminist theorists, including liberal feminists, remain wary of the traditional forms of liberal politics and liberal political theory. Liberalism evidences an overarching concern to promote individual liberty. It generally does so by establishing (legal) boundaries between independent individuals in order to proscribe illegitimate interference by government or society. Consequently, liberal theory is primarily concerned with securing individual rights through the rule of law.

In much liberal theory, this law is understood to be promulgated by a limited, neutral government whose legitimacy derives from a social contract. The social contract establishes governmental rule through the uncoerced agreement of independent and autonomous individuals who wish to escape the anarchy of a state of nature. Many feminists claim that liberalism's origins in social contract theory belie its masculinist tendencies. The charge is that liberalism focuses on the male concern for the protection of individual rights and independence while ignoring the feminine concern for the sustaining of relationships and community. Most starkly put, the charge is that "liberalism has no place for women *as women*."[57] Women must think and act like independent men to fit in a liberal world.

Feminists argue that the reason liberalism in general, and liberalism based on social contract theory in particular, has such a tough time with the obligations implicit in relationships and communities is that liberal theorists begin with the wrong premises. They assume the independent existence of autonomous (male) actors who negotiate a fair means of establishing and maintaining a peaceful collective existence. Thomas Hobbes, John Locke, and Jean-Jacques Rousseau are early social contract theorists credited with outlining the original boundaries of liberal politics. A contemporary liberal theorist and philosopher, John Rawls, has carried on this tradition.

Rawls asks us to imagine ourselves in an "original position" that serves a similar purpose as the imagined state of nature in traditional social contract theory. The original position is not proposed as an actual or even imaginary historic event. It is simply an intellectual abstraction that clears the ground for theorizing. In the original position we find ourselves situated behind a "veil of ignorance." Behind this veil we remain unaware of our class position and social status, our race or religion, our abilities, predispositions, and propensities, and our natural strengths or weaknesses. Were everyone situated behind a veil of ignorance in the original position, Rawls argues, people would not be able to design principles of justice that favored their own individual conditions or attributes. Not knowing what place in society one occupied, one would establish a social contract that was as fair as possible to everyone. People situated in the original position would negotiate a contract that safeguarded individual rights and liberties, maintained equality of opportunity, fairly distributed basic goods, and ensured that those inequalities that did arise in society were arranged so that they somehow benefited the least advantaged.[58]

Rawls's theory of justice is a masterpiece of contemporary liberal political theory. From a feminist perspective, however, it has serious shortcomings. Like all liberal social contract theories, Rawls's work is primarily concerned with maintaining the greatest autonomy possible for individuals who negotiate with each other from positions of rivalry. People negotiating in the original position are fearful of each other's freedom. Like the inhabitants of the state of nature, they are willing to give up some of their own autonomy in exchange for the increased security of an ordered social life. A feminist thinker explains the problem with such assumptions:

> Giving theoretical primacy to contract relationships and the choices made by independent individuals is possible only by imagining a 'state of nature' made up of unrelated adults. But no one is born that way. Our first and most fundamental human relationships are those of trust and dependence as infants, and any society that will reproduce itself has to create the conditions under which such diffuse obligations will be satisfied. If mother-and-child, rather than adult male, is seen as the basic human unit,

creating community does not seem so fraught with difficulty, nor does competition seem the archetypal human emotion.[59]

The way we imagine ourselves and theorize our past—from a masculinist perspective of competitive, autonomous individuals in a state of nature or from a feminist perspective of communities held together by naturalized obligations—plays a significant role in deciding how we construct our collective present and foresee our collective future.

Feminist theorists seek to reconstruct the mores that ground our self-conceptions and our politics so that more women's voices might be heard and more feminine points of view taken into account. Many feminists have focused on the oppression that occurs when women's voices and perspectives are systematically ignored or suppressed. Other feminists are wary of any effort that describes women in the role of victim. The danger, they argue, is that by constantly portraying women as victims of oppression and men as their oppressors, these pernicious roles may actually be reinforced. The description of women as stripped of power, as no longer agents but merely passive recipients or depositories of the mores of a patriarchal culture, is neither historically accurate nor psychologically helpful. Women, it is suggested, should view themselves not as weaker victims but as equals, and occasionally as moral superiors. Moreover, many women already exercise the social, economic, and political power to back up these views.

Susan Moller Okin observes that as many as one out of every three households worldwide is headed by a single female and that these households experience a significantly higher rate of poverty than those headed by males.[60] Other feminists point to the fact that in many countries women bear by far the largest share of the daily workload both in the field and at home. In many societies, women carry out more than 70 percent of the agricultural work in addition to their domestic chores. Yet they still languish with lower levels of nutrition, education, social status, economic opportunity, and political power. Feminists are aware that these "facts" relating to the unjust conditions in which women live may be employed in different ways. To view women as casualties of a patriarchal world is to promote a debilitating "victim feminism." To focus on the feminine strengths and resources that have allowed women to prevail under such oppressive conditions—managing households, caring for children, carrying on work outside the home, and becoming politically active—is to promote a more invigorating "power feminism."[61]

The differences between men and women, when coupled with the exercise of power, often lead to inequality and injustice. Feminists take on the dual task of criticizing this oppression while celebrating the potential development and often the actual flourishing of women in the midst of such adversity. They also take on the difficult task of balancing the struggle for equality with the celebration of difference. The pursuit of gender justice is grounded in this balance. It is also grounded in the realization that the boundary between private and public realms is permeable and that the relationship between private and public realms remains a political one.

In their writings, most contemporary feminist theorists criticize both the enduring and oppressive legacies of patriarchy as well as the implicit assumptions, conceptual categorizations, and tactical maneuvers carried out by other feminists who, like them, seek to end patriarchal oppression. Feminist contestation of feminism constitutes the burden and privilege of a tradition of thought that has become sufficiently strong and rich to benefit from self-criticism.

The Politics of Class

François Fourier (1772–1837), a French socialist with a utopian project for farming communes, observed that the degree of woman's emancipation is the natural measure of the general emancipation of a society. Friedrich Engels (1820–95), a German thinker who moved to England to manage his father's textile factory, agreed with Fourier. Engels was following a long tradition among socialist and communist thinkers in advocating the equality of women. This tradition extends back 2,500 years. In the *Republic*, Plato proposes the creation of a communistic society in which women are fully emancipated and treated as equals. One suspects, however, that Plato's proposal might have been ironic. Engels was very serious.

Engels believed that the oppression of women would cease only after most other forms of oppression had ceased. Long after the slaves had lost their chains, the serfs had won their freedom, and wage laborers had gained their full economic rights, women in society would still remain second-class citizens. The end to their oppression, therefore, would mark the end of oppression in general. Engels was the long-time collaborator and friend of Karl Marx (1818–83), a German philosopher who became the most important theorist of communism. Apart from a few of Engels' later works, notably *The Origin of the Family, Private Property and the State*, and even fewer statements from Marx, however, the question of gender did not find a voice in the work of these thinkers. (Marx wrote a short journalistic essay in 1842 entitled "On the Divorce Bill," but this article argued *against* the liberalization of the divorce laws.) For the most part, Marx and Engels were preoccupied with other issues. Their major concern was not the emancipation of women but the emancipation of the working class.

For Marx and Engels, economic oppression, not sexism, was the most salient issue. To the extent that they were concerned with women's oppression, they presumed that gender inequality would be adequately addressed once economic injustices in society were resolved. Contemporary feminists largely disagree. They argue that issues of gender should not be conflated with or subordinated to class interests, however much they remain related concerns. By concentrating solely on the significance of (men in) economic production, feminists suggest, many socialists neglect the significance of (women in) biological reproduction.[62] A strict economic focus blinds them to the inherent injustice of patriarchy. However unwilling feminists are to conflate gender issues with economics, they are well aware of the political importance of economic oppression, which affects women more severely than men throughout the world. Thus many feminists have informed their thinking by studying Marxist theory.[63]

Karl Marx's concern with economic oppression was already evident in his youth. His early career as a journalist led him to confront the plight of the impoverished grape growers of the Moselle region of his native Germany and the plight of peasant wood gatherers who were forbidden to make use of the forests of the nobility. Steeped in German philosophy during his days as a student at the University of Berlin, Marx took on the task of theorizing the origins and dynamics of these economic disparities. In turn, he wrote broadly about the nature of labor, class interests, and class conflict in capitalistic society and the potential for a communist revolution to supersede it.

In an early work written in 1843 called "On the Jewish Question," Marx analyzed religious freedom, an issue of much interest in his day. More specifically, Marx examined the question of whether the Jewish people of Germany should be granted full political rights. Hitherto their religion had kept them from becoming political equals in the Christian German state. Progressive liberal thinkers at the time suggested that the remedy for this injustice entailed a full separation of church and state. Religious belief should become a wholly private affair, rather than a matter of state sanctioning and enforcement. With state religion abolished, liberals believed, the traditional religious rationale for excluding the Jews from politics would no longer be valid. Jews, like any other religious group, would gain their full political rights.

Marx acknowledged that this liberal solution constituted an advance over the Christianized German state, which was a remnant of theocratic feudal times. Yet he argued that the liberal proposal did not go far enough. It is here that we first glimpse Marx's genius and the kernel of his radicalism.

Marx argues that making religion a private affair would not fully emancipate the Jews. Nor, for that matter, would it further the emancipation of Christian Germans. Political emancipation, Marx argues, is not a final emancipation. In the liberal state, one gains "religious liberty" to be sure. But one is not "liberated from religion." An adequate emancipation would entail the end of religious belief altogether.

Why should Marx care whether anyone is religious or not? What possible *political* significance could one's private religious beliefs have, assuming the state and church are adequately separated? Religion had great political significance for Marx because of the comprehensive nature of political life. Religious belief, Marx holds, is a symptom of a political life stripped of its full potential. Following the argument of a contemporary thinker named Ludwig Feuerbach, Marx maintains that religious belief is rooted in our dissatisfaction with the conditions of existence. Our earthly suffering, scripture promises, will be compensated for by heavenly happiness. But religious scripture is not written by the hand of God, Marx observes. It is written, and believed, by human beings who are unable to fulfill their desires in this life and thus imagine a God who will reward them in an afterlife. In his famous phrase capturing this thesis, Marx writes that "religion is the sigh of the oppressed creature, the sentiment of a heartless world, and the soul of soulless conditions. It is the *opium* of the people."[64] According to Marx, religion is an anesthetic that dulls our sense of earthly pain and oppression and produces delusions of a blissful beyond. The problem with such a drug is that it saps our drive for social reform and hence keeps us from bettering our present conditions here on earth. That is a political concern.

Alienation and Revolution

In keeping us from understanding the true nature of our present conditions and working for their betterment, Marx writes, religion fosters *alienation* (the German word is *Entfremdung*, literally "estrangement"). Alienation keeps us strangers from ourselves, from our world, and from our full development as human beings. It signals the extensive gap between humanity's condition and humanity's potential. Marx writes:

> The abolition of religion as the *illusory* happiness of men, is a demand for their *real* happiness. The call to abandon their illusions about their condi-

tion is a *call to abandon a condition which requires illusions.* The criticism of religion is, therefore, the *embryonic criticism of this vale of tears* of which religion is the *halo.* ... The immediate *task of philosophy,* which is in the service of history, is to unmask human self-alienation in its *secular form* now that it has been unmasked in its *sacred form.* Thus the criticism of heaven is transformed into the criticism of earth, the *criticism of religion* into the *criticism of law,* and the *criticism of theology* into the *criticism of politics.*[65]

For Marx, the struggle against religion is the necessary forestage to a more extensive struggle against oppressive and alienating social and political conditions.

Religion is not so much the problem itself as the symptom of a larger problem. The unpoverished conditions under which people suffer stimulate the need for the emotional and spiritual opiate of religion. Poverty, however, is not the sole issue, otherwise wealthy individuals would never be religious. The real problem, of which religion is merely a symptom, is the general dissatisfaction with earthly life. Being satisfied with one's condition on earth is not simply a matter of having enough money never to suffer from material want. To be truly satisfied one must achieve one's full potential as a human being, and human beings, for Marx, do not live by bread alone. They are primarily social and political animals who need to live as integral parts of communities. Social alienation, which keeps us from achieving our full potential as political animals, is the ultimate cause of our dissatisfactions. The alienation that results from poverty is effectively the by-product of a deeper alienation inherent in the injustices that disrupt and destroy human communities.

Poverty, at least in the modern age, is itself a symptom of the deeper malaise of class society. The chief concern for Marx, therefore, was not *"naturally existing* poverty," which he believed had all but disappeared in the industrial nations of his time. The chief concern was "poverty *artificially produced."* This artificial poverty was the direct consequence of the *"disintegration* of society."[66] In modern times, Marx argues, poverty is a product of the gross economic inequality that exists between different classes of people. A class society is a society chiefly defined by its economic cleavages and its resulting economic injustice. A society grounded in economic injustice is a disintegrated society. It is disunited, filled with antagonisms, torn by conflicts, and saturated with alienation.

Marx's concern with social alienation stems from his assessment of human nature. Marx assumes that humans are in essence "species beings." Humans are inherently collective or communal in nature. To achieve their full potential, Marx reasons, human beings would have to establish a truly communal life. Throughout history, however, fear and greed have pitted human beings against one another. A world of scarce resources has made one person's gain another person's loss. As a result, the world became populated by self-interested individuals, or groups of individuals, who dominate and exploit one another in their endless pursuit of wealth and power. In failing to live collectively harmonious lives, human beings become alienated from their species being. They no longer identify themselves—their knowledge, skills, and achievements —with humanity as a whole. Instead, they perceive themselves as living in competition and conflict. This alienation is suffered by rich and poor alike. But for the poor, scraping out a living in the sweat of their brows, the suffering is compounded owing to their extreme material want. Their suffering is not only emotional, psychological, and spiritual but also physical.

Marx suggests that the working poor are alienated in multiple ways. First, workers are alienated from the products of their labor. These products do not constitute a lasting tribute to the virtues of workers, as a painting testifies to the skill of the artist and becomes a prized possession. Instead, the goods produced by workers belong solely to the capitalist who employs them. The capitalist treats the products of labor as mere commodities to be bought and sold for profit in the marketplace. They have no intrinsic value for the workers themselves and have only an instrumental, economic value for the capitalist. Second, workers are alienated from the processes of labor. The division of labor in society forces them to perform menial and uninteresting work, such as assembly-line production, that cannot exercise their full potential as creative, thinking, feeling human beings. Third, workers are alienated from their fellow human beings. Always threatened by poverty and the loss of their means of subsistence, workers view capitalists as exploiters and fellow workers as competitors for scarce jobs. Fourth, workers are alienated from nature. Caught up in the system of capitalist production and its endless pursuit of profit, the earth ceases to be a cherished home. Instead, it becomes a storehouse of resources to be ruthlessly extracted and transformed into saleable products. Finally, Marx observes, workers become alienated from themselves. Viewed as labor power by the capitalists, workers eventually come to think of themselves as commodities to be bought and sold in the market for the price of wages.

The solution to the problem of alienation is social revolution. Only revolution, Marx believed, could wipe out class distinctions, economic injustice, and the various forms of alienation they create. To succeed in this endeavor, a social revolution would have to abolish private property. The abolition of private property is crucial because the right to acquire private property fosters the unequal accumulation of wealth. The unequal accumulation of wealth fosters the unequal exercise of power based on wealth. And the unequal exercise of power based on wealth leads to the development of an inegalitarian, hierarchical and alienated society. Thus the theory of communism, Marx wrote, "may be summed up in the single sentence: Abolition of private property."[67]

Without private property there would be no economic distinctions to divide society into classes. In a society without class divisions, where property was held in common and equally shared, human beings could realize the fullness of human life unsullied by want, greed, or exploitation. Moreover, communistic life after the revolution would not only be free of economic conflict. Marx believed that it would be free of all social conflicts, including those between the sexes. For Marx, conflicts are symptoms of social alienation. Like differences in religious belief, all sources of conflict will disappear, Marx argues, once the social divisions inherent in an alienated economic existence are ended.

Ideology

Marx's belief that the right economic and social conditions would put an end to all human conflict and dissatisfaction was grounded in his rejection of German idealist philosophy, particularly the philosophic idealism of G.W.F. Hegel (1770–1831). Idealists argue that individuals have an innate freedom of thought and will. They also believe that the realm of ideas (thought and understanding) constitutes the true engine of history. Action follows from thought, which is fundamentally free. History is the product of such thought-provoked action.

Marx, in contrast, was a materialist. He argues that human beings are distinguished from other animals not because they have ideas but because they produce their own means of subsistence by way of organized labor.[68] Idealism actually inverts reality, according to Marx. Ideas are the effect, not the cause, of the material conditions in which humans live in their workaday lives. Marx famously states that "life is not determined by consciousness, but consciousness by life."[69] What one thinks, values, and believes, in other words, is a function of one's economic and social environment. The type of society one lives in and the class of which one is a member largely determine one's identity. Hence greed, selfishness, and all other human vices could be abolished, Marx holds, if individuals were raised in the proper social environment.

History, Hegel argued, is the systematic unfolding of the *Idea* in time. While Marx rejected Hegelian idealism, he retained Hegel's perspective about progressive historical development in order to meld it with Feuerbach's materialism. The result was a labor-based theory of history that maintained that society developed progressively through periods of revolutionary upheaval and adjustment. Marx concluded that all history was the history of class conflict and that class conflict in his day had developed to the point of requiring a final, transformative revolution.

Marx not only criticized the idealist tradition but also attempted to explain its development in terms of its own material conditions. The idealist belief that freedom of thought and will allows one to determine one's beliefs, values, and identities, Marx argues, is itself a product of the particular social and economic conditions under which idealists live. Specifically, idealism is the product of a society that has, through the division of labor, separated those whose work is primarily mental from those whose work is primarily manual. Those who engage in mental labor generally exercise most of the power in a society because they control the means of production or are strategically aligned with those who do. By internalizing the effects of their social power, mental workers come to believe that the realm of ideas is not only independent from, but actually constitutes a greater historical force than, the material conditions of life. Owing to their preponderant influence in society, their ideas about the independence of ideas become widely disseminated and accepted as universal truths. The ideas of the ruling class in a society, Marx observes, become the ruling ideas of that society.

Marx calls these ruling ideas *ideology*. An ideology is a system of ideas that distorts or inverts reality but becomes widely accepted as true owing to the power of those whose interests these ideas primarily serve. When poor and powerless people are duped into holding beliefs and adopting values that best serve the interests of their exploiters, ideology is to blame. Marx describes these victims of ideology as having a *false consciousness* that keeps them from understanding and pursuing their true interests. By justifying economic inequalities and social hierarchy, ideology provides the ruling class with a rationale for its power and privilege while disseminating among the working class a set of beliefs and values that makes them complacent with their hardships. Industrial workers with false consciousness believe that they have freely contracted with employers to give a fair day's labor for a fair wage. In actuality, Marx suggests, these workers are being systematically exploited by a parasitic economic system that has, owing to its cooptation of religious leaders and intellectuals, produced a powerful ideology. While the capitalists get rich owing to their workers' hard labors, the workers, who are the actual producers of the capitalists' wealth, remain oppressed and impoverished. Ideology keeps workers from recognizing this injustice.

A successful ideology defines reality to serve particular (upper class) interests while at the same time ensuring that those (from a lower class) who suffer under this definition of reality willingly accept it as true. Ideology is important to Marx because it explains how an exploited class of people is kept in submission when it would be in its interest to engage in revolutionary activity. Nevertheless, Marx maintains that revolution cannot be staved off forever, regardless of how powerful the ideology created by the ruling class is. The reason has little to do with the power of revolutionary ideas, such as those Marx himself propagated. In this regard, Marx was consistent with his materialist premises. Not changes in thinking and beliefs, but changes in material conditions are what really counts. A brief look into Marx's theory of history will demonstrate why.

History and Class Conflict

As a materialist, Marx argued that thoughts, morals, religious beliefs, and social relationships are all products of the "forces of production." The forces of production are the material and social conditions that allow us to produce our means of subsistence. The forces of production include the means of production, that is, the raw materials and technology at hand, as well as the mode of production, also known as the relations of production, which refers to the social organization of labor. The mode of production is the economic structure under which people make their livings. The mode of production changes over time, synchronized with the technological development of the means of production. With changes in the means and mode of production come changes in the social and political values and beliefs that the means and mode of production create as ideological supports.

At certain points in history, as technological innovation (means of production) proceeds apace, the economic structure (mode of production) fails to keep up. The values, beliefs, and social relations that issue from this economic structure appear increasingly unjust. When this occurs, a society becomes ripe for social revolution. The revolution topples the old mode of production and institutes a new one better suited to the means of production currently in place. In turn, the entire *superstructure* of cultural, political, and legal relations is catapulted forward so as to become realigned with the *base* formed by the current level of technological and economic development.

The entire history of humankind, for Marx, may be described as a history of technological and economic change and the social revolutions that follow from it. Thousands of years ago, when the means of production were based on primitive methods of agriculture, the mode of production was based on slavery. Slavery was deemed necessary to satisfy the demands of free men in a world where making ends meet was extraordinarily labor intensive. Improvements in agricultural methods during medieval times brought about relations of serfdom. Serfs owed allegiance, service, and payments to their lords, but maintained certain hereditary rights and supported their families by their own labor. In turn, the development of such technology as spinning jennies and steam engines created the need for independent laborers to work in city factories. The feudal social relation of serfdom was abolished. Wage labor, a money economy, and the system of capitalism developed in its stead.

Marx projected this historic link between the means and relations of production into the future. The further development of technology under capitalism, Marx speculated, would allow for a vast production of wealth sufficient to eliminate poverty. Poverty would no longer be the natural, unavoidable condition of the majority of humankind. To the extent poverty continued to exist, it would be artificially produced by the class divisions in society. Eventually, the large working class, or *proletariat,* would come to understand that the cause of its suffering was its unnecessary exploitation by a much smaller capitalist class, the *bourgeoisie.* The proletariat would organize and revolt, overturning the present economic system, ending the privileges of the bourgeoisie, and putting an end to all class distinctions. A communist society would be born in which every form of inequality would disappear.

With the arrival of the highest phase of communistic society, Marx proposes, humanity would end alienation in all its forms. No longer would individuals be estranged from the products or processes of their labor, from one another, from nature, or from themselves. Each individual would rediscover its species being and freely and unresentfully contribute to the common good. No longer would the limitations of equality under the law or even equality of opportunity constrict individuals' needs and growth. Equal rights, which Marx calls "bourgeois rights," actually constitute a "right of inequality." Because bourgeois rights recognize and accept the inequality of individual endowments, those with the greatest intelligence and strength, or the greatest ruthlessness, cunning, and inherited wealth, rise to the top of bourgeois society. Equal rights thus actually protect and promote social inequality. In communist society, concrete needs, not abstract rights, determine social relations. In turn, labor ceases to be a necessary burden to life. It becomes instead life's "prime want." Labor becomes the means of self-fulfillment. In such an unalienated society, Marx suggests, all would joyfully contribute what they could to the common good and none would go without. The banner hanging over this utopian world would read, "From each according to his ability, to each according to his needs!"[70]

As a youth, Marx was already inclined toward such utopian hopes. In 1835, he reflected on his own future, writing in a school essay that

> the main principle, however, which must guide us in the selection of a vocation is the welfare of humanity, our own perfection. One should not think that these two interests combat each other, that the one must destroy the other. Rather, man's nature makes it possible for him to reach his fulfillment only by working for the perfection and welfare of his society.[71]

Marx's understanding of human nature—his definition of human beings as species beings—structured his economic, social, and political theory.

Though collaborating with Engels extensively, Marx was the primary source of ideas as well as the chief writer. Engels himself recognized this. Indeed, he provides us with the best summary of those ideas that belong "solely and exclusively to Marx" and constitute the core of Marxism. Karl Marx, Engels wrote, discovered that

> economic production and the structure of society of every historical epoch necessarily arising therefrom constitute the foundations for the political and intellectual history of that epoch; that consequently (ever since the dissolution of the primeval communal ownership of land) all history has been a history of class struggles, of struggles between exploited and exploiting, between dominated and dominating classes at various stages of social development; that this struggle, however, has now reached a state where the exploited and oppressed class (the proletariat) can no longer emancipate itself from the class which exploits and oppresses it (the bourgeoisie), without at the same time forever freeing the whole of society from exploitation, oppression and class struggles.[72]

Because all history is the history of class struggle, history as we know it effectively ends with the communist revolution. That is not to say that technological innovation ceases or time stops. Nonetheless, the book of history, traditionally written with the ink of blood and strife, can finally be closed because the engine of class struggle disintegrates once its source, economic want and injustice, is abolished.

Marx believed that anything that helped bring about the end of alienation and class conflict was a good thing. He therefore considered capitalism a good thing. It helped bring about the vast production of wealth that abolished the "natural" state of poverty and at the same time created the "artificial" poverty that would foment an emancipatory revolution. Though he praises its historical role in bringing about communist society, Marx sharply criticizes capitalism on all other counts at every possible turn. In capitalistic society, he believed, alienation achieves its greatest depths.

The problem of alienation is grounded in the division of labor, most significantly the division between mental and physical labor that keeps people from developing well-rounded lives. In a society where individual interests do not correspond to collective interests, this division is unavoidable. In a competitive marketplace, one is forced to do what one can to earn a living. Many will be reduced to the mind-numbing drudgery of repetitive physical labor. In the future communist society, in contrast, work would no longer be a regrettable necessity. It would become a cherished form of self-expression. A rigid division of labor and harsh economic needs would no longer force one to engage in certain activities and abstain from others.

Marx writes:

> In communist society, where nobody has one exclusive sphere of activity but each can become accomplished in any branch he wishes, society regulates the general production and thus makes it possible for me to do one thing today and another tomorrow, to hunt in the morning, fish in the afternoon, rear cattle in the evening, criticize after dinner, just as I have a mind, without ever becoming hunter, fisherman, shepherd or critic.[73]

Marx argues that in capitalist society we are burdened with narrow economic identities, rigidly circumscribed by an unjust division of labor. We are what we do (for a living) and little else. In communist society, our identities would be neither rigid nor static. We would be free to change them at will. There is, no doubt, something extremely appealing, even intoxicating, about this freedom, especially when its exercise promises fully developed individuals and a harmonious society.

Early theories of communism are to be found in Plato's writings, among the early and medieval millenarian Christians, in the writings of Thomas More (1478–1535), in the works of the Diggers and Levellers during the English Civil War and the Puritan Revolution (1642–48), in the writings of Claude Henri de Saint Simon (1760–1825), Robert Owen (1771–1888), Charles Fourier (1772–1837), who provided inspiration for the communistically organized Brook Farm in Massachusetts), and in the work of Auguste Comte (1789–1857). Marx, however, was critical of these thinkers for their idealism. Marx insisted that communist society would be born only out of particular historical conditions and revolutionary struggle. It would not emerge from wishful thinking or isolated acts of altruism based on idealist premises. Hence Marx criticized his socialist and communist predecessors for being utopian.

Yet Marx's own thought is surely utopian. Are we to believe that the greed, selfishness, and lust for power that have stained the pages of history with so much blood and tears can ever be fully eliminated from the human heart? Can what Marx called the "muck of the ages" really be wiped away for good by means of revolutionary activity? Will technology actually bring us to the point where life does not demand a certain amount of undesirable labor? Common sense suggests not.

There is, as well, good reason to worry whether such a world as Marx envisions would be desirable even if it were possible. The social and governmental power needed to ensure that individuals are nowhere exploited and that inequalities never arise would be so extensive and absolute as to amount to totalitarian control. Those holding such absolute power would likely not employ it virtuously or give it up without a struggle when called to do so. One might be particularly suspicious of the "vanguard" of revolutionaries that Marx believed would take control during the transitional period between the dissolution of the bourgeois state and the formation of the communist society.

The anarchist Bakunin, like Marx, hoped that exploited workers would rise up against the bourgeois state. But unlike Marx, Bakunin was suspicious of the dictatorship of the proletariat, however temporary its proposed tenure. Any revolutionary elites acceding to power, Bakunin warns, "will no longer represent the people, but only themselves and their claims to rulership over the people." Bakunin concludes that "those who doubt this know very little about human nature."[74] The revolutionary ideals of an elite vanguard, Bakunin held, mask a lust for power that will never exit history's stage. Karl Marx, taking this criticism rather personally, counseled Bakunin to "send all his nightmares about authority to the devil."[75] Apparently a nerve had been struck. As we reflect on the totalitarian regimes of this century that claimed Marx as their inspiration, Bakunin's understanding of human nature and his worries about power appear vindicated.

We can nonetheless appreciate Marx's many theoretical insights. Although Marx exaggerates the role played by the division of labor and shortchanges the many other relationships that affect us, he does illuminate how our economic role in society substantially shapes our identities. He also illustrates how ideology plays a role in legitimating unjust economic structures and relations. By reading Marx, we may better understand how we are blinded or constrained by our social circumstances and the identities we take on within them, whether as women or men, laborers or business people, students or teachers, religious believers or atheists.

This is not to suggest that we are complete prisoners of our social circumstances or material conditions. It would be taking on the worst and foregoing the best in Marx to believe so. Marx was a materialist, but he was not a fatalist or a strict economic determinist. He did not hold, or at least did not consistently hold, that our material conditions completely determine what we shall value and believe, and what we shall struggle to protect or overturn. Marx concluded that "circumstances make men just as much as men make circumstances."[76] The latter clause of this phrase should not be ignored.

Certain Marxist theorists, beginning in the nineteenth century, argued that Marx never was an economic determinist but that Engels's influence often made it seem so. We may, with this in mind, appreciate Marx's own criticism of fatalistic materialism. This naive and undynamic materialism maintains that "men are products of circumstances and upbringing, and that, therefore, changed men are products of other circumstances and changed upbringing." This is well and good, Marx observes, but we must not forget "that it is men who change circumstances."[77] In other words, while Marx insists that we are products of the environment, and more specifically products of the technological and economic environment, he also insists that we have the opportunity, as social and political beings, to transform our environment. Not only modern but also postmodern theorists have effectively employed Marx as a guide in this effort.[78]

Communism versus Socialism

Marx advocated the pursuit of a completely unalienated existence through the revolutionary abolition of private property. As a communist, Marx largely limits our capacity to change our environment to revolutionary practice. Yet Marx himself began his career not as a revolutionary communist but as a reform-oriented socialist, and his work has contributed greatly to the socialist thought of the last century.

Socialists generally do not advocate the revolutionary abolition of private property. They prefer strong governmental regulations that restrict the sorts of private property that can be owned, the means by which wealth may be produced and obtained, and how much wealth one can produce and obtain relative to one's fellow citizens. In an effort to temper class distinctions without abolishing private property altogether, socialists generally advocate highly progressive systems of taxation that limit the rate at which wealth may be accumulated and redistribute it so as to alleviate poverty and ensure equality of opportunqity. Frequently socialists advocate that the government, as the representative of the society as a whole, own the means of production by which certain basic goods and services are produced. Public ownership of key means of production, socialists believe, will ensure that society is never held hostage by capitalists for the provision of its basic needs.

Unlike communists, socialists generally do not believe in the necessity of social revolution. Gradual reform is possible. They believe that incremental change, a process of social evolution, may produce a just society in the future without overturning the full panoply of material conditions upon which the current society operates. It has been said, with this in mind, that communists are simply socialists in a hurry. But there is more to the distinction between communism and socialism than a matter of patience. Like liberals, socialists worry that many important individual rights and freedoms would be quashed in a violent revolution. These rights and freedoms, if sacrificed to revolutionary zeal, might never be fully resuscitated. Unlike communists, socialists are skeptical about the possibility of achieving a fully egalitarian society free of all forms of alienation. Therefore they are willing to tolerate many forms of private property, the social inequities these produce, and the frustrations of gradual change, in order to safeguard individual liberties.

For many contemporary socialists, the goal is not so much to overthrow liberalism as to transform it through greater democratic participation and social equality. For instance, Ernesto Laclau and Chantal Mouffe, socialists of a postmodern temperament, maintain that "the task of the Left therefore cannot be to renounce liberal-democratic ideology, but on the contrary, to deepen and expand it in the direction of a radical and plural democracy."[79] As "post-Marxists," Laclau and Mouffe seek to move "beyond the theoretical and political horizon of Marxism" in order to locate the socialist struggle for economic equality within the wider and deeper struggle for greater democracy.[80]

Even those unwilling to give up the Marxist banner, such as political theorist Ralph Miliband, suggest that the promotion and safeguarding of certain liberal rights may go hand in hand with greater social equality. Miliband argues that "political equality, save in formal terms, is impossible in the conditions of advanced capitalism. Economic life cannot be separated from political life. Unequal economic power, on the scale and of the kind encountered in advanced capitalist societies, inherently *produces* political inequality, on a more or less commensurate scale, whatever the constitution may say." In capitalistic societies, civil and political liberties are often "a mere cloak for class domination."[81] Miliband acknowledges nonetheless that "the civic freedoms which, however inadequately and precariously, form part of bourgeois democracy are the product of centuries of unremitting popular struggles. The task of Marxist politics is to defend these freedoms; and to make possible their extension and enlargement by the removal of their class boundaries."[82] The question, then, is whether these class boundaries are to be removed by means of revolution or by the slower processes of democratically-based reform.

If the latter course is taken, then Miliband's neo-Marxism amounts to socialism. Indeed, it may even approach a highly progressive form of liberalism, as the struggle for greater social equality remains grounded in an overarching concern for individual rights and well-being. Many liberal theorists endorse a "democratic welfare state" wherein the market is regulated "to reduce or ameliorate the socially adverse effects of essentially self-interested exchanges." In turn, "universal education" is advocated along with "a level of material well-being that is sufficient to enable [all] people to live at least minimally 'respectable' lives." These reforms are deemed necessary to provide the "means for everyone to attain full membership in society."[83] Economic equality, therefore, is not the goal for progressive liberals and socialists. Instead, economic security is the means toward realizing the goal of greater political equality.

Critical theorists of Marx who wish to make good use of his insights often observe that progressive social reform is a viable alternative to revolution. One might also suggest that revolutionary practice may be fruitfully understood in ways Marx never intended. Practices may be considered revolutionary without entailing large-scale social upheaval. Revolutionary practice might also include the individual's attempt to do what Todorov maintains Columbus could not do: escape from the self in order genuinely to discover the other. Perhaps it is a revolutionary event whenever we learn to speak in a different voice, hear through different ears, or see through different eyes. In many situations, there is no substitute for collective action, whether oriented to revolution or reform. Righting certain wrongs may be impossible on a piecemeal, individual basis. Yet developing one's own abilities to perceive things from others' perspectives may both pave the way for necessary collective action and temper its excesses.

In an early essay, Marx wrote that we should strive to achieve a condition in which our senses themselves become "directly in their practice theoreticians."[14] He meant to suggest that once we escape rigid (economic) identities that tightly constrain experience, we may see and hear the world in new and radical ways. Theory, in this sense, is itself revolutionary or at least potentially so. It prompts us to construct or borrow lenses that enable new perspectives.

There is an old Buddhist saying that when a pickpocket meets a wise man, he sees only his pockets. The moral of the story is that, like the pickpocket, we may miss many opportunities for valuable experiences and a fuller life if we remain too set in our ways. Having a rigid identity is like being set in one's ways. Our identities, as unavoidable as they are and as useful, stimulating and beneficial as they may at times prove to be, are dangerous if adopted uncritically. Identities may produce a sort of false consciousness, or to speak less dramatically, a set of constricting lenses. They may keep us from seeing expansively and from pursuing our full potential as human beings. That is because our identities, whether they be religious, racial, sexual, or economic in nature, frequently integrate us within certain communities by means of separating us out from others.

Marx predicted a final resolution to the politics of class through the revolutionary creation of a communist society. But there are no straightforward answers or final resolutions to the problems posed by collective human existence. The politics of identity—how we communicate and interact with others based on how we understand ourselves —is not a puzzle to be solved. It is an ongoing process of negotiation.

Marx offers valuable insights into the nature of human alienation. Yet his political legacy is troubled. At his best he offers both a sustained argument for increased human equality as a means to fuller, richer lives and a cogent explanation of why this equality has not yet been realized. At his worst he plays into the hands of those who, under the guise of pursuing equality, would destroy freedom, shackle individuality, and stifle difference. To explore ideology critically, for example, challenges prejudices that serve to perpetuate injustice. To attribute false consciousness to another person, however, suggests that one knows a person's interests better than that person herself does or can. This is a potentially antidemocratic assumption. The totalitarian communist regimes of this century testify to its danger. The greater economic equality that was achieved in these regimes was paid for in the coin of political inequality as absolute rulers presided over largely powerless subjects.

R.H. Tawney (1880–1962), a British historian and social theorist, offers one of the most concise statements about the limits of the socialist quest for equality. He writes:

To criticize inequality and to desire equality is not, as is sometimes suggested, to cherish the romantic illusion that men [and women] are equal in character and intelligence. It is to hold that, while their natural endowments differ profoundly, it is the mark of a civilized society to aim at eliminating such inequalities as have their source, not in individual differences, but in its own organization, and that individual differences, which are a source of social energy, are more likely to ripen and find expression if social inequalities are, as far as practicable, diminished.[15]

The question that Tawney's remarks beg, of course, is what diminishment of social inequalities remains practicable?

A good start is had by saying that it is not appropriate to diminish social inequalities if this effort suppresses more difference than it cultivates. Translating this handy rule of thumb into a political program specific enough to bear public scrutiny and sustain democratic implementation is a formidable task. It is the task of translating a theory of justice into a social practice.

Suggested Readings

Marimba Ani. *Yurugu*
Shlomo Avineri. *The Social and Political Thought of Karl Marx*
Simone de Beauvoir. *The Second Sex*
Mary Belenky et al. *Women's Ways of Knowing*
Seyla Benhabib and Drucilla Cornell, eds. *Feminism as Critique*
Mary Daly. *Gyn/Ecology*
Dorothy Dinnerstein. *The Mermaid and the Minotaur*
Carol Gilligan. *In a Different Voice*
Nancy Hartsack. *Money, Sex, and Power*
Karl Marx and Friedrich Engels. *The Marx-Engels Reader*
John Stuart Mill. *The Subjection of Women*
Ralph Miliband. *Marxism and Politics*
Susan Moller Okin. *Justice, Gender, and the Family*
Anthony Pagden. *European Encounters with the New World*
Carole Pateman. *The Sexual Contract*
John Rawls. *A Theory of Justice*
Michael Ryan. *Marxism and Deconstruction*
Charles Taylor. *Multiculturalism and the Politics of Recognition*
Tzvetan Todorov. *The Conquest of America*
Michael Walzer. *Spheres of Justice*
Wub-e-ke-niew. *We Have the Right to Exist*

6

Statecraft and Soulcraft

he politics of identity is central to postmodern political thought because the self is no longer accepted as a "given," that is, as a stable entity with an innate set of known or knowable characteristics. The assumption is that the social environment molds the identities of individuals, creating their interests, values, desires, and behavior. Postmodern theorists are concerned with the manner in which power shapes citizens and produces certain sorts of subjects.

This is not a totally novel approach to politics. In important respects, ancient Greek political theorists, notably Plato, also maintained that different sorts of citizens or subjects are produced by the social and political structures under which they live. But the ancient Greeks were neither as radically perspectivist nor as radically constructivist as postmoderns. They also employed a different vocabulary. In describing the relationship between the political realm and the character of its citizens they spoke not of identity but of the soul. Whereas contemporary postmodernists might say that politics pertains to the creation and contestation of identities, therefore, Socrates maintained that politics is "that concerned with the soul."[1] Differently constructed political regimes yield differently constructed souls. For the ancient Greeks, statecraft was a form of soulcraft.

Politics and Philosophy in Ancient Greece
The Greeks believed that legislators involved in the creation and maintenance of the city-state were effectively engaged in the ordering of the souls of its citizenry. This ordering of souls in the classical world was understood to be a shaping of character. It was a form of education, namely, an education in virtue. For this reason, both Plato and Aris-

totle agreed that education constituted the greatest part of politics and was the primary task of the legislator. Plato goes so far as to suggest that the responsibility for a people's wickedness lay not with the people themselves but with the politicians responsible for their education and government. "In such cases," he states, "the planters are to blame rather than the plants."[2] He complains that even the greatest of Athens' political leaders, such as Pericles, frequently pandered to the citizenry's base desires rather than educating them properly and ordering their souls.

In the absence of a proper education in virtue, an extensive legal system becomes necessary to control vice. Yet the attempt to rule citizens with heavy-handed legislation, Plato suggests, is like trying to kill the Hydra by cutting off its head. In Greek mythology, every time a head of the Hydra was cut off, two more grew in its place. Likewise, every time a law is enacted to restrain a particular vice, other vices emerge to take its place, requiring yet more laws. If souls are not properly crafted, laws and punishment can only alleviate the symptoms of decay and postpone catastrophe. Laws cannot produce justice; only an education in virtue can produce justice. Plato went so far as to suggest that a truly just city could only be created if everyone over ten years of age was first cast out. The remaining youths, bearing uncorrupted souls, could then be strictly mentored in the life of virtue.

The philosopher's first task, according to Plato, is to put his own soul into order. A well-ordered soul is one whose parts are harmoniously organized so that reason rules over passion and appetite. Plato suggests that the philosopher may also take on the task—or may be compelled to take on the task—of ordering the souls of his students and fellow citizens. Greek philosophy was the practice of performing reconstructive surgery on the soul. The philosopher's chief surgical instrument was reason.[3] Were the job of mending souls well done, Plato believed, the harmony *within* individuals would produce a harmony *between* individuals. Effectively, Plato combined modern and postmodern orientations to suggest that a concern for the construction of *identity* allows for the better regulation of *interaction*. That is to say, well-ordered souls produce a well-ordered city. The name Plato gives to this order, both within the soul and within the city, is justice. Hence the subtitle given to the *Republic* is *On the Just*

Statecraft is a form of soulcraft, and soulcraft, the ancient theorists agreed, is also a form of statecraft. That is to say, just as the structure and (educational) institutions of the political realm mold the characters of its citizens, so the character of citizens determines what sort of political regime will be formed and maintained. An uneducated citizenry cannot adequately organize its collective life. Good statecraft depends on the virtues of its citizens. This is where the philosophers become involved. They engage in the shaping of virtuous souls. Education is their most important task. Nevertheless, because an ill-organized collective life will, in time, have deleterious effects on the characters of the citizenry, particularly on the youths whose souls are most susceptible to influence, philosophers must also engage in political theory. They must determine the nature of the good regime.

What is the relation between the political and philosophical activities that produce, respectively, just cities and just souls? Plato's *Republic* depicts Socrates and a number of discussants constructing a hypothetical political regime, a "city in speech." The dialogue begins, however, with a conversation oriented to discovering justice in an individual, the harmonious order of a single soul. Socrates suggests that the individual soul is too small and obscure to see into its nature without aid. Magnifying lenses are required. The construction of a city in speech is proposed as a heuristic means to view justice at a sufficiently large scale. From the middle of Book II onwards, the largest portion of the dialogue focuses on the justice of the city, the soul writ large. Only at the end of Book IX are we explicitly reminded of our starting point, that founding the city in speech was only meant to make the investigation of justice within the individual soul a little easier. The entire theoretical enterprise of structuring and organizing the city-state was simply a "pattern ... laid up for the man who wants to see and found a city within himself."[4] Despite the time and effort spent discussing the nature of the just political regime, the person who knows what is best for himself, Plato concludes, "won't mind the political things." He will concern himself solely with "his own city," that is, with the microcosmic city of his soul. An unjust city, like an unjust soul, Plato maintains, is at war with itself. In the end, Plato seems most concerned with helping people put an end to inner strife, encouraging them to avoid all external entanglements.

Is the *Republic* primarily a political program for the just state or a philosophic program for the just, well-ordered soul? If the latter, was it necessary for Socrates to spend so much time talking about the city when his concern all along was the private realm of the psyche? It has been suggested that Socrates' proposal to found a city in speech was simply a devious way of securing the abiding interest of his politically ambitious discussants. Perhaps his sole purpose was to shape their souls through philosophic dialogue. The only way he could get them to stick around long enough for this sculpting of character, however, was to entice them with the prospect of becoming the theoretical founders of a new city-state. If this is true, then the *Republic,* like many of Plato's other dialogues, is an ironic piece of writing. It is not wholly serious or straightforward in its political proposals. We return to the question of irony in the next chapter.

Reason in the Soul and State

Philosophy literally means the love of wisdom. Plato tells us that it is an expression of a lack. The lover of wisdom seeks wisdom because he does not already possess it. As Socrates suggests, no one who is truly wise desires wisdom, for no one seeks to become what he already is. Only God, not the philosopher, is truly wise.[5] Though the philosopher is not wise, neither is he wholly ignorant. For the philosopher seeks wisdom above all, while the ignorant man does not even know enough to do that.

The route to wisdom and divine insight, Plato states, is through reason. Reason is the spark of the divine in man; it is what separates man from the beasts. All communication between gods and human beings takes place through the intermediary of reason. Reason, however, is not the only force within us. There are also the passions and appetites, which seek to go their own way. These passions and appetites, Plato suggests, should be put to good use and kept well in tow. Otherwise inner anarchy will arise and nothing much can be accomplished. An ordered soul, for Plato, is one in which reason rules unchallenged. Its power subjugates the passions and appetites, like the strength of a charioteer whose firm grip on the reins keep the horses running straight and true.

The means to develop and strengthen reason is by way of a type of conversation called dialectic. Dialectic, also known as the Socratic method, begins when someone asks a simple question about some fundamental issue. One might ask, for instance, What is the nature of justice? All answers given in response are subjected to further inquiry, which uncovers their unstated assumptions and subsequently submits these assumptions to yet further analysis. In this way, dialectical argument proceeds from opinion to opinion, revealing the vulnerabilities and inconsistencies of each.

At the end of the dialectic process, one usually finds oneself back where one started. The original question still stands unanswered. But one is no longer able to avail oneself of all those subsidiary opinions, beliefs, and assumptions that formerly gave one a sense of stability and promised to provide solutions. At this point, an admission of ignorance is required. This admission is the prerequisite for knowledge. Now the path is cleared. The mind is no longer cluttered with a hodgepodge of groundless opinions that lead nowhere. Instead, one may rely on reason to catapult one into the realm of knowledge.

Plato suggests that moral and political truths are of the same eternal and unchanging nature as mathematical truths. Such truths can only be apprehended through the intellect by way of reason. Dialectic clears the intellect of the debris of prejudice and opinion so that true knowledge may be gained. Now, however, we are confronted with a paradox. Only by achieving mastery over one's appetites and passions, which foster faulty opinions and prejudices, can one follow the rule of reason. Yet only by following reason can one secure "immunity" from the appetites and passions.[6] In other words, only those with well-ordered souls are capable of ascending through dialectic to knowledge. Yet only those who already have knowledge know how to order their souls. As Plato remarked in one of his letters, knowledge of the Good can be engendered with the careful use of reason, but only in a soul that is itself "naturally" good.[7]

A basic order in an individual's soul seems to be a precondition for philosophy to carry out its dialectic work. Indeed, in the *Republic* Socrates appears to choose his partners for conversation based on his sense of which souls are "naturally" good and hence have the potential for further philosophic ordering. Socrates states that the function of speech is to influence the soul. The speaker must know the kinds of souls he is addressing, however, in order to tailor his speech to get the desired results.[8] Very disorderly souls are presumably not worth the bother. Socrates' decision to carry out the project of constructing the city in speech in the *Republic* was based on his pleasant surprise at the natural orderliness of the souls of those available to take part in the conversation, namely Adimantus and Glaucon, the older brothers of Plato.[9]

In the *Republic* and other dialogues, Plato affirms that human beings are reincarnated. Before being born or reborn, they are allowed a glimpse of the divine. This experience is mostly forgotten at birth, though remnants of it linger in memory. If Plato is taken at his word about reincarnation, then every human soul shares some basic degree of order because it has been privileged to behold cosmic order at the end of a former life. Having gazed at true being, a soul necessarily becomes reincarnated in human form.[10] Its glimpse of the cosmic order, however, does not guarantee a philosophic disposition. Very few individuals remember their glimpse of true reality. Once born into this life, most human beings smother the divine spark under opinion and belief rather than kindle it into the raging fire of knowledge. For the select few, philosophers help fan the flames. The philosopher finds a suitable soul and sows the seeds of knowledge using the tools of dialectic.[11] Dialectic reasoning is the philosophic art that leads "the best part of the soul up to the contemplation of what is best among realities."[12] Dialectic turns souls around so that they may face the truth.

This is the soulcraft of Platonic philosophy. Since education is the better part of politics, this Platonic soulcraft is effectively a form of statecraft. Socrates considered it a relatively safe form of politics. If he had engaged in standard political practices, Plato observes in the *Apology*, he would not have lived as long as he did. Indeed, his efforts at crafting souls eventually landed him in a court of law facing charges of impiety and corrupting the youth. Athenians took their religious and political mores seriously, and they were not about to see them altered. Socrates, at seventy years of age, was condemned to death. Plato's writings may be interpreted as attempts to vindicate the means and ends of Socratic soulcraft against what he perceived to be the injustice of Athenian statecraft.

In the *Republic*, statecraft is explicitly modeled on a kind of aristocratic soulcraft. The role of reason in the city is modeled on its role in the psyche. Just as reason should rule over the passions, so the rational part of society should rule over the spirited and appetitive parts. As embodied in the rule of the philosopher king, reason ensures the happiness of the whole city just as the rule of reason in the well-ordered soul ensures the happiness of the individual. Justice in the man and the city is the same, namely, the authoritative rule of reason. Hence the best-ordered city is "the city whose state is most like that of an individual man."[13] Despite Socrates' early suggestion that the city in speech was to serve as a model of justice for the soul, the effect of the dialogue is for the individual soul to serve as a model of justice for the city.

Plato suggests that political structures mirror the order or disorder found in the souls of their citizens. He proposes that there are as many types of political regimes as there are types of souls. Aristocracy corresponds to the soul that loves goodness and justice; timocracy to the soul that loves honor and glory; oligarchy to the soul that loves wealth; democracy to the soul that loves freedom and pleasure; and tyranny, the worst of all regimes, to the soul that loves domination.

The best regime is not the democratic one, according to Plato. He believes that the democratic love of freedom leads to anarchy, and anarchy eventually leads to tyranny. Democracy, Plato admits, is the "fairest regime," owing to the beautiful complexity and diversity of its life. The problem is that democracy's celebration of political freedom leads to disorder in souls. The defense of liberty deteriorates into the toleration of license. Democratic freedom amounts to the freedom to be irrational, to let the passions and appetites rule supreme. Rather than promote a freedom that amounts to licentiousness, Plato prefers monarchical or aristocratic rule that maintains strict authoritarian control. In the *Laws*, Plato writes that nobody must get into the habit of acting independently. All men and women must always be under command of a leader who instructs their actions "to the least detail." Freedom from such control, Plato writes, must be expelled "root and branch from the lives of all mankind."[14] This form of authoritarian regime is not considered a tyranny by Plato because the leaders are actuated by reason rather than the desire for domination. In the best-ordered regime, Plato maintains, philosopher kings speak the authoritative voice of reason and cultivate in the souls of citizens an abiding respect for it.

The Politics of Unity and Plurality

Many political theorists, starting with Aristotle, have criticized Plato's attempt to model the political realm on the workings of the soul. The problem, Aristotle observes, is that the political realm is defined by its plurality or diversity, while the individual soul is defined by its organic unity. Reducing plurality to unity is a dangerous ambition. It is neither easy to achieve nor easy to maintain. Indeed, to realize this ambition Plato's philosopher kings must resort to the propagation of myths and "noble lies." The citizens must be tricked into believing that the rigid caste system that structures their society is the creation not of humans but of infallible gods. So duped by what amounts to an ancient form of ideology, the citizens of the *Republic* allow the philosopher kings to rule unhindered and unquestioned.

Even in Plato's much more practical work, *The Laws*, we find that the laws are accepted by the citizens uncritically. "All should agree, without a dissonant voice," Plato writes, that the laws "are all god-given and admirable, flatly refusing a hearing to anyone who disputes the point."[15] Inquiry into the merits of the laws is strictly forbidden, except for private conversations elders may hold with magistrates. Here reason also rules supreme, becoming embodied in the laws themselves.

Theorists throughout the ages have worried about the concentration of power that the rule of philosopher kings would entail. Montesquieu writes that "constant experience shows us that every man invested with power is apt to abuse it, and to carry his authority as far as it will go.... To prevent this abuse, it is necessary from the very nature of things that power should be a check to power."[16] Montesquieu's insight became the basis for the American system of "checks and balances" between executive, legislative, and judiciary branches of government.

With a similar concern, Benjamin Constant (1767–1837), a French-

Swiss political thinker, maintained that whenever unlimited power was exercised, regardless of who wielded it, the results were unfortunate. The problem, he states, rests not with the holder of power but with the amount of power held. "There are weapons," Constant writes, "which are too heavy for the hand of man."[17] Perhaps the most famous statement of this sort was made by the English historian and moralist Lord Acton (1834–1902), who observed that "all power tends to corrupt, and absolute power corrupts absolutely." Like Montesquieu and Constant, Acton cautions us against the unintended yet unavoidable consequences of the concentration of power. The American religious and social thinker Reinhold Niebuhr (1892–1971) argued in this vein that democracy was the only viable solution to the problem of power. "Man's capacity for justice makes democracy possible," Niebuhr said, "but man's inclination to injustice makes democracy necessary." Democratic controls on political leaders ensure that power—and hence the corrupting effects of power—will be limited.

As knowledgeable and good as Plato's philosopher kings may be, one must worry that absolute power would corrupt them as well. Plato, of course, was not unaware of this danger. That is why he proposed tyranny to be the worst of all regimes. That is also why Plato suggested that the philosopher would not of his own free will seek power. True philosophers like nothing better than to philosophize. They are concerned with the order of their souls, not the ordering of the city. Political power is a dangerous burden and an unwanted distraction. Were the philosopher to rule, then, it would be because he was literally forced to rule by citizens who recognized his wisdom and wished to benefit from it. If the philosopher agreed to take the helm of the ship of state, in other words, he would do so not for the love of power but to fulfill his obligation to the city.

Even under such a benevolent despot as Plato's philosopher king, however, the concentration of power might work its mischief. This mischief need not come from a leader who relishes an excess of power. Indeed, Plato's rulers live a Spartan lifestyle, with few amenities and none of the trappings of wealth. The mischief might come from below, from a people who suffer a dearth of power. We might expand on Acton's well-known adage by saying that a lack of power also tends to corrupt, and an absolute lack of power corrupts absolutely. To be constantly subjected to power while remaining wholly powerless oneself is to be transformed from a responsible citizen into a resentful slave. A political realm built on resentment is ripe for revolution.

Aristotle offered the first of many challenges to Plato's modeling of the city on the soul. These criticisms are in order because Plato's reductive analysis courts the danger of despotism. In some respects, however, Plato's effort fails because in drawing his analogy between the political realm and the soul he actually ignores key parallels. Most important, he neglects to observe the political analog of dialectic reasoning. Dialectics, Plato states, is the art of discerning "unity and plurality" as they exist in the nature of things.[18] Yet Plato fails to discern the inherent plurality of political associations. In turn, dialectic engages in the search for philosophic order through discussion that is grounded in an admission of one's ignorance. Yet Plato does not sufficiently explore the type of political order that would arise through discussion grounded in the admission that no one has, or could have, all the right answers. Had Plato done so, he might have proposed democratic practices to be analogous to dialectic ones.

A critical mind is imperative for the dialectical activity of the philosopher. Uncritical belief in words eventually leads one to be "misologic," to despise rational argument, in the same way that uncritical belief in people may lead one to be misanthropic, to despise humankind. The inevitable disappointment and sense of betrayal that comes when one's uncritical beliefs or celebrated heroes let one down, Plato observes, produce a deep suspicion and hatred of all knowledge and all people. Cynicism takes root in the soul.[19] Yet Plato does not foresee that political cynicism might result from citizens' uncritical belief in noble lies and myths and philosopher kings. Plato's philosophy is characterized by the rule of reason and the art of dialectic. His proposed political realm retains the rule of reason. But little room is found for the dialectical art of open debate in his polis.

In the next two sections of this chapter, we examine in greater detail political concepts of primary importance to the Western tradition of politics and political theory. Freedom (or liberty) and reason or (rationality), are examined because, as Plato already demonstrated, they inhere in a tensioned relationship in both the state and the soul. Freedom and reason not only link the private and public realms but ensure that both realms may thrive in justice.

Feminists and non-Western theorists might contend that the attention paid to the concepts of freedom and reason within the tradition of political theory speaks more to the Western, masculinized nature of that tradition than to the inherent centrality of the concepts to political life. Perhaps obligation and empathy, not freedom and reason, lay closer to the core of our political existence. Readers are encouraged to explore this possibility. Nonetheless, if statecraft and soulcraft are indeed kindred activities, then political theorists must grapple with the natures of freedom and reason and explain their relation to justice. Admittedly, this theoretical investigation can only provide its illumination at the cost of leaving certain other concepts and relationships in the shadows.

The Life of Liberty

Freedom is a good thing. Indeed, in the history of the Western world few other aspirations have sponsored more philosophical meditations, political theorizations, social struggles, revolutions, and wars than the quest for freedom. Patrick Henry gave voice to the American revolutionary sentiment with his famous declaration, "Give me liberty or give me death." Thomas Jefferson reflected that "the tree of liberty must be refreshed from time to time with the blood of patriots and tyrants. It is its natural manure."[20] For Henry and Jefferson, liberty was something that made life worth living. Liberty was also something for which it was worthy, and occasionally necessary, to die. In this century, President John F. Kennedy concurred. In his inaugural address he said: "Let every nation know, whether it wishes us well or ill, that we shall pay any price, bear any burden, meet any hardship, support any friend, oppose any foe to assure the survival and the success of liberty."

The pursuit of liberty is often held to be a modern concern. It certainly has been celebrated in modern times as in no other. Yet the pursuit of liberty has a long history. It goes back at least two and a half millennia, to the time when the ancient Greeks first developed democracy, the only political regime grounded in the principle of freedom. The Greeks' extensive dependence on slaves, moreover, made freedom both a palpable good for some and a sought-after ideal for others.[21]

After surveying the origins and development of the Western philosophic tradition, Hegel concluded that "the history of the world is none other than the progress of the consciousness of freedom."[22] Likewise, the well-known theorist of medieval thought, A.J. Carlyle, wrote "it seems evident that the history of civilization during the last two thousand years is primarily the history of the development of liberty."[23] Quite likely these retrospective assessments were colored by the modern enchantment with liberty. But their generalizations are understandable. Undoubtedly, freedom has become one of our most cherished prizes today.

As with many other things in life, however, we have to ask of liberty whether there can be too much of a good thing. "At its best, the valorization of personal liberty is the noblest achievement of Western civilization," sociologist Orlando Patterson writes. Yet he goes on to observe that "at its worst, no value has been more evil and socially cor-

rosive in its consequences, inducing selfishness, alienation, the celebration of greed, and the dehumanizing disregard for the 'losers,' the little
people who fail to make it."[24] Does too much individual liberty present
a threat to the political community? What limits, if any, should be
placed on our freedom?

Clearly there must be some limits. With none in place, as Hobbes
foresaw, anarchy would prevail. Unless we believe, as some anarchists
do, that in the absence of all governmental institutions individuals
would never harm one another, we are forced to consider placing limitations on the exercise of liberty lest societal relations deteriorate into a
state of war. That is not to say that individual liberty and collective
welfare battle each other in a zero-sum game. An increase in one does
not always signify a decrease in the other. On the contrary, individual
liberty and collective welfare are often mutually reinforcing. In many
respects, and for most practical purposes, one cannot be had without
the other.

Edmund Burke (1729–97), a conservative British political thinker,
believed freedom to be "a blessing and a benefit" for the individual no
less than for the community. Liberty, he goes on to say in his Letter to
the Sheriffs of Bristol, "is a good to be improved, and not an evil to be
lessened. It is not only a private blessing of the first order, but the vital
spring and energy of the state itself, which has just so much life and
vigor as there is liberty in it." Yet liberty, Burke acknowledges, is dangerous if taken too far. Aristotle lamented that Plato's radical idealism
had the effect of making the best the enemy of the good. Likewise,
Burke warns that political values are not meant to be all-or-nothing
achievements. Political values such as liberty are not to be likened to
"propositions in geometry and metaphysics which admit no medium,
but must be true or false in all their latitude." With the pursuit of liberty, as in most political affairs, compromises are in order.

Burke continues:

> Social and civil freedom, like all other things in common life, are vari-
> ously mixed and modified, enjoyed in very different degrees, and shaped
> into an infinite variety of forms, according to the temper and circum-
> stances of every community. The *extreme* of liberty (which is its abstract
> perfection, but its real fault) obtains nowhere, nor ought to obtain any-
> where; because extremes, as we all know, in every point which relates ei-
> ther to our duties or satisfactions in life, are destructive both to virtue and
> enjoyment. Liberty, too, must be limited in order to be possessed.[25]

Here Burke may well have been recalling the French philosopher

Michel de Montaigne (1533–92), who observed that "we can grasp virtue in such a way that it will become vicious, if we embrace it with too
sharp and violent a desire."[26] The virtue of freedom turns to vice if
taken too far. Practically speaking, liberty should be understood as the
freedom to adopt appropriate limits, rather than a freedom from all
limits. For Burke, we are qualified to exercise liberty in exact proportion to our disposition and capacity to restrain our own appetites.

In cautioning his British compatriots against what he believed to be
an extremist celebration of liberty in the French Revolution, Burke
wrote that "the effect of liberty to individuals is that they may do what
they please. We ought to see what it will please them to do before we
risk congratulations." When the French revolutionaries emblazoned
Liberté at the top of their banners, Burke feared that their passionate
pursuit would not be sufficiently moderated to preserve the collective
welfare or to safeguard the basic rights of individuals. Burke was right.
Yet in this case, revolutionary zeal developed in response to monarchical zeal. The revolutionaries, extremists though they were, were responding to an extreme situation. They believed themselves to be following Jefferson's dictum of refreshing the tree of liberty with the blood
of tyrants. The tyrants in question were King Louis XVI and the French
aristocrats. The king of France along with much of the nobility eventually paid for their long-held power and privilege with their heads. The
revolutionaries' unmoderated pursuit of liberty was a response to the
deprivations suffered by the common people under a regime that, in an
equally unmoderated fashion, had monopolized liberty for a king and
his court.

The idea that liberty must be limited in order to be possessed is perhaps most easily illustrated by the issue of free speech. Freedom of
speech is one of the most fundamental and most cherished liberties in
modern democracies, and particularly so in the United States. Without
freedom of speech, democracy could not exist. Yet even in the case of
this fundamental liberty, restrictions necessarily apply. Freedom of speech
must be limited to prevent its abuse whenever that abuse immediately
harms others. As Justice Oliver Wendell Holmes argued in the 1919
case of *Shenck* v. *United States,* "the most stringent protection of free
speech would not protect a man in falsely shouting 'fire' in a theater
and causing a panic." Such an irresponsible exercise of free speech
would create a "clear and present danger" to the lives of individuals
who might become injured in the panicked scramble of theatergoers to
vacate the premises. Freedom of speech is not a freedom to say anything to anyone in any place.

One might argue, however, that freedom of speech should not be so restricted. Perhaps it is the responsibility of listeners to decide when "Fire!" is shouted in earnest and when it is a malicious joke. Yet even those who defend the individual's right to lie maliciously generally admit that some restrictions apply to how and when one may speak in certain circumstances. Rules of debate must be enforced within discussion-oriented or decision-making bodies. These rules undeniably limit freedom of speech. They determine when one may speak and how long one may speak. They may also limit what one may speak about. For example, in formal debate one must generally speak to the issue at hand, rather than arbitrarily raise new issues.

These rules limiting the exercise of our linguistic freedom do so in order to make such freedom possible and meaningful in the first place. One cannot truly exercise one's freedom of speech, whether at a town meeting or in Congress, if another speaker simultaneously chooses to exercise his freedom of speech or loudly bang on drums. Freedom of speech means more than the right to speak; it includes the right to be heard (though not necessarily listened to attentively or taken seriously). In order to be heard, others must, at least temporarily, restrict their own freedom to speak. As Montesquieu writes, "liberty is a right of doing whatever the laws permit, and if a citizen could do what they forbid he would be no longer possessed of liberty, because all his fellow-citizens would have the same power."[27] We often think of liberty as the ability to flaunt rules, laws, and boundaries, as the right to do whatever we care to do, heedless of others. Yet such abstract liberty has little political merit or application because it is impossible for people to share.

Freedom of speech, like all freedoms, can be misused. Liberty is a potentially dangerous thing. Since the time of Plato, political theorists have taken on the task of determining exactly how much liberty is beneficial, and when, how, and where it should be limited. The problem is made particularly troublesome because the word liberty means different things to different people at different times. Hegel himself found the concept of liberty to be "indefinite, ambiguous, and open to the greatest misconceptions."[28] Indeed, historians of ideas have gathered hundreds of meanings for the words liberty and freedom. We explore a few of the more prominent ones.

Positive and Negative Liberty

In Western political thought, two distinct meanings of liberty have attained preeminence: positive liberty and negative liberty. The eighteenth-century German philosopher Immanuel Kant was perhaps the first to differentiate "positive" and "negative" senses of the word freedom in his work *The Metaphysic of Morals*. T.H. Green, a nineteenth-century British political theorist, greatly popularized the distinction. Subsequently, the contemporary British political theorist Isaiah Berlin revitalized discussion and brought the terms into the mainstream with his lecture "Two Concepts of Liberty."

Berlin wished to distinguish positive liberty from negative liberty because he thought the former concept to be treacherous. Making clear distinctions between the two concepts, he hoped, would prevent their meanings from becoming conflated. If misunderstood and misused, Berlin warned, words like liberty and freedom might acquire an "unchecked momentum and an irresistible power over multitudes of men that may grow too violent to be affected by rational criticism."[29] Here Berlin, like Burke before him, was thinking about the relationship between the liberty advocated by Rousseau and the bloody events of the French Revolution carried out in his name. Berlin was also thinking about the liberty advocated by Marxists in the then still powerful empire of the Soviet Union. Berlin's criticism of positive liberty was meant to militate against these extremes. Negative liberty was less dangerous than positive liberty, Berlin believed. It also served as a corrective to the excesses of its counterpart.

By adopting the label *negative* for a form of liberty, Berlin does not mean to suggest that it is bad or injurious. Negative liberty is negative only in the sense that it refers to something pernicious that is prevented rather than to something beneficial that is achieved or gained. What is being prevented is external constraint on our individual choices or actions. Negative liberty means freedom from interference or confinement. One is negatively free as long as one is neither physically restricted nor violently coerced (say, at gunpoint) from speaking or taking action. What is negative about negative liberty, then, is that it denotes an *absence* of constraint.

Negative liberty constitutes an open space within which an individual may pursue his desires unhindered by the impositions of others. For this reason, negative liberty is closely aligned to the notion of privacy. It signifies a private realm over which the individual exercises complete jurisdiction. It denotes a personal sovereignty over behavior and belief. This private realm is shielded from all external interference, whether that of the church, state, or society. In this vein, John Stuart Mill, one of the foremost advocates of negative liberty, argues that individual freedom requires protection not only from monarchic and oligarchic power but from democratic power as well. Freedom is threatened, in other words, not only by the power of the few but also by the power of the many.

In modern society, Mill worried, individual freedom was in particular danger of being undermined by the coercive power of social mores. Employing the famous phrase of Alexis de Tocqueville, Mill wrote of the impingement of personal freedom caused by the "tyranny of the majority." Against this threat, Mill penned his famous essay *On Liberty*. Its purpose was to establish a

> very simple principle, as entitled to govern absolutely the dealings of society with the individual in the way of compulsion and control, whether the means used be physical force in the form of legal penalties or the moral coercion of public opinion. That principle is that the sole end for which mankind are warranted, individually or collectively, in interfering with the liberty of action of any of their number is self-protection. That the only purpose for which power can be rightfully exercised over any member of a civilized community, against his will, is to prevent harm to others. His own good, either physical or moral, is not a sufficient warrant.[30]

We should note that for Mill this principle holds only for "civilized" communities. He believed that compulsion might be warranted and justified when advanced imperial nations, such as Britain in Mill's own time, governed less developed nations such as India.

The principle of negative liberty might be grounded, as A.V. Dicey later suggested, on the notion that "every person is in the main and as a general rule the best judge of his own happiness. Hence legislation should aim at the removal of all those restrictions on the free action of an individual which are not necessary for securing the like freedom on the part of his neighbors."[31] The only justification for constraining an individual is that he is inflicting some harm or deprivation on others. In all other matters, freedom ought to prevail.

To preserve negative liberty the individual must assert mastery over his immediate environment, effectively shielding thoughts and beliefs, words and speech, allegiances and associations, movements and deeds from external interference. For Mill, therefore, liberty is evident whenever "over himself, over his own body and mind, the individual is sovereign."[32] Negative liberty generally includes an individual's rule not only over his body and mind, however, but also over his personal possessions. Most negative libertarians consider private property to constitute an extension of the self.

The argument for this claim was first made by John Locke in his "labor theory of property." Locke suggests that private property arose within a state of nature even before the formation of political society. In principle, everything was originally held in common. Once effort was exerted by an individual to gather, hunt, cultivate, or appropriate land or the things that grow or are found on it, however, this land or these things became the property of the laboring individual. Property exists because individuals invest their labor into natural resources. Through labor, Locke argues in his *Second Treatise of Government*, the self may effectively extend its sovereignty beyond the reach of its own limbs, establishing dominion and ownership over what previously had been ownerless.[33] Following Locke's theory, negative libertarians maintain that to be free is to be the master of one's private domain. To be free means that no one is allowed to trespass on, appropriate, or otherwise constrain one's body, mind, or property.

Positive liberty, in contrast to negative liberty, is not a freedom from constraint or interference but a freedom to do or achieve something. It signifies not an absence but an attainment. To be positively free is not simply to remove all physical restraints hindering bodily movement, mental expression, or the use of one's private property. It also entails possessing the means necessary to accomplish a particular task at hand. These means may be physical, mental, social, economic, or political.

Apes, for instance, are negatively free to write critical commentaries on Shakespeare's poetry. No one is physically preventing their doing so. Apes are not positively free to engage in literary criticism, however, for they lack the intellectual means with which to accomplish the task. Likewise, a person is negatively free to repair his automobile if no one prevents him from doing so by, say, locking him indoors. He is only positively free to repair his automobile, however, if, along with the opportunity, he has the knowledge, skill, and tools necessary to complete the task. Positive liberty thus requires more than the absence of constraint. It also requires the capacity or ability to accomplish specific tasks or fulfill specific desires.

Positive libertarians argue that it does not make sense to say that someone is free to do something if actually doing it remains an impossibility for him. Most of us are not free to travel back in time, for instance, though no political constitution or legal code forbids it. Likewise, for the positive libertarian, the acrophobic person (someone intensely or obsessively fearful of heights) is not free to walk across a high bridge, even though no one is preventing him from doing so. While the acrophobe may truly want to walk across the bridge, his fear of heights disempowers him. For the acrophobe, the positive freedom to cross high bridges is only truly gained once his debilitating fear of heights is overcome or controlled.

To be positively free, in other words, is to be self-directed and capable of realizing one's will. For this reason, Isaiah Berlin identifies positive liberty as a kind of mastery over the self. Positive liberty entails pursuing a goal or abiding by a law of one's own choosing or making. The obstacles to this self-direction or self-legislation may come either from concrete things in the external world or from intellectual, emotional, or psychological shortcomings in oneself.

For the negative libertarian, deciding whether freedom exists for a particular person is a relatively straightforward affair. One simply observes if there are any physical constraints that prevent the person from speaking, acting, or enjoying his private property. In the absence of such constraints, one concludes that this person is free. For the positive libertarian, deciding whether freedom exists for a particular individual is more complex. First, one must find out what the person wants to do (e.g., write a critical review of Shakespeare, fix an automobile, or cross a bridge). Then, one must find out if in fact the person is capable of fulfilling his desire. The problem is further complicated if one holds, as most positive libertarians do, that what an individual believes he needs or says he wants is not always what he *really* needs or wants.

Imagine a person who, under the pernicious control of a hypnotist, furiously rubs his eyes every time the name "Plato" is mentioned. If asked why he is rubbing his eyes, the person would respond, as per instructions given under trance, that his eyes itch. Now if this person happens to attend a lecture on ancient political philosophy, his eye-rubbing might become so intense as to cause physical injury. Clearly this would not be in his best interest. Is this person truly free not to rub his eyes whenever the name of Plato is mentioned? The strict negative libertarian would answer yes, as no one is physically forcing him to rub his eyes. For the positive libertarian the answer is clearly no, as the victim of hypnosis has neither the ability to refrain from rubbing his eyes nor is it in his best interest to rub them.

This talk of hypnosis may seem far-fetched. Moreover, certain negative libertarians, such as J.S. Mill, would probably claim that being in a hypnotic trance does not meet the criterion of having sovereignty over one's own mind. Suppose, then, the cause of one's self-destructive action is not an external agent (the hypnotist) but an internal weakness. It is commonly said, for example, that people can become slaves to their passions or slaves to their addictions to tobacco, alcohol, or other drugs. The idea is that one can lose one's freedom not simply because another person constrains or controls one's movements but because in some palpable sense one loses self-control.

In the *Republic*, Plato speaks of those who are ruled by, rather than rule over, their appetites and passions. The good life is one in which reason, not desire, gains the upper hand within the soul. Those who are ruled by their appetites and passions believe themselves to be free because they do whatever they want to do. Plato, however, describes them as slaves because in abandoning reason they do not know how to pursue their best interests. Indeed, they do not know what their best interests are. Even Rousseau, who had a more charitable opinion about natural impulses and passions than Plato, held that man only achieves liberty by becoming "truly master of himself." The "mere impulse of appetite," Rousseau stipulates, "is slavery."[34]

This point may be made even more politically relevant, to recall Marx, by substituting for the victim of his own appetites or addictions the victim of ideology. For Marx, an exploited worker who strongly supports the laws that protect private property and the accumulation of capital is not really free. The worker has been duped to support a political and legal system that violates his interests and leads to his ruthless exploitation. A false consciousness keeps the worker from actively pursuing his own good, which would be better served by fomenting revolution. Like the libertines criticized by Plato, the victims of ideology described by Marx are particularly resistant to true liberation because they already believe themselves to be free.

To be positively free one must not simply be unhindered by external constraints from doing what one wants to do. One must also be unhindered by internal constraints from pursuing one's best interests. Internal constraints may consist of beliefs, attitudes, values, predispositions, and deficiencies in aptitude that prevent one from securing one's objective interests. Examples of such constraints would be posthypnotic suggestions, irrational impulses, appetites, passions and phobias, weaknesses of character, false consciousness, ignorance, lack of skill, and shortsighted judgment. Such internal constraints prevent the exercise of positive freedom.

For the most part, positive libertarians are not interested in our freedom to fix cars, traverse bridges, or escape malicious hypnotists. They are interested in politics. More specifically, they are interested in each individual's freedom to exercise his share of power in the ordering of collective life. Negative liberty is primarily a private liberty grounded in individual rights. It is historically identified with the liberal tradition and pertains to the protection of citizens *from* government. Positive liberty is primarily a public liberty that pertains to the involvement of citizens *in* government. It is historically identified with civic virtue and popular self-rule, values that developed within the republican tradition, first in ancient Rome and subsequently in the city-states of the Italian Renaissance. Positive liberty is a disposition for civic virtue coupled with the opportunity to put this disposition into practice through self-government.

The negative libertarian maintains that one is free if one is not interfered with when one speaks or acts. The positive libertarian maintains that one cannot be considered free if, despite the above-mentioned opportunities, one remains wholly ignorant of political affairs or if one is not disposed to participate in them. While no laws or authorities may actually keep one from exercising one's political rights to speak out about public concerns, to organize, to vote on issues or for representatives, or to run for office, the fact may be that one does none of these things because one has been socialized into a state of apathetic passivity or cynicism. Thus internal constraints such as irrational beliefs and feelings, or a lack of knowledge and skill, effectively strip one of the positive liberty to exercise civic virtue in self-government.

Balancing Positive and Negative Liberty

From the perspective of the positive libertarian, negative liberty is only the precondition for true freedom. Negative liberty is a necessary but not a sufficient condition for the full exercise of freedom as it is manifest in actual political participation. Positive liberty is not so much a state of affairs (the absence of constraint) as an event, namely, the event of exercising one's capacities, particularly one's political capacities, in one's best interests.

Jean-Jacques Rousseau, one of the early modern advocates of positive liberty, insists that freedom is only ever obtained when people take their collective lives into their own hands. Freedom is evidenced in the actual exercising of political capacities. Criticizing the representative system of English government, Rousseau writes in *The Social Contract* that "the people of England regards itself as free; but it is grossly mistaken; it is free only during the elections of members of parliament. As soon as they are elected, slavery overtakes it, and it is nothing. The use it makes of the short moments of liberty it enjoys shows indeed that it deserves to lose them."[35] Freedom, Rousseau insists, is a form of sovereignty, and sovereignty cannot be represented. It must be exercised directly. Far from minding one's own business and staying at home, everyone in a truly free society "flies to the assemblies" to let his voice be heard and to take part in the legislative affairs of the commonwealth.

Cicero (106–43 B.C.), the Roman orator and statesman, maintained that "to be free one must become a slave to the law." Rousseau, following Cicero, agrees that freedom means abiding by law. He insists, however, that the law one obeys must be of one's own making. Logically, Rousseau argues that those who live collectively exercise their freedom through collective lawmaking. Those who do not participate in the making of laws that govern society forgo the opportunity for self-legislation and hence the opportunity for freedom. Freedom first emerges in the public realm when each contributes to the governing of that realm. Through collective self-governance, human beings realize their greatest potential for liberty.

Positive liberty, one might then say, is the freedom to be the most one can be. Attaining this goal entails abiding by the laws of one's own making that best serve one's interests. As an isolated ideal for individuals, engaging in self-legislation and self-mastery seems unproblematic. It appears obvious, for instance, that the acrophobic person who cannot legislate himself to walk over high bridges is not as free and hence not as fortunate as someone who does not bear the burden of this obsessive fear. The problem arises when we examine positive liberty in social and political life. Can we assume that the citizens engaged in self-legislation are identical in their interests, desires, and needs? Historically, Berlin notes, this assumption has been made by positive libertarians, and with some catastrophic results. The quest for positive liberty, Berlin observes, has typically led to a "prescribed form of life" that often served as "a specious disguise for brutal tyranny."[36] A brief look at the political thought of Jean-Jacques Rousseau will illustrate Berlin's point.

Rousseau, like Hobbes, posits the making of a social contract that effectively politicizes a prior state of nature and puts an end to anarchy. For Rousseau, this social contract constitutes a real loss of freedom. Rousseau conceives the anarchical state of natural man—that is, man prior to the advent of private property and government—in much better terms than does Hobbes. He criticizes Hobbes for equating the state of nature with a state of war. This equation is made possible, Rousseau states, because Hobbes projects onto natural man all the degenerate traits, such as the lust for power, that are first created by society. In the original state of nature, Rousseau suggests, the instincts of primitive humans were largely benign. As a result, their world remained mostly free of hostility. Only "civilized" man is the prideful, acquisitive, power-hungry individual that Hobbes describes.

Except for purposes of mating, Rousseau suggests, primitive human beings lived as isolated individuals and had few worries. The primitive man could be found "satisfying his hunger at the first oak, and slaking his thirst at the first brook; finding his bed at the foot of the tree which afforded him a repast; and, with that, all his wants supplied."[37] Not caring about others, and particularly not caring what others thought of him, Rousseau's primitive finds his freedom in the absence of external constraints and rests content with the satisfaction of minimal needs. A stranger to envy or pride, he has no cause to covet his neighbors' goods and finds little to quarrel about with anyone he meets.

The liberties gained by entry into social life, that is, the freedom from fear of violent death and the freedom to own property, actually mark the end of a greater "natural liberty" according to Rousseau. Social life in general, and property relations in particular, entail a panoply of rules and regulations. "Man is born free; and everywhere he is in chains," Rousseau observes.[38] The newborn child, like the primitive man of the state of nature, is unburdened by the restrictions, both legal and moral, that constrain the behavior of his socialized elders.

Despite his sharp criticism of social life, Rousseau does not believe that we could or should revert back to noble savages anarchically running about in the wilderness with nothing to our names, or for that matter, without having names. Such unmitigated individual freedom has been lost forever. Absolute negative liberty, in other words, is impossible for social man. Society necessarily burdens its members with rules that dictate much of what they can and cannot do, where they can and cannot go, how they can and cannot act. Ideally, as J.S. Mill suggested, these restrictions would simply keep individuals from harming each other. But in a densely populated, technically advanced society there are few actions or endeavors that could not be construed as potentially harming others. In economic affairs, for instance, one person's gain often amounts to another's loss, as the scarcity of resources and consumers pits competitors against each other. In turn, industrial processes often pollute the environment and release noxious substances. Thus health itself has become a public issue, whereas in former ages it was largely a personal concern. To be a political animal today—with all the rules, regulations, and responsibilities that political life entails —means giving up a great deal of one's natural negative liberty.

Rousseau acknowledged that the natural liberty of the primitive individual was forever lost. He nonetheless believed that social man had developed a worthy substitute, namely, positive liberty. To achieve positive liberty, however, one's integration in society must become more, not less, extensive. The alternatives for Rousseau were stark and clear. "The source of human misery is the contradiction between man and citizen," he writes. "Give him wholly to the state or to himself ... if you divide his heart you tear him apart."[39] In other words, our choices are limited to two. We might yearn for absolute negative liberty as experienced in the mythical state of nature, but our efforts to reestablish it would be in vain. Alternatively, we might strive to cultivate positive liberty within a highly politicized and unified society. What we lose in individual (negative) liberty we gain in political (positive) liberty. Were we, in turn, to forgo this positive liberty by not participating in the democratic process, Rousseau warns, we would be deprived of freedom altogether. To endure social constraint without exercising political liberty is to be little better than a slave.

There is, then, no going back for Rousseau and only one way forward. Once contaminated by the envy, pride, greed, and lust for power that is inevitably cultivated in society, the individual can no longer experience the easy contentment of the isolated savage. Having developed the egoism, what Rousseau called *amour-propre*, endemic to social life, man can never again be given wholly to himself. Rousseau proposes that we therefore give ourselves wholly to the state, transforming our individual egoism into a collective egoism. Ideally, *amour de la patrie*, love of one's country, would replace *amour-propre*, or love of self.

The prospects for this transformation, Rousseau laments, are not very good. In large part, this is because the remnants of negative liberty exercised in society have been reduced to economic egoism, that is to say, the freedom to own and amass property and wealth. If positive, political liberty is to redeem social life, it must first turn self-interested, egoistic individuals into a community of patriots who realize that their greatest freedom arises in acting for the common good.

Rousseau holds that it is in every individual's best interest to serve the interests of the people as a whole, even if one believes or feels otherwise. Positive liberty is the desire and ability to adopt the interests of society at large as one's own. If, in asserting one's personal will, one contradicts these social interests as expressed by the "general will" of the people, one is by definition acting against one's own better interests and against oneself. Hence one is also acting unfreely. Thus Rousseau famously states that in our political lives we may be "forced to be free." When false beliefs cloud our vision, we realize our true liberty only by being forced to act in conformity with the general will.

In many ways, Rousseau anticipates Marx, who also suggests that bourgeois (negative) liberty amounts to little more than the freedom to be selfish. Negative liberty for the wealthy and powerful means the freedom to amass wealth and power. For the poor and powerless, it amounts to lives of misery with scant opportunity to exercise their full potential as human beings. While Rousseau's patriotic remedy is primarily grounded in political equality, however, Marx's revolutionary remedy is primarily grounded in economic equality. Positive liberty, Marx suggests, emerges only once we become emancipated from the class relations that alienate us from our neighbors. Collective freedom is discovered by abolishing private property.

In 1958, when Berlin lectured on the two concepts of liberty, he was concerned with the actual and potential abuses of positive liberty. At that time, he could write that the view of those who reject negative liberty and favor its positive counterpart "rules over half our world."[40] He was thinking about the Soviet empire and "the great clash of ideologies" that dominated his time. Today concerns have changed. History has effectively rechanneled many of the Marxist yearnings for positive liberty, and swept away their institutional perversions. At the same time, the pursuit of positive liberty remains very much alive, though it is seldom manifested in revolutionary zeal for communism. Instead, the pursuit of positive liberty is evidenced in efforts to cultivate citizen politics and develop more participatory democracies.

Positive liberty aims at a fuller realization of the human potential. This is its glory, but also its danger. A liberty that seeks to achieve great things may do great harm. If one's object is to shepherd everyone into the promised land, then one may be tempted to force those who would rather lag behind or take a different route to march in lockstep. Negative liberty does not aspire to such grand, collective projects. Far from seeking the eradication of egoism, it establishes our right to be egoistic. Far from realizing our full potential as human beings, negative liberty may be experienced, at least according to Hobbes, by animals and plants. It is simply the absence of constraint. By these standards, negative liberty may not seem like much of an achievement at all. Isolation on a desert island would bring about its greatest realization.

In a social setting, however, negative libertarians believe that freeing individuals from external constraints will best facilitate their flourishing. Human beings are naturally ambitious and creative. The task at hand, negative libertarians argue, is to allow individuals the space to achieve their greatest potential, not to dictate what that potential is. As long as the rules of the game are fair and people are let alone to take responsibility for their lives, great heights will be attained.

A society grounded solely on negative liberty, nonetheless, would be a pretty harsh place. The negative liberty to go one's own way under one's own steam also entails the danger of falling between the cracks or being left behind. In the jungle, the fate of those less fortunate or less favored is sealed. They become food for the strong. In society, however, most believe that those who stumble and fall deserve aid. Perhaps we should solely rely on human beings' natural charity to ensure that the less fortunate are humanely cared for. Negative libertarians maintain that a society that is both grounded in negative liberty and cultivates, but does not legislate, charity, is the most for which human beings may hope.

Is justice adequately served, however, if the pursuit of freedom is not balanced with the pursuit of equality? Consider the fact that poverty has an adverse affect on the intellectual and emotional development of children. Lower IQs and greater fear and anxiety are evident in children who chronically or even occasionally live in poverty.[41] Poverty and lack of education also correlate with lower levels of integration and participation in the political system. The problem is very real today. Child poverty has risen in the United States to levels two to four times higher than in other highly industrialized nations. Currently, one in five children in the United States lives below the poverty line. About 20 million Americans, with the vast majority of these being children, suffer from malnutrition, that is, the chronic shortage of nutrients needed for growth and good health.[42] Equality under the law, as we earlier observed, does not always translate into equality of opportunity. Although the rules of the game may be the same for all, a political system grounded solely in negative liberty and voluntary charity is unlikely to create a level playing field for its children. If history is any guide, the children of the disadvantaged will face a markedly uphill climb during their life journeys. Thus the innocent suffer from inequities grounded in the social order. They will not receive according to their due.

Those who advocate positive liberty do not, and need not, advocate social and political programs as radical or extreme as either Rousseau or Marx. They may hold positive liberty to be only one among many goods, including negative liberty, that need to be realized. Nor would all positive libertarians agree that other goods, such as civil rights, need to be sacrificed in order to achieve greater positive freedom. One may advocate increased participation in politics as a good in itself, as a form of positive liberty crucial to democratic life, and staunchly uphold the individual rights and freedoms typically championed by negative libertarians. Indeed, many positive libertarians argue that we can only fully take advantage of our individual political rights—say, our right to free speech or freedom of association and assembly—once we have sufficiently developed and expressed our capacity for political participation. Arguing for the development of "strong democracy," political theorist Benjamin Barber writes: "To be free we must be self-governing; to have rights we must be citizens. In the end, only citizens can be free. The argument for strong democracy, though at times deeply critical of liberalism, is thus an argument on behalf of liberty."[43] Positive liberty, in this instance, is both an end in itself and the means by which negative liberties may become more fully realized and more vigilantly protected.

Likewise, negative libertarians do not necessarily hold that negative liberty is the only good for which to strive. Freedom means freedom from constraint, many would argue, and it is a good. But justice is also a good, and establishing justice might at times require a diminution of (negative) liberty. Still, negative libertarians insist that we make clear conceptual distinctions between liberty and other values, such as justice. Once these distinctions are made, we may better judge which values are to be realized at the (partial) expense of others. To underline this point, Isaiah Berlin observes that we force children to go to school. In so doing, we constrain their negative liberty for the purpose of elevating another value, namely, the growth of knowledge and the diminution of ignorance. According to Berlin, one must acknowledge and accept this sacrifice of liberty.

Positive libertarians might suggest that in forcing children to attend school we are actually increasing their positive liberty because a child's freedom is effectively enhanced by the growth of knowledge that allows more informed and mature choices and decisions. Negative liberty sacrificed to achieve certain other values, such as knowledge or justice, is less a freedom lost than a greater freedom gained.[44] Positive libertarians do not make the neat conceptual distinctions between freedom and other values that negative libertarians insist on. At the same time, they appeal to our intuitive sense that someone cannot be considered at liberty to take advantage of opportunities if he remains wholly ignorant of their existence.

Negative libertarians subordinate positive to negative liberty for practical reasons. The positive political liberty to participate in government, many negative libertarians insist, is not an end in itself but the only tried-and-true means of protecting negative liberties. Samuel Johnson advocated this position in its starkest form, claiming that "political liberty is good only so far as it produces private liberty."[45] John Locke held a similar view.[46] Democratic participation, by this account, simply serves the goal of ensuring that despots or tyrants who would threaten our private liberties do not come to power. To paraphrase Thomas Jefferson, the tree of liberty must occasionally be fertilized with the blood of tyrants and patriots and continuously watered with the sweat of active citizens.

Negative libertarians need not hold positive liberty to such a limited role. Positive political liberties may be held to be good in themselves, though potentially dangerous if left uncontrolled and taken to extremes. Isaiah Berlin clarified his own position in this regard. He writes:

> The only reason for which I have been suspected of defending negative liberty against positive and saying that it is more civilized is that I do think that the concept of positive liberty, which is of course essential to a

decent existence, has been more often abused or perverted than that of negative liberty.... Certainly the weak must be protected against the strong.... Negative liberty must be curtailed if positive liberty is to be sufficiently realized; there must be a balance between the two.[47]

In the ostensible attempt to secure positive liberty for its citizens, by defining their citizens' "true interests," totalitarian states have trampled much negative liberty and personal freedom underfoot. As Berlin acknowledges, however, a world of wholesale negative liberty, like a Hobbesian state of nature, would disable most from exercising and enjoying their freedom.

In such a world, each individual theoretically would have the absolute negative liberty to do as he pleases short of directly harming others. In practice, however, only the very powerful would have the strength and security to make use of their liberty. There would be freedom to discriminate but no freedom from discrimination. There would be freedom to accumulate wealth but no freedom from poverty. There would be freedom to pursue power but no freedom from domination. Negative liberty, like positive liberty, is certainly not immune to abuse. A balanced pursuit of positive liberty and negative liberty may best mitigate the susceptibility of each to excess.

Mastery and Liberty

Positive libertarians equate freedom with mastery, namely, one's mastery over desires, passions, and any other obstacles to self-realization. As Durkheim observed, "to be free is not to do what one pleases; it is to be master of oneself."[48] Negative libertarians are also animated by a pursuit of mastery. Negative liberty, we recall, identifies freedom with the individual's mastery over his immediate environment, over his private life and property. The difference is that for negative libertarians sovereign control is exercised by the individual; for positive libertarians it is collectively mediated. With this in mind, political theorist William Connolly observes that "mastery is the route to freedom" for both "individualists" (negative libertarians) and "collectivists" (positive libertarians).[49]

What is wrong with seeking control? Is there any reason that we should not identity freedom and liberty with mastery? Actually there is nothing wrong with mastery and control in itself, or with the positive and negative liberties that incorporate it. The danger lies in the limitless pursuit of mastery, and this limitless pursuit may be abetted by straightforwardly equating freedom with mastery.

Reflect for a moment on the historical effect of this equation on the natural environment. Human mastery over the earth has certainly taken its toll. Many ecologists worry that if the extension of human power and control is not kept within limits the natural world as we know it may soon cease to exist. Countless species have become extinct and thousands more are threatened. Millions of acres of ancient forests are being leveled and their populations of plants and animals destroyed each year. As humanity extends its power and control across the lands and seas and skies of the planet, the ecological catastrophe grows, undercutting the earth's capacity to support many forms of life, including our own. No small part of this environmental devastation, one might argue, is fostered by a love of freedom that is too closely identified with mastery.

Already in ancient Greek and biblical times, freedom was equated with dominion over the earth. There is little in positive and negative liberty that militates against this equation. Positive libertarians have celebrated the mastery of nature as a testimony to humanity's higher rationality. The positive libertarian's attempt fully to actualize the human potential typically asserts the human prerogative to dominate the natural world. Negative libertarians, in turn, have fostered the mastery of nature in no less degree owing to their concern with the sovereign rights of property owners. Nature, incapable of bearing rights of its own, relinquishes all claim to protection, respect, or care except insofar as it is accorded sanctuary under the aegis of private property. And private property, negative libertarians maintain, may be disposed of as its owner sees fit, unconstrained by anything save perhaps the obligation of its efficient exploitation.

Benjamin Constant, for instance, argues that the liberty of moderns is to be chiefly found in their right "to dispose of property, and even to abuse it."[50] John Locke believed the abuse or wasting of property to be unjustified. He argued not for the protection of nature, however, but for its more efficient exploitation. Hence Locke justified the colonists' forceful expropriation of aboriginal American land without recompense, owing to the natives' inadequate exploitation of it. According to Locke, leaving land unexploited was equivalent to wasting it, and in wasting their land, the natives forfeited all rights of ownership and defense. "Land that is left wholly to Nature," Locke writes in the *Second Treatise of Government,* that hath no improvement of Pasturage, Tillage, or Planting, is called, as indeed it is, *wast[e];* and we shall find the benefit of it amount to little more than nothing."[51] Here, again, a freedom equated with mastery bodes ill for the preservation of the natural world.

Opposed to both positive and negative freedom is a third kind of freedom that cannot be equated with control or mastery. The German philosopher Martin Heidegger (1889–1976), who was much concerned with the pernicious effects of modern technology, developed this concept of freedom. He explicitly characterizes it in opposition to positive and negative liberty. For Heidegger, freedom is not a form of control but a "letting be." Freedom lets people and things be themselves. It reveals them in their uniqueness. It constitutes a witnessing of difference. (Heidegger is thus a seminal figure for postmodern theorists.) According to Heidegger, freedom is closer to guardianship than control. It is discovered primarily in caring for the world and in caring for our place in the world. We enjoy our freedom as solicitous witnesses of reality rather than as its manipulators and masters.

Unfortunately, Heidegger did not explain the political ramifications of his philosophic understanding of freedom. Moreover, his arcane vocabulary and links to Nazism make him an unlikely choice for political inspiration.[52] Nevertheless, one of Heidegger's students, Hannah Arendt (1906–75), did employ Heideggerian themes to develop an explicitly political understanding of freedom untethered to mastery.

Arendt, a Jewish intellectual, fled Nazi Germany to Paris in 1933 and moved to the United States in 1940 where she began a distinguished career as a political theorist. In her essay, "What Is Freedom," Arendt takes issue with traditional Western notions of liberty. She holds that the nature of freedom has generally been misconstrued owing to a prevailing philosophical tradition that equates freedom with the mastery of will. Arendt suggests that freedom is not a kind of sovereignty. It neither signifies the absence of individual constraint, as negative libertarians claim, nor the willpower to achieve or control one's desires, as positive libertarians claim. In direct opposition to the common notion of freedom as the unconstrained opportunity to exercise one's will and fulfill one's wants, Arendt suggests that freedom pertains neither to the motivations we have to pursue a goal nor to the final achievement of a goal. Freedom, she argues, is not at all an individual or collective achievement of willpower. It is a public event that escapes individual and collective control.

For Arendt, freedom primarily appears in the open spaces of the political realm whenever the actions of citizens intersect and create new relationships. This creative interaction is inherently unstable and unpredictable. What humans discover when they act in concert is that freedom becomes manifest in the very novelty of the results and relationships. Far from being controllable and predictable, political action, Arendt states, is closer to the nature of a miracle. In action, by way of freedom, the new and the unforeseen occurs. Our political institutions allow us both to witness this freedom in action and to provide for its safeguarding.

Sovereignty is the capacity to control the outcome of action. Like mastery, it is commonly understood to be a condition of freedom. Arendt holds that sovereignty—whether exercised by the individual or the collectivity, that is, whether exercised as negative liberty or positive liberty—actually signals the absence of freedom. She writes:

> Under human conditions, which are determined by the fact that not man but men live on the earth, freedom and sovereignty are so little identical that they cannot even exist simultaneously. Where men wish to be sovereign, as individuals or as organized groups, they must submit to the oppression of the will, be this the individual will with which I force myself, or the 'general will' of an organized group. If men wish to be free, it is precisely sovereignty they must renounce.[53]

Arendt's understanding of freedom is unsettling because it cuts against our common assumptions.

As a political translation of Heidegger's philosophical notion of freedom, however, Arendt's understanding of freedom is illuminating. Like Heidegger, Arendt maintains that freedom evaporates once it is possessed by a sovereign power. Political freedom emerges most fundamentally in the creating and caretaking of a public realm, a *res publica,* in which the novel interactions of unique individuals transpire. Safeguarding this public realm, accomplished through the words and deeds of active citizens, cannot be reduced to mastery, control, or sovereignty of a personal or collective nature. Rather than establish control or mastery over the outcome of our actions, freedom allows the unexpected to arise. It is a letting be of the future and its potential for novelty. And it is a letting be of others, of human plurality and its potential for difference.

In today's world, where the caretaking of local and global ecologies becomes an increasingly important task, such an understanding of freedom may fruitfully supplement its positive and negative counterparts. It is difficult to see how this concept of freedom as a "letting be" could wholly substitute for negative or positive liberties. Our freedom to "witness" reality would quickly lapse into fatalism and leave us open to oppression if we did not also exercise our private and public liberties to shape that reality according to our interests. What Berlin concedes of positive liberty, then, one might unbegrudgingly affirm for negative liberty as well as for a liberty divorced from mastery: their exercise may lead to dangerous abuses, and they are prone to excess, yet held in balance they remain essential for a decent existence.

The Life of Reason

Within modern Western societies, the most common foundation for mores is reason, or rationality. One might also point to religious faith or the authority of tradition as a grounding for the rules and principles that guide and regulate collective life. The fact remains, however, that the last court of appeal before which competing mores are usually presented, advocated, and defended is that of reason. If action is not reasonable or rational, it may be tolerated when it causes no harm to others. But it will not be celebrated as a model of appropriate public behavior.

In modern times, social and political life began to justify itself in terms that were both publicly accessible and independent of transcendent authority. Appeals to the gods, their earthly vicars, or heroic figures of days gone by, though not illegitimate and generally in lip service, could no longer justify the principles structuring collective life. The separation of church and state and the rise of democratic culture spelled an end to systems of authority and tradition, whether religious, monarchical, or aristocratic in nature, that once served as the bedrock for social and political life. In their stead, reason asserted itself as the basic stuff from which the foundations of society could be built. The language of reason became the *lingua franca*, the vernacular of a democratic, scientific, and secular age.

Political life, in short, is primarily analyzed, assessed, and accounted for in the language of reason. As a contemporary political theorist observes, "if we had to choose a single normative standard for the understanding and evaluation of liberal democratic political systems, the one that would get the farthest would be neither liberty, nor fairness, nor neutrality, nor utility, nor pluralist bargaining, but instead would be the ideal of rational practice."[54] Another contemporary political theorist writes that "modern states are not 'communities of shared meaning' in any simple sense, they are associations of more or less reasonable people ... whose reasonableness we wish to respect and whose allegiance we hope thereby to engage."[55] This theorist goes on to observe that what makes for good public policy, morality, and law within the modern state is its grounding in reason, which is to say its "capacity to gain widespread agreement among reasonable people moved by a desire for reasonable consensus."[56] If, as these theorists suggest, reason and rational practice are the mainsprings of modern politics, then determining the precise meanings of these terms becomes imperative.

As voluminous writings in the history of philosophy testify, precise and stable definitions for reason and rationality have proved elusive. Indeed, political theorists have carried on a debate about the meaning of reason and rationality for more than two millennia. The matter is no nearer to being settled today than it was in the ancient Greek *polis*. The challenge has been recently been taken up by postmodern theorists. Michel Foucault writes that "the central issue of philosophy and critical thought since the eighteenth century has always been, still is, and will, I hope, remain the question: *What* is this Reason that we use?"[57] In large part, the importance of reason in Western political thought, and in particular modern Western political thought, arose because of its intrinsic relation to other core political values, namely, law and liberty.

Over 2,000 years ago, Plato described law as the embodiment of reason. Law holds political communities together. Reason thus allows for social and political order. This understanding of the cohesive and moderating qualities of reason remains widely shared today.

In the modern world, liberty and law are similarly linked. They are mutually reinforcing. Liberty and law stand together for negative libertarians because law ensures that the liberties of some do not illegitimately interfere with the liberties of others. Without law, negative liberty may theoretically exist for all, but only the most powerful could practically enjoy it. "Where there is no law," Locke concisely states, "there is no freedom."[58] Positive libertarians also equate liberty with law. They maintain that liberty consists in abiding by a law of one's own making. As Rousseau states, "obedience to a law which we prescribe to ourselves is liberty."[59]

Liberty is created and preserved by law. Law, in turn, is created and preserved by the exercise of reason. Hence the existence and exercise of reason is a necessary condition for the existence and exercise of liberty. Without the former, the latter would not arise and could not persist. Reason allows for the widespread enjoyment of negative liberty by establishing laws that forbid encroaching on another's life or property. For positive libertarians, to be free is to be self-legislating, and the only human faculty capable of setting itself laws and controlling the appetites and passions is reason.

What, then, is this reason that gives us law and liberty? Like Plato, Aristotle believed that freedom was best established and bounded by law and that law should be the embodiment of reason. Like Plato, Aristotle believed that reason should legislate the appetites and passions of the soul just as it should legislate the citizens of the polis. Unlike Plato, however, Aristotle did not locate the faculty of reason in a single caste, namely, the philosophers. Nor did he believe reason to constitute an abstract, purely intellectual faculty within the soul. Reason, for Aristotle, was a practical faculty as well. He spoke of practical reason or prudence, in Greek *phronesis,* as that faculty of the soul that blended the capacity for abstract thought with the capacity to make judgments about the concrete world.

Prudence allows practical understanding and judgment because it is grounded in experience. Prudence allows one to act at the right time, in the right place, in the right manner, for the right reason. It achieves this feat by integrating abstract knowledge of the way things should be (e.g., ideals and principles) with practical assessments of the way things actually are.

Aristotle believed that practical reason was exercised not only by philosophers but by a wide range of the citizenry. People gain use of the faculty of reason through their involvement in day-to-day affairs. The best judge of the fit of a pair of shoes, Aristotle suggests, is not the cobbler who makes them but the person who wears them. Likewise, the best judge of government is not the official who runs it but the citizens who live under it. Being a subject of government and a participant in a collective order forces one to exercise one's practical judgment on an ongoing basis. Thus is practical reason developed among all who negotiate the life of politics.

Aristotle admitted that the best *possible* regime would be a monarchy (or aristocracy) in which the philosopher king(s) ruled supreme. This would also be a very dangerous regime, however, unlikely to arise and easily corrupted once established. The best *practicable* regime, both easier to achieve and more stable once in place, Aristotle called a *polity.* A polity is a mixed regime that incorporates both aristocratic and democratic principles. The stability of this regime is due in large part to the widespread cultivation of practical reason. In the polity, a large segment of the population actively exercises reason in the day-to-day affairs of managing the ship of state. Upholding the prejudices of his day, however, Aristotle maintained that women and slaves should be excluded from politics along with children because they were naturally deficient in reason.

As the disagreement between Plato and Aristotle demonstrates, reason and rationality, like liberty and freedom, have no single, settled meaning. Yet deciding just what reason and rationality should mean —like the determination of the meaning of liberty and freedom—is a serious affair with important political consequences. If, for instance, we hold reason to be a purely intellectual faculty, one that only philosophers fully exercise, we may be persuaded by Plato's argument for the establishment of an aristocratic or monarchical system of rule. If we believe that reason is also a practical faculty, one that everyone exercises in his daily affairs, we may be persuaded by Aristotle's argument for the establishment of a more democratic system of rule. In turn, if we think that reason inheres not only in men but also in women, we may be persuaded that patriarchal rule is illegitimate in any of its forms.

In questioning the status of reason, Foucault asks: "What are its historical effects? What are its limits, and what are its dangers? How can we exist as rational beings, fortunately committed to practicing a rationality that is unfortunately crisscrossed by intrinsic dangers?" Foucault goes on to say that he does not mean to criticize rationality per se, but only to demonstrate "how ambiguous things are."[60] William Connolly likewise observes the inherent instability of words such as reason and rationality, words that constitute the "terms of political discourse." These terms are subject to endless contestation. Their contestation is not merely an academic affair; it has practical consequences. Connolly writes that "the language of politics is not a neutral medium that conveys ideas independently formed; it is an institutionalized structure of meanings that channels political thought and action in certain directions."[61] By structuring the language of politics, political theorists effectively channel thought and action. Contesting the meanings and uses or words such as reason and rationality is the *sine qua non* of political theory.

There are at least as many different definitions of reason and rationality as there are definitions of liberty and freedom. One might examine the contemporary feminist challenge to "masculine rationality" and the effort to establish the groundwork for a "feminist rationality."[62] One might critically engage Western rationality as a whole, a form of rationality, according to African-centered theorists, that attempts to "explain all of reality as though it had been created by the European mind for the purposes of control."[63] One might investigate concrete historical efforts to achieve a "higher reason" or "higher rationality," as was evidenced by the American counterculture movement in the 1960s and 1970s.[64] Alternatively, one might explore theoretical constructions of higher rationality, such as Jürgen Habermas's espousal of a "communicative rationality" that promotes social and political change through open communication.[65] The possibilities are virtually endless. We shall limit ourselves here to the cursory examination of three concepts of rationality. These concepts are respectively shaped by economic, political, and ecological concerns. Political reason and ecological reason, we discover, inherently challenge the hegemony of economic reason in our times.

Economic Reason

The British economist John Maynard Keynes wrote that "the ideas of economists and political philosophers, both when they are right and when they are wrong, are more powerful than is commonly understood. Indeed the world is ruled by little else. Practical men who believe themselves to be quite exempt from any intellectual influences are usually the slaves of some defunct economist."[66] Keynes exaggerates the power of economic theories and theorists, but perhaps not by much. People often act on principles little examined and follow conventions seldom challenged. In the modern Western world, a large portion of these principles and conventions are economic in nature.

Economic principles and conventions structure a wide range of our individual and collective thought and behavior, including aspects of social and political life not formally economic in nature. The dynamics of the "market" and the laws of "supply and demand," for example, are often used to explain the relationship between voters and candidates or between teachers and students. Economic principles and conventions gain widespread currency in our thought and speech because they are perceived to mirror the dictates of rationality. So much of modern life may be accounted for in economic terms because rational thought and economic thought have become virtual synonyms. As one political theorist writes: "Economic rationality is the dominant form of reason in contemporary industrial society—and, arguably, the defining feature of those societies."[67] What is the nature of this economic rationality, and how did it come to exercise such tremendous influence in the modern world?

One of the first theorists to examine the growth of economic rationality was Max Weber. Weber declares his chief concern to be the investigation and explanation of "rationalism" in the Western world.[68] Yet he never clearly defines reason or rationality. Better said, Weber refuses to give reason or rationality a single definition. Over a dozen distinct meanings for the terms have been charted in his writings.[69] Weber approaches the concept of rationality in different ways at different times for different purposes. He justifies this contextual approach by noting that "a thing is never irrational in itself, but only from a particular rational point of view."[70] Likewise, the rational is only ever rational from a particular perspective. The definition of rationality, therefore, largely depends on one's point of view.

Despite the multiple forms that modern rationality assumes in different historical and cultural settings, Weber leads us to believe that they all bear a unifying essence. There is, as it were, an ideal type of rationality. The process of rationalization, Weber writes, is always a function of the "striving for order."[71] Rationality constitutes an attempt to gain either a "theoretical mastery of reality" or a "practical mastery of the world."[72] Rationality pursues mastery by means of selecting among possible alternatives according to objectively calculable criteria of relative worth. In other words, rationality allows one to secure the best means to one's ends by systematically measuring the costs and benefits of various actions and opportunities. Rationality is synonymous with calculability. It is opposed to spontaneity and unpredictability. To rationalize something is to make it amenable to mental or physical control.

The most fascinating quality of rationality for Weber is its capacity to systematize and routinize what would otherwise remain quite unpredictable and disorderly. The mystery of the earth's creation or the impenetrable enigmas of human drives, for instance, may be rationalized through theology and religious rituals. With this in mind, Weber suggests that Calvinism, a form of Protestantism developed by the French (and later Swiss) theologian John Calvin (1509–64), marks the highest reach of religious rationalization.

Calvinists believe in predestination. Predestination means that God decides for each man and woman, even before his or her birth, whether he or she will go to heaven or hell. What an individual attempts or achieves in life can neither win salvation nor ensure damnation. Only the hand of the Almighty can tip the scales. Salvation is attained only by the grace of God. What one does in earthly life—the performance of rituals, the offering of sacraments, or the doing of good deeds—cannot alter one's ultimate fate.

Calvinists originally adopted the doctrine of predestination because they thought that it was prideful of human beings to believe that they could gain eternal salvation through their own means, effectively tying God's hands. Ironically, the Calvinists' belief in predestination did not lead to the fatalism or passivity one might expect. Calvinists believed that if a person was "chosen" for salvation, he would evidence this enviable status by way of his devotion. He could not help but display his "calling." Of course, no one *really* knew who was chosen for salvation. But this uncertainty only strengthened the Calvinists' resolve. In an effort to prove to themselves, and to others, that they were among the chosen few, Calvinists embraced a strict life of duty. They fervently devoted themselves to a vocation so that not a moment of life was wasted and they were never left idle. If one were truly among the chosen few, one would presumably always have good deeds to do. Even brief periods of idleness would suggest that one was not predestined for a heavenly afterlife or would at least give oneself pause to reflect on the uncertainty of one's fate.

For the Calvinists, Weber writes, good works became "technical means, not of purchasing salvation, but of getting rid of the fear of damnation."[73] Devotion to work became a way of convincing themselves and others that salvation was secured. The key was always to remain in full control of one's time and actions. The enemy of this religious rationalism was not so much the *enjoyment* of life itself as its *spontaneity*. For it is "impulsiveness" and not pleasure per se that evidences a life untethered to the mandate of duty. Thus Calvinism turned "with all its force against one thing: the spontaneous enjoyment of life and all it had to offer."[74] The Protestant ethic developed out of the need to routinize life. A steadfast and calculated devotion to duty became of paramount importance.

The great irony is that this attempt to heighten religious devotion produced an increasingly *secular* work ethic. The deprecation of spontaneity and the celebration of duty led to a preoccupation with work for its own sake. This quickly became translated into a preoccupation with the accumulation of wealth for its own sake, regardless of the pleasures it could afford. This preoccupation, Weber suggests, was the impetus for capital accumulation and the development of capitalist economies.

Weber explains how rationality in the modern, Western world became primarily an economic concept. Under the regimen of a Protestant work ethic, rationality became chiefly identified with the economic actor who engages in the secular, self-interested, and instrumental pursuit of wealth.[75] Weber's thesis, it should be noted, has been contested by historians who point out that capitalism began to develop centuries before the Protestant Reformation occurred. The fact that capitalism also developed in non-Protestant countries, such as Italy, further undermines Weber's thesis.[76] Despite its historical and cultural inaccuracies, Weber's work bears such originality and such tantalizing twists of logic that it has secured the reputation of a peerless piece of theorizing.

Weber rightly rejected the notion that the vast diversity of modern individuals could somehow be described as having a unitary "group mind" that operated in accordance with "a single formula."[77] Nonetheless, he maintained that economic rationality was indeed a predominant feature of modern life. Adopting this Weberian understanding, certain social scientists propose that all human thought and behavior, to the extent that it is 'rational,' is amenable to economic analysis. Social science becomes a matter of explaining the decisions and choices people make in terms of their rational efforts to minimize the costs they pay and maximize the benefits they receive. As one well-known social scientist observed, "we can fit anything into a loosely 'economic' framework if we are sufficiently hospitable to different kinds of 'reward' and 'cost.'"[78] From this point of view, any thought or behavior that merits the label of being rational may be reduced to an economic calculation.

To analyze behavior in terms of economic rationality is not to assume that everyone always acts selfishly in an attempt to accumulate wealth. As Weber demonstrated, economic rationality originally arose in the service of God, not mammon. Likewise, contemporary theories of economic rationality are not built on the assumption that all actors are driven by unmitigated economic self-interest. The goals of the economically rational person need not be egoistic, venal, or even financially oriented. The economic actor simply pursues the greatest amount of value with the least expenditure of effort and resources. The economic actor, as Anthony Downs writes, is interested in "maximizing output for a given input, or minimizing input for a given output."[79] The logic of economic rationality holds even when the content of the input and output remains unspecified. As Downs demonstrates, economic rationality can be usefully employed to explain how, with the least expenditure of time and resources, politicians seek to maximize votes and voters seek to maximize the benefits of voting. The ends that the "cost/benefit" analyses of politicians and voters serve may be either egoistic or altruistic. Likewise, one's rational efforts to earn the most money with the least effort might serve a wholly altruistic purpose if one chooses to donate one's income to charity. Alternatively, the output one seeks to maximize might be a friend's academic test scores, and the input one seeks simultaneously to minimize would be the time spent studying together.

Rather than assume that individuals are selfish, theorists of economic rationality assume that individuals behave in ways that are "wholly determined by the endeavor to relate means to ends as efficiently as possible."[80] Not *selfishness* but *efficiency* is the key characteristic. Assuming that individuals are selfish, however, certainly simplifies the application of economic rationality as a tool of social science inquiry. If actors are assumed to pursue the maximization of personal wealth (or personal power), one's theory gains a level of parsimony not otherwise achievable. Yet this assumption is not strictly necessary.

Theorists of economic rationality also need not assume that people are endowed with superhuman capacities for achieving high levels of efficiency. Social scientists have modified their theories to account for situations where the rational actor's effort to relate means to ends most efficiently is neither easy nor completely successful owing to the complexities and confusions of life. Herbert Simon, an organizational theorist, is widely recognized for initiating these modifications by introducing the notion of "bounded rationality." Simon's point is that the rational actor seldom if ever actually selects the most efficient means to achieve given ends. Instead, he selects those means found satisfactory given his cognitive limitations, the availability of information, and the constraints placed on his time and resources. The rational actor is engaged not in maximizing but in "satisficing" values, that is to say, in achieving satisfactory rather than optimal results. The rational actor satisfices, Simon bluntly states, because he does not have "the wits to maximize."[81] Likewise, Anthony Downs considers an actor to be rational not because he always achieves his goals with the least expenditure of effort, but because he "moves toward his goals in a way which, *to the best of his knowledge,* uses the least possible input of scarce resources per unit of valued output."[82]

The "glory" and "power" of economic rationalist theory, one political scientist observes, is evidenced in "its ability to imply a great range of testable hypotheses from few assumptions."[83] Indeed, political scientists have productively employed economic rationalist theory in very elegant and very ingenious ways. The glory and power of economic rationalist theory, however, wedded as it is to the virtue of parsimony, is significantly undermined as the bounded nature of rationality increases the number and intricacy of assumptions that the theorist has to make.

Simon insists that there is little alternative to sacrificing some parsimony in order better to understand human behavior in a complex world.[84] An early collaborator of Simon, James March, goes beyond exposing the cognitive limitations of the rational actor.[85] He proposes that the rational actor not only frequently fails to employ the most efficient means but also fails to pursue stable goals. Actors may exhibit an "ambiguity of preferences."[86] If preferences or goals are ambiguous or unstable, then efficiency in attaining them is by definition impossible. One cannot get to one's destination by the most direct route if one does not know where one is going.

With regard to political life, March's assumption about the ambiguous and unstable nature of preferences or goals is particularly apt. Politics is an activity that goes well beyond the efficient pursuit of stable, preconceived interests. That is because politics involves the shaping and reshaping of interests and desires and the formation and transformation of identities. The commonsense belief that attitudes and interests determine our behavior must also be questioned and qualified. The reverse is often true. Behavior frequently shapes attitudes and interests.[87] That is to say, what we do often determines what we want as much as what we want determines what we do. In the former case, one cannot most efficiently pursue one's goals through instrumental action because goals only become formulated in the midst of action.

Political action shapes preferences and goals. Rationality in politics, then, has something to do with the formation of interests and goals, not simply their efficient pursuit. We may better understand the relationship of reason to politics by returning to ancient Greece to explore further the multifaceted nature of rationality.

Classical Reason

Although Weber insisted that rationality is multifaceted, his work focused on the powerful and seemingly inevitable tide of modern economic rationality. This tide largely submerged the classical (Platonic and Aristotelian) and medieval (scholastic) understandings of substantive reason. Substantive reason is not restricted to devising efficient means to serve given ends. Substantive reason is capable of determining what the ends of action ought to be. Plato, we remember, held that reason should rule over the passions, determining what the nature of the good life was and setting us on the path toward it. Reason determines what the *goals* of life should be as well as what *means* are required to secure these goals. The rise of economic rationality in the modern era left reason only the latter, instrumental task.

David Hume (1711–76), the Scottish skeptical philosopher, famously reversed Plato's understanding. Hume writes in his *Treatise of Human Nature* that "reason is, and ought only to be, the slave of the passions, and can never pretend to any other office than to serve and obey them."[88] Following Hume, Bertrand Russell insisted that "reason has a perfectly clear and precise meaning. It signifies the choice of the right means to an end that you wish to achieve. It has nothing whatever to do with the choice of ends."[89] Herbert Simon, in developing his theory of bounded rationality, accepted this modern understanding. He maintains that "reason is wholly instrumental. It cannot tell us where to go; at best it can tell us how to get there. It is a gun for hire that can be employed in the service of any goals we have, good or bad."[90] Plato, Aristotle, and the medieval scholastics acknowledged that reason had an instrumental side to it. Unlike many modern theorists, however, the ancients did not think that instrumental rationality was the only form of rationality or even the most important form.

Aristotle suggests in the *Nichomachean Ethics* that reason pertains to more than the efficient pursuit of economic self-interest. Aristotle accepts the common understanding that reason is the capacity that allows thinking—and particularly inferences, judgments, and decisions—to achieve greater consistency. This capacity presides not simply or even primarily over economic thought, but over thinking about the nature of the human good as a whole. Unlike those who pursue passing pleasures, the person of reason strives to live the good life. Reason is not simply a calculative means to achieve sundry ends. Reason pertains to the human capacity to evaluate, understand, and participate in a social and cosmological order. As such, reason has a particular political relevance.

Jean-Pierre Vernant, a classical scholar, writes that "when Aristotle defined man as a 'political animal,' he emphasized what differentiates Greek reason from today's reason. If in his eyes *homo sapiens* was *Homo politicus,* it was because Reason itself was in essence political."[91] Aristotle considered the *polis,* or city-state, to be a self-sufficient association of citizens that allows for the pursuit of justice and the practice of virtue. He maintained that human reason serves this inherently political purpose. The *polis,* Aristotle writes, originally arose as a means of satisfying basic human needs, such as the provision of food, shelter, and security, needs that are only possible, or at least easier, to secure in a community. Nevertheless, the *polis* exists, Aristotle reminds us, not only to make life possible but to make the good life possible.

The good life is defined as the life of reason. The practice of reason not only determines the means to the good life, it also determines its content. And the content of the good life, it turns out, includes the practice of reason. The practice of reason itself is constitutive of the good life. Aristotle maintains that the good life cannot be instrumentally pursued or mastered. Its achievement is found in its very pursuit. Right action does not simply produce the good life, as a means to an end. To act rightly *is* to live the good life. Since right action is action informed by reason, the good life, according to Aristotle, consists in an active life of reason.

Reason is a civic virtue. Aristotle maintained that reason, like virtue in general, is achieved only through its practice. The practice of virtue, moreover, constitutes its own reward. Hence the exercise of reason is a substantive good, rather than merely an instrumental good. The expression or practice of this civic virtue is at the same time its cultivation and enjoyment.

Like the virtue of self-knowledge, the civic virtue of reason is developed only when we subject our convictions and values to public contestation. What holds for the development of virtue holds for the development of what Aristotle called "character" and what we have spoken of, somewhat more expansively, as "identity." The only way to build a virtuous character or construct a worthy identity is to participate self-consciously in social and political life. For Aristotle, the individual develops a virtuous character by engaging in social and political action that demands the exercise of reason.

This political participation is not reducible to carrying out cost/benefit calculations. Nor is it rational in the Weberian sense of allowing sovereign control or mastery. As one theorist explains Aristotle's thesis, the political agent or actor

> is constituted through the actions which disclose him both to others and to himself as the person that he is. He can never possess an idea of himself in the way that the craftsman possesses the form of his product; rather than his having any definite 'what' as blueprint for his actions or his life, he becomes and discovers 'who' he is through these actions. And the medium for this becoming through action is not one over which he is ever sovereign master; it is, rather, a network of other people who are also agents and with whom he is bound up in relationships of interdependency.[92]

In like manner, Hannah Arendt relies on Greek thought to illustrate how political action (and speech) discloses "who" we are. This "who" is not a sovereign entity. It is part of a "web of human relationships," a web that allows for the expression of freedom through public action.[93] As political actors we reveal ourselves as participants and agents of a collective performance rather than sovereign producers or authors of our own story. That is why, for Arendt, the "meaning" of a political deed lies in its actual performance rather than its achievement of a particular goal.[94] The ancient Greek philosopher and biographer Plutarch (A.D. 46–120) wrote that "they are wrong who think that politics is like an ocean voyage or a military campaign, something to be done with some end in view, something which levels off as soon as that end is reached. It is not a public chore to be got over with; it is a way of life."[95] Politics, for the ancients and many of their modern interpreters, is not only an instrumental endeavor but also a performative exercise.

Politics, which is defined by Aristotle as the practice of practical reason, is performative because the exercise of reason is performative. Reason is performative, rather than merely instrumental, because one practices it not only as a means, but also as an end in itself. That is why electing representatives is not the same thing as engaging in political debate and action, despite the fact that representatives might more efficiently secure one's interests. As one classical political theorist puts the Aristotelian point, politics is a partnership in virtue, and you cannot designate someone to be virtuous for you.[96] In the efficient production of commodities or the efficient administration of bureaucracies, means and ends are easily separable. In politics, however, these lines of separation are not so clear. Hence there is a difference, for Aristotle, between a craftsperson who *makes* something and a citizen who *does* something. *Poiesis*, or craft production, is not the same as *praxis*, or political action. Aristotle stipulates that "production has its end beyond it; but action does not, since its end is doing well itself."[97] *Praxis* is self-fulfilling because it signifies the incorporation of reason into the world.

Participation in politics engages one in a process whereby individual and collective identities become contested and constructed. In a truly political life, therefore, one cannot solely pursue the maximization of preconceived interests and goals because one is entering into a process whereby goals and interests, along with values and identities, become shaped and reshaped, formed and transformed. Like a participant in a dialogue, the political actor necessarily involves himself with others in the cooperative determination of a course of action and a destination.[98] With this in mind, Jürgen Habermas has proposed that rationality in political life is achieved by "removing restrictions on communication" so that all may participate in "public, unrestricted discussion, free from domination."[99] This identity-transforming political communication is at one and the same time an instrumental means of achieving ends, a means of determining the substance of these ends, and an end in itself, that is to say, an intrinsic aspect of the good life.

Karl Popper argues that rationality in science is chiefly evidenced not in the unwavering maintenance of dogmatic belief, but in the openness of theoretical positions to contestation.[100] Likewise, rationality in politics is chiefly evidenced not in the unremitting pursuit of preconceived interests and values but in the openness of one's interests and values to contestation and transformation. The politically rational individual accepts the ambiguity and instability of interests and values because they are grounded in an identity that is itself the object of ongoing evolution.

Following in the footsteps of Anthony Downs and Joseph Schumpeter,[101] many theorists of economic rationality assume that politics may be described in terms of the aggregate effects of instrumental voting and office seeking. Votes are analogous to dollars that citizens spend efficiently in an effort to reap the biggest electoral rewards. Politics is reduced to a marketplace where rational buyers (voters) and sellers (candidates) strike their bargains. The elegance of this economic theory of politics is truly appealing. It may serve admirably as a heuristic tool for analysis. But economic rationalist theory ignores the performative aspect of politics and the substantive aspect of rationality. In doing so, it fails to recognize that politics is largely defined by the contestation and construction of individual and collective attitudes, interests, values, and identities.

An analogy may clarify the point. Cats will patiently wait for hours in front of mouse holes, ostensibly having decided that the chance of satiating their hunger with a capture justifies the time invested in motionless loitering. After observing this phenomenon for some time and charting out these observations, one might construct an elegant theory that illustrates the respective value cats place on their time and the satiation of their appetites. One could then predict how cats would act on the basis of this cost/benefit analysis given the relative scarcity of mice, mouse holes, and hours in a day. Yet any such theory would distort the nature of cats and their activity of mouse hunting. Cats value the stalking of prey regardless of its value as food. Placed in a room teeming with mice, cats will initially kill and eat their fill. Then they will kill a few more mice but forgo their consumption. Finally, they will spend their time stalking mice across the room while ignoring those that scamper over their forepaws.[102]

The point is not that people are genetically programmed to engage in politics for its own sake, as cats are presumably programmed to engage in stalking and hunting. Still, politics is not simply about who gets what, when, and how. It is also about exercising one's political nature as a member of a collectivity and having one's interests and identity emerge therefrom. That is what Aristotle meant by calling human beings political animals.

Albert O. Hirschman's investigation of the psychological dynamics of public action nicely supports this thesis. Hirschman writes:

> The implication of the confusion between striving and attaining is that the neat distinction between costs and benefits of action in the public interest vanishes, since striving, which should be entered on the cost side, turns out to be part of the benefit.... The best illustration is perhaps the phenomenon of *pilgrimage*.... Obviously, it would make no sense to categorize the travel as the cost of the pilgrimage, and the sojourn and prayers at the holy site as benefit. The discomforts suffered and perils confronted during the trip were part and parcel of the total 'liminal' experience sought by the pilgrim, and the distance from the site often acted as a stimulant to the decision to go forth rather than as a brake.[103]

Hirschman's point is that political action is not reducible to economic analysis. It is, at least in part, a performative endeavor. What is crucial to politics is the ongoing process, not simply the final product.

The instrumental pursuit of self-interest in an intrinsic part of political life because it is an intrinsic part of human life. Humans, like all other animals, actively seek their own welfare. But the instrumental pursuit of self-interest is not the whole of politics. Politics includes the self-fulfilling exercise of civic virtue, particularly the civic virtue of reason. The contestation and construction of individual and collective identities that occurs in political life is part of that exercise.

Ecological Reason

Environmental issues consistently rank near the top of people's concerns and a "strong environmental ethic" is evident within the public at large. Nonetheless, opposition to specific measures to protect the environment is often equally strong when such measures involve "personal sacrifice" or specific costs to the individual. The general attitude is that "someone else should bear the burden."[104] How do we explain these seemingly contradictory positions?

Theorists of economic rationality have an explanation. Public environmental goods, such as clean air or water, are said to be "nonexcludable." That is to say, if they exist, everyone benefits. People will accrue the benefits of a healthier environment regardless of whether they personally make a contribution to its preservation. Faced with this fact, economically rational actors will opt to "free ride" on the efforts of others. Letting someone else bear the burden is quite rational from an economic perspective. It allows one to gain benefits at virtually no cost. As such, it constitutes the height of individual efficiency. Competition within the marketplace, theorists of economic rationality further maintain, ensures that those who behave in an economically rational manner will survive and those who are less efficient will fail.[105] The conclusion follows that economic success in life depends on shunning personal responsibility for environmental care.

Environmental theorists observe that modern society in general and American society in particular "was conceived, born, and bred on the principles of economic rationality."[106] Yet these theorists strongly disagree with the assumed rationality of much self-interested economic behavior. They insist that our ecological viability and survival as a species rests squarely on our escaping the conceptual and practical constraints of a narrowly conceived rational self-interest. Economically rational individuals seeking to contribute as little as possible to environmental preservation while maximizing their benefits in the marketplace will place too great a demand on the earth's capacity to sustain life. Their economic success will thus undermine the very conditions of life that allow their practices in the first place. That, environmental theorists point out, is not very rational. Environmental theorists therefore provide their own definition of rationality. Not the efficient pursuit of economic gain but an expansive orientation to sustainable living constitutes the key feature of an ecological rationality. To be sustainable, human life must nurture rather than undermine the interdependent relationships that characterize the earth's ecologies.

In addressing the root causes of our ecological straits, Al Gore laments that "the future whispers while the present shouts."[107] With similar concerns, Robert Heilbronner speaks of the "inverted telescope through which humanity looks to the future."[108] The metaphors are apt. The impression the future makes on us is faint. That which is distant in time remains distant in concern. Indeed, under the guidance of economic rationality we would maximize our pleasures and profits today and let tomorrow take care of itself. As the future becomes the present, however, the lack of concern for it returns to haunt us in the form of severe environmental degradation. Environmental theorists reject definitions of rationality that pertain to securing one's interests at the expense of future generations. A frequent slogan employed by environmentalists is "We have not inherited the earth from our parents, we borrow it from our children." Implicit in these words is a form of rationality animated by a concern for the future.

Economists maintain that a key feature of human beings is their "positive time preference." Goods currently available are valued more than the same goods available at a later date. Hence evils that affect us today are addressed immediately while those that will affect us tomorrow, or will affect our grandchildren's children, are ignored. The future becomes "discounted." Summarizing the ecological ramifications of economic rationality, political theorist John Dryzek writes: "This form of reason is less than compelling in the ecological sphere, if only because a system may be judged economically rational while simultaneously engaging in the wholesale destruction of nature, or even, ultimately, in the total extinction of the human race. The latter result holds because of the logic of discounting the future."[109] The farther something is in the future, the greater is its discount and the weaker is its whisper. The voice of economic rationality, on the other hand, loudly announces the means to secure our current interests.

Discounting the future is viewed as good economics. But it is bad ecology. As Theodore Roszak observes: "Our habit has been to regard the future as the carpet under which environmental degradation gets swept. It is called 'externalizing' the costs, meaning writing them off to our children's, children's, children's.... Out of sight, out of mind."[110] When the costs of resource depletion and pollution are externalized to future generations, and the concerns of these future generations are discounted by present-day decision makers, ecological catastrophe looms. Those who deny the severity of the ecological crisis have charged that

"much of the modern environmental movement is a broad-based as-
sault on reason."[111] Yet environmentalists do not so much denigrate
reason as challenge the hegemony of a particular form of reason. Environmental theorist David Orr writes that "a humane version of sustainability will [not] come about solely as the result of 'economically rational' behavior. It will only come about as the result of a higher and
more thorough rationality."[112] Environmental theorists advocate the
transformation of rationality.

John Dryzek has made one attempt to sketch out the features of a
higher and more thorough ecological rationality grounded in sustainable practices. Dryzek examines a number of forms of rationality, including what he calls political rationality, which is concerned with securing collective goods. Although Dryzek does not consider political
rationality to be a performative practice, he does believe that it is more
fundamental than economic rationality because politics provides the legal and material foundation on which economic activities take place.
Without this foundation, economic activity could not exist. Therefore
political rationality has priority because "a logical antecedent of a
value must be accorded at least equal standing to that value." Dryzek's
argument for ecological rationality follows the same logic. He writes:

> The preservation and enhancement of the material and ecological basis of
> society is necessary not only for the functioning of societal forms such as
> economically, socially, legally, and politically rational structures, but also
> for action in pursuit of *any* value in the long term. The pursuit of all such
> values is predicated upon the avoidance of ecological catastrophe. Hence
> the preservation and promotion of the integrity of the ecological and ma-
> terial underpinning of society—ecological rationality—should take prior-
> ity over competing forms of reason in collective choices with an impact
> upon that integrity.[113]

In short, ecological rationality is of overriding importance because it
does not discount the future and hence does not undercut its own or
any other future rational activities by way of its present operation.

One might argue that a component of any higher and more thorough ecological rationality would be its substantive and performative
nature, as suggested by the classical theorists of reason. But citizens
may enjoy and gain benefits from collective activities as ends in themselves in a way that still degrades the environment. The fact that an
action is carried out for its own sake does not mean that the action is
ecologically sustainable. The attitude of "chicken today, feathers tomorrow!" may be held by someone who eats his chicken noninstru-

mentally, for the pure delight of eating it. Still, today's delight will not address tomorrow's hunger. Likewise, the question of ecological sustainability is only adequately addressed once rationality, whether instrumental, substantive, or performative, includes a distinct focus on the future.

One means to gain this future focus is for long-term ecological and social costs to be figured into the prices paid for goods and services. This is known as full-cost accounting. If the goods and services we consume today are not priced to account for the environmental costs of their production, delivery, and disposal, then our present savings are effectively gained at the expense of future generations. These future generations will find their resources depleted and their environment degraded. Only a rationality that prompts one to make decisions from the standpoint of a political community sufficiently extended in time can marshal itself against the ecological destructiveness of short-term economic efficiency. The so-called invisible hand that the Scottish classical economist Adam Smith (1723–90) said was wisely guiding the free market decidedly lacks a green thumb. Our freedom in today's market commits future generations to paying extensive ecological reparations.

Environmental theorists also emphasize the interdependence of human life across the globe, noting that there is but one earth to be shared by all. What makes dollars and sense for the rational economic actor seeking to maximize his own benefits may lead to disaster for society and the biosphere. This comes as no surprise to theorists of economic rationality, who admit that "individual rationality is not sufficient for collective rationality."[114] The insufficiency arises because individuals may accrue economic benefits at a relatively low price by fobbing off costs on their neighbors.

Environmental theorists reject any concept of rationality that pertains only or primarily to securing individual interests at the expense of the interests of neighbors. They are interested in fostering transpersonal and transnational sensibilities.[115] The politics they practice tends to be global in intent, if not always in origin and effect. Thinking globally is as important to them as acting locally. Competitive struggles between individuals and nations are generally considered counterproductive to the goal of preserving the environment. That is because military or economic victories often bear within them an ecological loss for all concerned, victors no less than vanquished.

A global orientation forms a natural complement to the future focus of environmental theorists. There are both moral and practical reasons for this complementarity. Morally speaking, the justification for the rights of future generations is difficult to separate from the justification for the rights of those beyond national borders.[116] Once we acknowledge that we have an obligation to those incapable of actively representing their ecological interests for temporal reasons (i.e., they will live in the future), we are hard pressed to justify excluding from consideration those who are incapable of actively representing their ecological interests for geographical reasons (i.e., they live in another country). In both instances, obligations exist to preserve the environment for people who do not have the present capacity to demand that we live sustainably.

For Americans, the issue is particularly salient. If present trends continue, an American born in the 1990s will produce in his lifetime more than 4 million pounds of atmospheric and solid wastes. He will consume more than 55,000 pounds of animal products, use up 1.5 million pounds of minerals and the energy equivalent of 4,000 barrels of oil. This rate of consumption and waste is between ten and one hundred times higher than the rate at which the world's other people consume and dispose of resources.[117] It cannot be sustained. Were all the world to consume and waste resources at this rate, environmental collapse would be imminent.

Environmental theorists, in sum, argue that ecological rationality is a form of reason that extends one's obligations and concerns both in time and in space. The practical complementarity between a global orientation and a future focus is reinforced because local environmental sustainability has become increasingly dependent on the earth's ecological viability as a whole. That is to say, the environmental benefits we seek for ourselves, or for our compatriots and progeny, are becoming increasingly difficult to secure without also ensuring some level of global environmental protection. Eliminating the use of ozone-destroying chemicals in the United States will not help us much, for instance, if other countries do not similarly change their practices. Ensuring a healthy environment within national borders, in other words, increasingly entails the extension of ecological care and the promotion of ecological mores beyond national borders. The requirement to reach beyond ourselves for a global sensibility is thus grounded in the ecological principle of interdependence.

Environmental and political theorist Lester Milbrath observes that "a central axiom of environmentalism is, We can never do merely one thing. We must learn to ask, for every action, And then what?"[118] The question "And then what?" pertains to the unintended effects of actions on those who are distant in time and distant in space. The geographically nonlocalizable nature of many environmental problems (e.g., ozone depletion or the greenhouse effect) and the temporally nonlocalizable nature of other environmental concerns (e.g., the loss of biological diversity or the accumulation of nuclear waste) have spatially and temporally expanded our political obligations. One would hope that they have also expanded the political rationality that will facilitate fulfilling these obligations.

The 1986 catastrophe at the Chernobyl nuclear power plant in the Ukraine, which spread radioactive contamination as far as Sweden and Ireland, demonstrated that national borders can no longer mark the boundaries of responsible government. Likewise, individual life spans are equally unable to contain the effects of ecologically destructive behavior. The extinction of a species in our generation will rob all future generations of that species. Extinction is forever. Likewise, high-level radioactive waste must be stored in sealed containers for thousands of years to prevent toxic contamination of the environment. Plutonium may remain toxic for hundreds of thousands of years, which is to say, for about fifty times longer than any civilization has yet survived, and five times as long as *homo sapiens* have been on earth. We might, with this in mind, retrieve the wisdom of certain American native people whose rules of governance were said to be made with the welfare of seven generations in mind—a foresight quite sufficient given the environmental repercussions of their levels of technological development and population density. Today, however, the demands on reason have been markedly increased.

Assessing the changes occurring within contemporary society, a geographer observes that "the history of social change is in part captured by the history of the conceptions of space and time, and the ideological uses to which those conceptions might be put. Furthermore, any project to transform society must grasp the complex nettle of the transformation of spatial and temporal conceptions and practices."[119] Environmental theorists argue that rationality itself, one of our core political concepts, must become transformed to account for our changing relationship to space and time. Rationality must become increasingly farsighted and foresighted to keep up with a civilization that is increasingly powerful, expansive, and interdependent.

R.H. Tawney once observed that economic ambitions may be good servants, but they made very bad masters. One might say the same thing about economic rationality. It may serve our purposes well enough, when our purposes are well known and narrowly defined. Yet it cannot produce overall, long-term benefits for the individual or for the collectivity. And it cannot tell us much about the good life.

One of the "flaws in mainstream economics," David Orr writes, is that "it lacks an ecologically and morally defensible model of the 'reasonable person,' helping to create the behavior it purports only to describe."[120] If our efforts to describe human behavior reduce all human action to the product of instrumental economic calculations, we may be stifling the development of more sustainable rational behavior. Key to this development is the theoretical formulation of an ecologically defensible model of rationality. If there is something called ecological justice, it would find its sponsor in this kind of reason.

Suggested Readings

Harnah Arendt. *Between Past and Future*
Aristotle. *Nichomachean Ethics*
Benjamin Barber. *Strong Democracy*
Isaiah Berlin. *Four Essays on Liberty*
C.M. Bowra. *The Greek Experience*
Lester Brown. *Building a Sustainable Society*
Edmund Burke. *Reflections on the Revolution in France*
F.M. Cornford. *Before and After Socrates*
Anthony Downs. *An Economic Theory of Democracy*
John S. Dryzek. *Rational Ecology*
Robyn Eckersley. *Environmentalism and Political Theory*
Michel Foucault. *The Foucault Reader*
Jürgen Habermas. *Toward a Rational Society*
Joel Jay Kassiola. *The Death of Industrial Civilization*
C.B. Macpherson. *The Political Theory of Possessive Individualism*
John Stuart Mill. *On Liberty*
Baron de Montesquieu. *The Spirit of the Laws*
Plato. *Crito, Gorgias, Laws, Phaedo,* and *Republic*
Jean-Jacques Rousseau. *The Social Contract* and *Discourses*
Mark Sagoff. *The Economy of the Earth*
Leslie Paul Thiele. *Timely Meditations*
Max Weber. *The Protestant Ethic and the Spirit of Capitalism*

7

Ideology and Irony

Francis Bacon attempted to furnish humankind with a new, scientific route to knowledge. It entailed the expunging of all biases, mistaken premises, and false methodologies that had accumulated in human learning over thousands of years. "I have purged and swept and leveled the floor of the mind," Bacon wrote.[1] This is precisely what the scientific elite who rule the technocratic utopia described in Bacon's novel *The New Atlantis* set out to do. On this pristine foundation, a sturdy edifice of knowledge is built using only the tools of reason, the methods of science, and the materials of the sensible world. In this manner, Bacon hoped to achieve "the enlargement of the bounds of Human Empire, to the effecting of all things possible." It was a grand scheme.

Key among the prejudices that Bacon hoped to expunge were what he called the "idols of the marketplace." These were mistaken beliefs that "crept into the understanding through the alliances of words and names," the kinds of misunderstandings that grow whenever people congregate and exchange stories. Putting the wrong labels on things, or making the wrong connections between these labels, led to bad thinking and faulty beliefs. To get one's language straight was the first and most important step toward straightening out one's mind. The straightening of minds, Bacon held, was the only way to put the world right.

Two hundred years after Bacon wrote about the idols of the marketplace, a French scholar and former nobleman, Antoine Destutt de Tracy (1754–1836), coined the word *ideology*. Destutt de Tracy was interested in educational reform and politics and worked at the prestigious Institute de France. In 1796, during the French Directory and after the revolutionary Reign of Terror, de Tracy developed his theory of ideology as a "science of ideas." This ideological science, de Tracy believed, would allow for a full knowledge of human nature through the empirical analysis of individual sensations and perceptions. His strategy was to focus primarily on language use among children and youth. Following the tradition of Francis Bacon (and the path of other empiricist thinkers such as John Locke, Helvetius, Holbach, and Condillac) de Tracy attempted to ground all human thought and action in reason and to ground reason in the precise use of language.

De Tracy's science of ideology set itself the ambitious task of eradicating all the false thoughts and beliefs in people's minds by correctly linking words to things and rationally grounding all concepts. This task was initiated with children, for children were assumed to be largely uncorrupted by the various idols of the marketplace. Employing a notion developed by John Locke, de Tracy maintained that the mind of the child at birth was a *tabula rasa,* a completely blank slate on which perceptions and ideas become engraved over time. Because language is the chief means humans have of expressing perceptions and formulating ideas, de Tracy hoped to ensure clear concepts, correct ideas, proper beliefs, and consequently good behavior by strictly supervising the use of language among those whose mental slates had yet to be marred by inappropriately cataloged experiences.

De Tracy proposed that France adopt a centralized and routinized form of education. Among other things, schools would strictly regulate their students' acquisition and use of language. This scientific organization of the schools was so systematic that under the supervision of the "ideologues" it was said that one could know at any time of the day what every French student was learning.

Initially, de Tracy's ideological science enjoyed official support and a certain measure of success. Napoleon (1769–1821), who had recently come to power, favored the "science of ideas" and venerated the work of de Tracy's Institute. The theories of the ideologues were widely promulgated in France and abroad. Thomas Jefferson and John Quincy Adams read and heartily approved of de Tracy's writings. In time, however, Jefferson and Adams abandoned de Tracy's science. After the failures of his war campaign in Russia, Napoleon also lost his interest in ideology. He became less concerned with lofty ideas and more concerned with the grisly task of holding on to power. He also found it increasingly necessary to court the favors of the Catholic church, which was reestablishing its traditional authority and was antagonistic to the progressive science of the modernists.

Eventually, Napoleon became severely critical of the ideologues, charging them with impracticality and idealism. Ideology, Napoleon accused, had become a "sinister metaphysics." The French emperor criticized the ideologues for the same reason that Francis Bacon had earlier criticized the scholastics. These were people who made "imaginary laws for imaginary commonwealths." The problem, Bacon charged, was that "their discourses are as the stars, which give little light because they are so high."[2] Though intended to illuminate the minds and direct the behavior of an entire people, Destutt de Tracy's science of ideas fell into disfavor and obscurity owing to its abstractness and failure to achieve practical results.

Under Napoleon, then, ideology became a pejorative term, denoting an unrealistic set of beliefs that was practically useless if not socially pernicious. This pejorative connotation of ideology was taken up by Karl Marx, who had studied de Tracy's works. Marx rejected de Tracy for the same reason that he rejected the German idealists. De Tracy assumed that ideas were more important than the forces of material production. He believed, with Saint-Simon, that the troubles of the social order arise from obscurities in theory and that the practical world could be straightened out if theorists would simply tidy up their own conceptual world. For Marx, however, conceiving, thinking, and intellectual matters in general, like politics, laws, morality, religion, and philosophy, constitute merely the "efflux" of material circumstances. Ideas and ideology, Marx held, are the effect, not the cause, of social conditions. Marx criticized de Tracy, as he had the German idealists, for inverting reality.

Building on Napoleon's denunciation of ideology, Marx employed the term to describe the false beliefs and values that legitimize the power of the ruling class. Ideology produces a distorted or false consciousness that serves the economic interests of this class. Marx recognized, however, that if all thoughts are products of material conditions, then even inverted, ideological thoughts must have material origins. He writes: "The phantoms formed in the human brain are also, necessarily, sublimates of their material life-process, which is empirically verifiable and bound to material premises. Morality, religion, metaphysics, all the rest of ideology and their corresponding forms of consciousness, thus no longer retain the semblance of independence."[3] Ideological thought arises directly from material conditions when these conditions demand a more advanced form of social organization than the ruling class will allow because its interests are best served by the status quo. That is to say, ideology is a system of false beliefs used to legitimate outmoded forms of social and economic relations. Marx speculates that if the economic mode of production could become realigned with the current means of production, putting an end to classes and class conflict, then ideology would no longer be needed. The proletarian revolution achieves this realignment. Thus the revolution eliminates ideology, replacing it with a true consciousness of humanity's species-being.

Over the century and a half since Marx wrote his major works, the term ideology has retained its pejorative connotation. It is generally used to describe a system of beliefs that distorts reality in order to justify or rationalize class interests. Engels claimed that Marxist thought escaped all ideology because it constituted a "scientific socialism." Critics have charged just the opposite. They claim Marxism is a highly ideological enterprise precisely because it abandons science and pragmatic thought for revolutionary ideals. In its pejorative connotation, then, ideology has often been used as a term of opprobrium against Marxism itself.

In time, ideology came to gain a broader, less pejorative connotation. Indeed, some forms of ideology were considered useful and good by Marxists. Vladimir Lenin (1870–1924), the Russian revolutionary and theorist, is largely responsible for this modification of the Marxist understanding of ideology. In support of his attempt to instigate a communist revolution in Russia, Lenin argued that ideology can be either good or bad, depending on the social class with which it is aligned. There are, however, only two choices: a proletarian, or socialist, ideology and a bourgeois, or capitalist, ideology. The latter, Lenin insists, distorts consciousness by upholding and justifying capitalist property rights. The former signifies a true consciousness that stimulates the revolutionary overthrow of the capitalist system.

Socialist ideology is necessary, Lenin argues, to combat bourgeois ideology and overturn the bourgeois mode of production. Creating and propagating socialist ideology becomes the job of revolutionary intelligentsia or "socialist theoreticians."[4] Hence Lenin understands ideology to constitute an important intellectual force of its own. Indeed, Lenin leads us to believe that ideology may at times become the primary force fostering revolutionary changes in class societies. This stands in marked contrast to Marx's claim that ideology is only the efflux of material conditions.

Lenin's understanding of ideology remains in wide use today. The term is still employed as Marx pejoratively employed it, that is, as an epithet implying that an individual's beliefs and values constitute rationalizations of her social power or class privilege. Yet ideology is also used as a relatively neutral term to denote any system of belief about society or politics, especially if this system of belief is action oriented and has clear political implications. Socialist or anarchist systems of belief that advocate revolution may be no less ideological than conservative systems of belief that justify and rationalize the power and prerogative of the upper class. College courses on ideology thus focus on a wide range of political beliefs and values. These typically include the "isms" that compose the traditional political spectrum—anarchism, communism, socialism, liberalism, conservatism, and fascism—along with nationalism, an ideology that promotes common ethnic, linguistic, or territorial identities, and even feminism, environmentalism, and religious fundamentalism.

The word ideology is less than two centuries old. Yet from time immemorial, individuals, classes, and castes have fabricated belief systems to justify either their rule over others or their revolutions. In the past, these belief systems were often grounded in religious doctrine. Social power and privilege were justified, for instance, as the will of God. Plato himself employed myths about the gods to legitimate the rigid caste system in his *Republic*. Medieval monarchs and their court scholars advocated the "divine right of kings" to legitimate their arbitrary and absolute rule. Although De Tracy's ideology originated as a secular force aligned with science and pitted against religious power and rule, many ideological systems of belief today seek religious grounding for their political projects.

For our purposes, we might define ideology as a set of coherent beliefs and values about history, nature, psychology, and society that conceptually and practically orders and organizes collective life. Importantly, ideologies are not simply any set of beliefs and values. The term ideology pertains only to those beliefs and values systematically connected to each other within some coherent scheme that reinforces and is reinforced by relations of power within society. As one political theorist observes:

> Ideology is *always* about power because it involves the determination of meaning and the legitimation of one set of meanings from among a competing field. In that sense, to talk of *political* ideologies is tautological, as the power aspect in all ideology is precisely its political element. And inasmuch as all ideology has a deliberate or unconscious impact on public agendas, it is political.[5]

The belief that only women have ovaries and wombs, along with the belief that only women can conceive and bear children, is a coherent set of beliefs but it is not an ideology. Nevertheless, these beliefs can be put to ideological uses—as any set of beliefs or values can—if they are employed to generate relations of power. They may, for instance, be used to legitimize a patriarchal society in which women's lives are restricted to home and family while men rule the roost and pursue business and politics.

Ideologies are usually detailed enough to elicit some form of practical commitment, say, to patriarchy or gender justice, equality or hierarchy, stability or change. But they are seldom so detailed as to spell out a specific program for political action. Ideologies, in other words, are broader and more comprehensive than partisan platforms but remain focused enough to stimulate collective behavior and commitments. Ideologies theoretically and practically situate us in the world by explaining what our role in collective life is and should be.

To become powerful social forces, ideologies must exhibit at least four features. First, they must be *comprehensive,* describing or explaining our place within nature, society, and history. Second, ideologies must be *consistent.* Their beliefs and values must be connected and coherent. Their elements must be systematically integrated so as not to contradict one another. Third, ideologies must be *plausible.* They must be realistic enough to mesh with commonly perceived social facts or commonsense understandings. Otherwise, they could not successfully elicit and organize beliefs and action. Finally, ideologies must be *useful,* serving the needs, advancing the interests and justifying the power or struggles of particular groups in society.

Some ideologies defend upper-class interests. Others justify collective struggle against class privilege or promote nationalist concerns. In any case, ideologies typically foster a hard-and-fast distinction between friends and foes, "good guys" and "bad guys," the "in-group" and the "out-group." In this way, clear battle lines can be drawn and strategies for action devised. For this reason, ideologies tend to create rigid identities that are exclusive of difference.

Escaping Ideology

As long as there are stakes to be won and lost in the game of politics, ideologies will develop and be put to use. As long as individuals and groups have particular interests that can be served by particular forms of social organization and political rule, their beliefs and values will be systematized in ways to justify these forms of organization and rule. Ideologies, in this sense, are key contributors to and depositories of the mores that order our individual and collective lives.

In the years following World War II, a number of intellectuals (such as Edward Shils, Raymond Aron, Seymour Lipsett, and most notably Daniel Bell) spoke about the "end of ideology." They believed that a general consensus had arisen, at least in the Western world, about the bankruptcy of communism and the immorality of unconstrained capitalism. The consensus was that free enterprise and liberal democracy, in tandem with a welfare system that served as an adequate safety net for the less fortunate, was too good and too stable a system to require revolutionary change or even significant reform. Consequently, they believed that a pragmatic politics aimed at the piecemeal technical solution of complex social problems could replace the simplified worldviews, apocalyptic visions, and strident claims to world-historic truths promulgated by ideologies of the past.

More recently, and with a Hegelian slant, Francis Fukuyama has written grandiosely about the "end of history."[6] Fukuyama's thesis is similar to that propounded by theorists a generation earlier who spoke about the end of ideology. Once again the claim is that the economic, technological, political, and moral achievements of liberal democracy and marketplace economics have made ideological visions and struggles obsolete.

To be sure, the global ideological struggle between communism and capitalism has all but disappeared. Yet ideological visions persist, and bloody ideological struggles—chiefly grounded in territorial, economic, ethnic, and religious claims—are in evidence throughout the world. The end of ideology is no more likely today or in the future than it was when Marx and Engels, echoing Saint-Simon, originally proposed to substitute a pragmatic "administration of things" for the strife-prone "government of men."

Ideology may be used as a relatively neutral term or even a term of praise, as when Lenin speaks effusively of "socialist ideology." Nonetheless, ideology always denotes the beliefs or values of particular groups or classes of people that advocate for their own interests. As such, an ideological view, though it typically lays claim to truth, neutrality, and universality, is not a particularly objective view. Ideology, for this reason, is frequently placed in opposition to truth, just as the word "ideological" is frequently used as a synonym for biased or self-serving.

To describe someone's views as ideological is to suggest that her system of beliefs and values was formed for the purpose of legitimating her (group's) advantages or claims within society. If all social and political beliefs and values serve the interests of those who hold them, and if they are formed precisely for this purpose, what legitimacy do these beliefs and values really have? For that matter, we might ask the same question of political theorists. Perhaps the political theorist is simply one ideologue among others. Perhaps political theories are simply ideologies dressed up in scholarly garb.

The German social theorist Karl Mannheim (1893–1947) was one of the first thinkers to address this sticky issue. In his treatise *Ideology and Utopia,* Mannheim suggests that all economic classes and ruling groups necessarily propound systems of beliefs that justify their social position and prerogatives. To assess and analyze the ideological link between thought and power, Mannheim practiced a "sociology of knowledge." The sociologist of knowledge analyzes the relationship between the claims to truth made by various social groups and their social status. The goal is to demonstrate that a group's claim to truth effectively derives from its need to protect and justify its social position and prerogatives.

Mannheim realized that a sociology of knowledge might be applied to the truth claims of the sociologist of knowledge, casting their validity into doubt. He sought to avoid this problem by suggesting that a group of people exists whose class position in society is not as "fixed" as that of wage-laborers or capitalists and who therefore remain largely "unattached" or "unanchored" to particular economic interests. This "*relatively* classless stratum" of individuals are the intellectuals. Since intellectuals are less attached to economic interests than traditional classes, Mannheim believed they might rise above the ideological fray and supply a more objective view of the world. Mannheim writes that "a group whose class position is more or less definitely fixed already has its potential viewpoint decided for it. Where this is not so, as with the intellectuals, there is a wider area of choice.... Only he who really has the choice has an interest in seeing the whole of the social and political structure."[7] In escaping rigid class structures, Mannheim proposes, intellectuals leave behind all the ideological baggage that others are forced to carry with them. Freed of this baggage, they may carry the torch for truth.

The problem with Mannheim's thesis is that it leaves itself open to the charge of being ideological itself in the most traditional sense of the term. As Marx and Lenin pointed out, each class attempts to portray its beliefs and values as neutral, objective, universal, free from hypocrisy, and beyond the taint of narrow self-interest. These claims are essential to all ideologies. They are, as it were, the key components of each ideology's public relations strategy. But ideologies are not simply lies people make up and propagate to protect their interests and privileges. They are complex systems of beliefs and values that people adopt and develop because they believe them to be true and worthy, not only for themselves but for others as well. The power of ideology is that it allows (classes of) individuals to believe that their inherently biased opinions are actually universal truths. Thus ideology is not something people systematically create one day in an effort to cover their tracks. Ideology is the natural and largely unconscious outgrowth of lives lived in particular social positions within a competitive social system.

When Mannheim makes the claim of objectivity for intellectuals like himself, he is therefore doing exactly what Marx saw capitalists doing for their class and what Lenin encouraged proletarians to do for their class. Mannheim's notion of the "unattached" intellectual, Marx and Lenin would say, is the most essential, legitimizing component of his ideology. It clearly protects the interests of intellectuals, the merchants of ideas. Intellectuals would not be taken seriously and could not easily practice their trade were their studies perceived as wholly self-serving endeavors.

Should we then deny that intellectuals, along with all other groups and individuals, can gain objectivity and neutrality in their views? Are all political theories that we might formulate or subscribe to simply biased derivations of our own (economic, ethnic, religious, or gender) interests? Regardless of how much we aim for truth and how impartial we strive to be, is everything that we think and say about society and politics equally ideological? Can anything we say or do rise above the self-serving prejudices that arise out of our particular social identities?

There are no wholly satisfying answers to these questions. Nevertheless, we may work through the dilemmas they pose by recalling the insights and excesses of the man who coined the word ideology. De Tracy rightly observed that language is a very powerful medium, that our ideas and behavior are in large part formed and transformed by the words we use to describe ourselves and our world. Yet de Tracy mistakenly supposes that we might develop some universal and neutral language to describe social and political life objectively. This streamlined language was intended to get beyond the contaminating forces of social position and hence to rise above political interests and disputes. The problem is that the language of politics is not amenable to such a program. Not only are the beliefs and values that we hold susceptible to biases, but the very words out of which these beliefs and values are constructed remain sources of dispute. The terms of political discourse —such terms as justice, freedom, and reason—are inherently subject to endless contestation.

The language of politics is not a neutral medium. It channels thought and behavior in particular directions. Following this line of thought, William Connolly adjusts the optical metaphor introduced at the beginning of this book. He observes that "the concepts of politics do not simply provide a lens through which to observe a process that is independent of them. As we have seen, they are themselves part of that political life—they help to constitute it."[8] The conceptual and terminological lenses through which we view political life, Connolly suggests, shape that life because they affect the way we think and act in the world.

Political thought, to employ the phrase of W.B. Gallie, is rife with "essentially contested concepts." The meanings of these concepts and the work they are supposed to do never gets resolved once and for all. These concepts are subject to ongoing dispute, as are the values and interests they represent and promote. Indeed, the words "politics" and "political" themselves remain essentially contested. They mean different things to different people who use them for different purposes at different times. Political words will always be subject to heated debate, the fragile and temporary outcome of which will likely serve some people's interests, bolster some people's beliefs and values, and reaffirm some people's identities, more than others.

The words and concepts traditionally employed to interpret, describe, or explain political life are like gatekeepers. They regulate how we describe or explain things and events and what sort of judgments, beliefs, or actions are deemed appropriate in relation to them. If we, in the manner of strict negative libertarians, limit the meaning of freedom to the absence of actual physical constraint, then we cannot speak of poverty as constituting a lack of economic freedom. This restriction may translate into increased political difficulties for underclasses in their struggle against economic deprivation. Alternatively, if we, following Marx, define the human being as a species-being, then this may lead to increased difficulty for those who wish to champion individual rights and avoid the "tyranny of the majority." Likewise, if we define reason instrumentally and economically, as a faculty for finding efficient means for given ends, then we cannot speak of people's goals as irrational even when those goals foster the collapse of political community or widespread ecological destruction.

The problem is not simply that our beliefs and values may be ideological. The problem is that language itself may be ideological. Almost any word may become an ideological tool. How, then, can we legitimately argue for our opinions when the very vocabulary out of which our opinions are constructed remains suspect? Would it not be hypocritical or duplicitous to suggest, at one and the same time, that political terms and concepts are never neutral and that our own terms and concepts nonetheless ought to be adopted? What does it mean to persuade others to accept an idea or moral position that one cannot ground in a firm, uncontroversial set of definitions and concepts?

It means that one is taking on the challenge of living as a political animal. In political affairs one necessarily make one's stand upon shifting foundations. The beliefs and values one promotes, the mores one propagates, the terms, concepts, and theories one employs, necessarily exist in tension with a vast network of competing beliefs, values, mores, terms, concepts, and theories. There will be agreement about many things and arguments about many more. There will, with any luck, be enough common understandings and commitments to make community possible and fulfilling. Yet there will never be terminological harmony, conceptual accord, or moral unanimity. Perhaps that is a good thing. The absence of contestation would likely only exist in what Aldous Huxley described as a brave new world, where genetic engineering and mind-altering drugs rob us of individuality, or in George Orwell's dystopic *Nineteen Eighty-four,* where the language of Newspeak stultifies originality and imagination and "thought police" enforce mental paralysis.[9] In these worlds, the very opportunity for political life has been erased.

George Orwell observed that "in our time, political speech and writing are largely the defense of the indefensible."[10] Orwell exaggerates his point to underline the corruption of public life. Nonetheless, political speech and writing are always defending or promoting something. At times, as Marshall McLuhan stated, "the medium is the message." What is being defended or promoted in political speech and writing are the particular uses or meanings of words and concepts. The defense and promotion of one's vocabulary, in other words, is an intrinsic part of politics. For better or worse, so is the criticism of others' vocabularies.

For those who wish to participate in political life, or in the life of political theory, there is no alternative to engaging in the politics of language. Connolly writes that "there is no contradiction in first affirming the essential contestability of a concept and then making the strongest case available for one of the positions within that range. That's politics."[11] Is all politics, then, infused with ideology? The answer must be a qualified yes. That is not to say that every definition or conceptualization is as good as any other because we have no means to discriminate between them. We should bring detailed historical and conceptual analysis to bear and strive for fairness and consistency. But, in the end, we have to argue our case without the benefit of stable foundations and without the hope of winning over one and all once and for all to our position.

A point of departure for our arguments might be established by rejecting beliefs, values, terms, concepts, and theories that pretend to be beyond contestation, as somehow natural and unchallengable in their meanings and significance. One might argue that such beliefs, values, terms, concepts, and theories, precisely by asserting their unchallengable objectivity and universality, are more ideological than those that acknowledge and endure their own contestability. That is to say, political thought and action may eschew ideology in the most pejorative sense of that word to the extent that it seeks understanding and fosters commitment without at the same time forbidding all challenge to it. If this is true, then the ironic result is that our political thoughts and theories only ever escape the deepest pitfalls of ideology when we acknowledge its pervasive presence.

All ideologies imply, and more extreme ideologies insist, that there is only one appropriate or correct lens with which to view social and political reality. This single-minded advocacy of a particular point of view has certain benefits. It may lead to insights that would not have arisen from a less dogged approach. The danger, however, is that ideology might blind one to more facets of political reality than it reveals.

Political theories employ conceptual lenses to develop and justify the mores that order, or should order, social life. That is to say, political theories organize ideas, principles, and facts into reasoned sets of propositions to gain both understanding of the political world and moral footing within it. These ideas, principles, facts, and methods of reasoning remain susceptible to ideological use and abuse. If political theorists remain self-conscious about their role as purveyors of conceptual lenses and propagators of mores, however, they may avoid the gravest threats of ideological thought.

Irony

It is fair to presume that all political theories are ideological to some extent. It is impossible for a theorist to view all things from all angles at the same time. No theorist can completely divorce her interests and biases from the language and the concepts she employs. That is not to say that political theories cannot or should not be grounded in sound reason. It is just that sound reason means different things to different people, as do most of the other concepts, principles, and methodological procedures on which a political theory might be based.

If the ideological tendency to view the world through a single lens is ever-present in political theorizing, so is an opposing tendency. We may call this opposing tendency *irony*. Unlike the ideologist, the ironist is not very self-assured. She acknowledges that there is no single best lens with which to view the world, or at least admits that she has failed to discover it. But this is not viewed as a shortcoming. Instead, it prompts the ironist to look through many lenses, gaining an increasingly expansive view of the world without committing to any particular set of concepts or values. The ironist reserves judgment and withholds support from ideological positions in order more deeply to explore and appreciate the inherent complexities and ambiguities of political life.

In the past, political principles were often grounded in faith and religious scripture. Today, they are ostensibly grounded in reason. But in what is reason, and our faith in reason, itself grounded? Ironists accept the essential contestability not only of the concepts and principles that guide political life but also of the epistemological categories, such as reason and rationality, that ground our concepts and principles.

It follows that irony is the natural accompaniment to the perspectivism of postmodern theorists. For the postmodernist, a "God's eye view" of the world is simply not attainable. One can see things only from particular perspectives. Perspectivism disallows authoritative statements about the world as a whole. It begets a kind of skeptical reserve, and skeptical reserve begets irony. Rather than search for a "final vocabulary" with which one might construct an objective description or definition of reality, the postmodern ironist engages in a perspectival rendering. She accepts, as Richard Rorty maintains, that many different "language games" are being played simultaneously in the competitive attempt to capture reality. There is no neutral vocabulary that might allow the ironist to decide once and for all how best to view, understand or speak about the world.[12]

Marx said that the bourgeois class, like all other classes before it, carried within it the seeds of its own destruction. Postmodernists suggest that all concepts, ideologies, systems of thought, and other epistemological categories carry within them the seeds of their own *deconstruction*. The ominous seeds, in this case, are the words, concepts, and other linguistic tropes on whose ever-shifting foundations the categories of knowledge are precariously built. Marx maintained that the revolutionary proletarian class alone did not carry within it the seeds of its own destruction. Hence the communist revolution was the last revolution the world was to witness. Postmodernists, in contrast, accept that the minor epistemological revolutions they inaugurate remain susceptible to the deconstructive efforts of others. For this reason, irony becomes a necessary demeanor. It allows one to tolerate the shaky foundations on which one's own beliefs, values, and way of life are built and welcome the inevitable undermining they will receive at the hands of others.

The ironist is often found irritating, owing to her habit of exposing the precariousness of other people's convictions. The ironist's deconstruction of other systems of thought, however, is prefaced or accompanied by a critical confrontation with her own convictions. Irony is always self-referential. Hence the postmodern ironist takes on a somewhat playful role in her work. Complete seriousness cannot issue from a foundation of self-doubt. This self-conscious skepticism was developed in modern times by Friedrich Nietzsche, whose "gay science" set the stage for the ironic playfulness of postmodernists.[13]

While the postmodern ironist adopts perspectivism, judging that there is no surefire means of attaining "objective" knowledge freed of all interpretive intrusions, she cannot dismiss the possibility that there may be some ultimate "truth" out there. The ironist lacks all certainty, including the certainty that there is no truth whatsoever. With this in mind, Michel Foucault speaks of leaving "as little space as possible" in his own research for assumptions about underlying truths that might ground knowledge once and for all. At the same time, he cannot exclude the possibility that "one day" such a truth will be discovered.[14] Foucault admits that "there is no way that you can say that there is no truth."[15] Thus the postmodern ironist engages in the pursuit of knowledge despite her skepticism.

Irony, though recognized as a key feature of postmodernism, is not its invention. Ironic political thought is also found in the early modern writings of Miguel de Cervantes (1547–1616), Jonathan Swift (1667–1745), and François Voltaire (1694–1778). Here it most often appears in the form of social satire, where various figures or causes are ridiculed and parodied in literary form. The philosophical roots of irony go back 2,500 years. Socrates was the first ironist. Many still consider him the greatest. In the original Greek usage of the term, an ironist was a fellow who leads others astray through rhetorical deception or sarcastic praise. The ironist (from the Greek *eiron*) was a dissembler. In a number of Plato's dialogues, such as the *Symposium,* the *Apology,* and the *Republic,* the word irony is applied to Socrates as a term of abuse.

In the *Republic,* the description of Socrates as an ironist is used in exasperation by Thrasymachus, who finds Socrates' dialectic argument to constitute a tiresome beating around the bush. Socrates does indeed move in dialectical circles, often to no apparent purpose. Yet there is a method in his madness. To get the conversation started, Socrates admits that he has nothing to teach. He then flatters those who lay claim to knowledge into sharing their bounty. This flattery is often perceived as a mockery, for his dialogue inevitably undercuts his interlocutors' claims to knowledge. Yet Socrates is ironic not so much because of what he presumes of others, but because of what he does not presume of himself. Irony, Aristotle states, is the opposite of boastfulness. The ironic person denies that which he is thought to possess. Socrates denies his own possession of knowledge. At the same time, Socrates is eager enough to poke holes in any inflated intellectual egos that come his way.

Socrates assumes that those who act with self-assurance must possess knowledge. In the dialogue *Euthyphro*, for instance, he comes across a young man who is about to prosecute his own father in a court of law. Socrates begins the dialogue by asking Euthyphro to explain how he knows that he is morally justified in carrying out his criminal prosecution. As in most of Plato's dialogues, the discussant's claim to knowledge quickly collapses during Socrates' relentless questioning. Embarrassed and resentful, Euthyphro rushes away to carry through his prosecution, despite its now demonstrated lack of epistemological and ethical legitimacy. Socrates is left behind to carry on his ironic thinking.

Socrates' irony validates the oracle's claim that he is the wisest of men. The only thing that Socrates knows is that he knows nothing. Thus he demonstrates that he knows at least one thing (i.e., that he really knows nothing), while other men do not even know that.

"Knowledge of ignorance is not ignorance," Leo Strauss remarks in his discussion of Socrates. "It is knowledge of the elusive character of the truth."[16] To be an ironist is to know that one knows nothing for sure. It is to know that truth is not something one can ever grasp, only something one can approach. As Socrates demonstrates, the ironist tirelessly seeks knowledge by critically exploring the claims to knowledge made by others. One engages in this exploration because a firm sense of the limits of knowledge is only ever gained by the pursuit of knowledge itself.

It has been said that a good education leaves much to be desired. The mark of a good education, in other words, is that the student is left with the desire for more education. Likewise, ironic knowledge leaves one with a good grasp of what one does not know, and that is always a great deal. This knowledge of one's own ignorance prompts the search for knowledge. But the search must take place with one's ultimate ignorance kept well in mind. For this reason, Socrates always begins his philosophical conversations from the ground up, forgoing the traditional beliefs, conceptual habits, common opinions, and unchallenged assumptions that mislead others.

Irony is often defined as saying the opposite of what one really means. Socrates is ironic, however, not so much because he does not mean what he says but because he does not fully know what he means. Socrates is never sure what he means because he is aware that the stable definitions of the words and concepts required for self-expression will disintegrate when given over to dialectic examination. Words have unstable meanings and concepts form ambiguous connections. Convictions based on words and concepts, the ironist understands, are built on sand.

Ideologies typically supply their bearers with straightforward descriptions of the social and political battles to be waged and hard-and-fast distinctions between the allies and enemies involved. Irony muddies the waters. The ironist does not deny that important social and political wars are waged in the world. Such struggles, moreover, may be necessary and most worthy. Still, the ironist suggests that battles need to be fought on many fronts simultaneously, that the distinction between allies and enemies is always ambiguous and subject to revision, and that some of the key struggles should occur within the self, as our very limited capacities for certainty and truth are forced to confront a world that will not stand still.

In Plato's *Republic,* Socrates recites the famous allegory of the cave. He tells of a long-time captive who mistakes dim shadows on the cave wall for reality. The captive eventually breaks free of his chains and climbs up out of the cave into the bright sunshine. Here, after being initially blinded by the light, he comes to perceive things as they really are.

The allegory of the cave is typically interpreted as evidence of Plato's elitist understanding that truth is available only for the very few who break free of the common opinions and perceptions of the mass of humankind and rise up to gain philosophic knowledge. This may be Plato's intent. Or perhaps there is another message. Perhaps Plato is being ironic. The actual words that Plato puts down on paper to describe the allegory of the cave, as all the words found in the *Republic* and his other dialogues, are very much like the shadows dancing on the cave walls. These words are, at best, dim reflections of things. Plato might be suggesting that his own words do not and cannot constitute an unmediated revelation of truth. Indeed, the *Republic* as a whole, like Plato's other writings, are like reflections of reflections, dim representations of a man's thoughts. How could we ever mistake them for truth?

From this perspective, Plato's writings are ironic because they demonstrate a self-critical understanding of their own limitations. Perhaps, indeed, they are not meant to persuade us of their truth with the rigor of a geometric proof. Perhaps the real message is that truth, be it philosophic or political in nature, can never be grasped through the obscuring media of words. It may only be glimpsed. It should be diligently sought by way of theoretical investigations but can never be seized.

An ancient Zen story tells of a teacher who directed students to look at the moon by pointing his finger. The young Buddhist monks, however, naively stared at their teacher's outstretched finger. Plato's words are like the teacher's finger. They point to knowledge but do not constitute it. More enlightened readers, Plato seems to suggest, will understand that his writings are merely heuristic devices, goads to further thought, and intimations of greater things to be remembered and pursued. Plato writes that "anyone who leaves behind him a written manual, and likewise anyone who takes it over from him, on the supposition that such writing will provide something reliable and permanent, must be exceedingly simple-minded; he must really be ignorant ... if he imagines that written words can do anything more than remind one who knows that which the writing is concerned with."[17] Only those who fail to understand Plato's irony will mistake his written words for the truth itself, like the Zen disciples who mistake the master's finger for the moon.

Perhaps one of the reasons Socrates himself never wrote down any of his thoughts (his student, Plato, did that for us) is that while the student can read a book, a book cannot read the student. Only the active philosopher can do that. Before engaging his discussants in dialogue, Socrates gives them a cursory inspection. He does this for two reasons. First, he examines his discussants in order to taper conversation to fit their needs. No book can do that. Second, he examines his discussants to determine if they are likely to be worth the effort of conversation. Only the philosopher can do that. As Socrates states, "once a thing is put in writing, the composition, whatever it may be, drifts all over the place, getting into the hands not only of those who understand it, but equally of those who have no business with it; it doesn't know how to address the right people, and not address the wrong."[18] Socrates talks rather than writes because he does not want people forever peering at the words his fingers scrawled when the intent was to get them to look up at the moonlit heavens.

Plato states in a letter that "no intelligent man will ever be so bold as to put into language those things which his reason has contemplated, especially not into a form that is unalterable—which must be the case with what is expressed in written symbols."[19] Plato, however, chose to write. Thus he was faced with the problem of distinguishing between suitable and unsuitable readers. One means of meeting this challenge was to write dialogues rather than formal treatises. In a dialogue, which consists of numerous voices, the reader is never completely certain who, if anyone, speaks for the author or for truth. Dialogue is well suited to irony.

The genius of Plato is found in the multiple levels at which his dialogues operate. If we adopt an ironic perspective, and understand Plato to have adopted an ironic perspective, then our former interpretations of Plato's politics—as guided by the pursuit of mathematical precision—must be reevaluated. We are left unsure of the extent to which Plato was serious about his political prescriptions for an authoritarian regime and rigid caste society. Infused with irony, Plato's works bear different meanings and messages. Indeed, not all his readers will receive the same lessons, leading to diverse interpretations of the same text. Thus Plato's foundational works of political theory are not as stable as one might at first presume. Indeed, they are less a foundation stone than a fertile field that nourishes originality in interpretation. In keeping with the world it evaluates, ironic political theory does not stand still.

Balancing Ideology and Irony

Wholly ideological thought is exceedingly rare. Wholly ideological thought could emerge only from a mind swept clean of all countervailing tendencies and confusions, incapable of original or independent thinking, and wholly ordered by a single, coherent system of beliefs and values. Perhaps it is only temporarily evident in those who have been successfully brainwashed.

Likewise, wholly ironic thought is rare. Indeed, it may not exist. To remain wholly ironic one's mind would have to be swept every bit as clean of former beliefs and values as the ideologist's. But the sweeping would have to be continual and unending, leaving the cleansed mind without any firm beliefs or values to fill the void. To be a complete ironist would entail switching lenses with such speed that nothing ever comes fully into focus. Everything would remain in flux. Everything would be muddied and confused. One could form no stable concepts, secure no attachments, and maintain no commitments.

Practically speaking, the complete ironist would be as a leaf in the wind, incapable of self-direction and settling nowhere. Since no one allows her life to be completely directionless, the pretension to be wholly ironic is hypocritical. One may be able to feign it in writing, but one could never attain it in living. Full-fledged irony can be rhetorically affirmed, but not practically achieved.

Like Thrasymachus, critics of postmodernism often find irony to be a hypocritical dissimulation. The ironist pretends to hover above firm convictions but, as critics suggest, she still lives much like the rest of us, tied to her beliefs and biases and, despite any pretensions to playfulness, usually quite serious in the pursuit of her interests. In other words, even the most radical ironist cannot completely escape ideology, those systematic sets of values and beliefs that help us order our social and political world. In the *Republic*, Socrates found it necessary to resort to telling myths so as to achieve order in the city. In postmodern times, the ironist also must fall back on a type of mythology. This contemporary mythology comes in the form of ideological convictions.

Ideological thinking provides us with relatively simple answers to complex questions. In order to elicit and justify specific forms of political behavior, ideology makes claims that it cannot fully defend. Ironic thinking, in contrast, confronts us with relatively simple questions that are left unsatisfied by complex answers. It undermines and destabilizes the very vocabulary and conceptual tools that we have at hand to make sense of the world. Whereas ideology offers a shorthand means of navigating life, irony reminds us that all paths are crooked and that our destination remains undecided.

Ironic thinking unsettles far more than it settles. Perhaps that is the result of all thinking. As Hannah Arendt observes, "thinking means that each time you are confronted with some difficulty in life you have to make up your mind anew."[20] This means that taking decisive action is difficult for those who think deeply. Thinking disturbs commitment. As poor Hamlet laments, "the native hue of resolution" is often "sicklied o'er with the pale cast of thought." It is often said that one thinks "through" things in order to "make up one's mind." To the extent that irony comes into play, however, thinking moves in circles and spirals rather than straight lines and leaves one's mind less tidy than before.

The ironist remains too unsettled to "take a stand." The ideologue remains too committed to "gain perspective." By making things seem simpler than they are, ideology promotes action. By demonstrating the complexity and ambiguity of the world, irony induces reflection. To the extent we live and work and speak and think in political communities, we are all ideologists and ironists to varying degrees. As actors, complete irony is impossible for us. As thinkers, wholesale ideology is impossible for us. Thinking interrupts acting just as acting interrupts thinking. Yet one might hope that thinking and acting would go hand in hand in political life.

One political scientist observes that "in a sense, all ideologies are substitutes for thought, and they get condemned for this reason; but they do not deserve condemnation. They are substitutes for thought in about the same way as the Ten Commandments are substitutes for thought."[21] Ideologies, like all moral systems, are shorthand guides to action. To act, one must cease to think ironically, at least for the moment. This does not mean that one must become a complete ideologue. We might momentarily abandon an ironic position not because our beliefs and values suddenly seem incontestable to us but simply in order to cope with the demands of life. We may do so because we find action necessary and desirable given a world that never stops turning. Despite inevitable doubts about the validity of our knowledge and the worthiness of our commitments, action of some sort is unavoidable. Hence we employ our assumptions, beliefs, and values as foundations for our action, however temporary and unstable these foundations are admitted to be.

By underlining the uncertainty of our knowledge, irony also underlines the uncertainty of our actions. Reading in the newspaper that a young athlete unexpectedly died of a heart attack or that a rich tycoon was robbed in the street and left without a dime for a phone call, one might say, "How ironic!" The irony lies not only in the frailty of human life but in the thwarting of even the greatest efforts to control its twists and turns. However one might shore up one's defenses against what Hamlet called "outrageous fortune," one often can do no better than expect the unexpected.

For the ironist of postmodern times no less than the ironist of ancient Greece, therefore, a certain sense of the tragic pervades action. The ancient Greeks were well known for their celebration of tragedy. Having a tragic sense meant accepting that humanity could not fully control its world or its fate. It meant accepting that a human being's reach necessarily exceeded its grasp and that each gain in the control and mastery of life had its price. Often this price was paid in human blood to the Olympian gods who did not like to see mortals become too prideful, or *hubristic.* Yet the Greeks celebrated a tragic sensibility because they believed that one could avoid tragedy only by narrowing one's concerns to a point that would constrict and demean what it meant to be truly and fully human.

Like postmodernists, the Greeks were not progressivists. Time, for the ancient Greeks, was not linear but circular. The golden age was not ahead of them but behind them. Postmodern ironists do not nostalgically yearn for a golden age of the past. Yet they remain informed by a tragic sensibility born of the insight that humans can neither escape from nor fully control the web of power that envelopes and shapes them. For Foucault, this tragic sensibility generated a "hyper and pessimistic activism." Despite their suspicion of all attempts to gain mastery, therefore, ironists need not abandon action altogether. They may even become hyperactive. Nonetheless, they acknowledge that the product of action is even more unpredictable than the product of thought.

For both ancient and postmodern ironists, the motivation for active engagement lies in the stakes of the game. Action is called for, first, because the fundamental liberty to lead one's own life always needs defending. Like Socrates, the postmodern ironist would be wise to defend the just laws of the land. These laws safeguard the basic rights of its citizens, including the right its citizens have to lead ironic lives. Second, action is also called for because our identities—who we are and shall become—are at stake. To choose not to act, in effect, is to choose to be acted upon. Not to act is to take no part in the formation and transformation of the mores that largely determine who we are and shall become.

Nietzsche, a perspectivist and deep ironist, acknowledged the appropriateness of the skeptic's statement, "I have no idea how I am *acting*! I have no idea how I *ought to act*!" Nietzsche also observed that the one cannot stop there. "You are right," Nietzsche responds to the skeptic, "but be sure of this: *you will be acted upon* at every moment!"[22] Even those who for skeptical reasons refuse to "do" anything are nonetheless always being "done." Even those who take no part in the social construction of identities are having their own identities constructed for them. With this in mind, Foucault followed Nietzsche in suggesting that we attempt to "invent" ourselves, that we make the effort to create ourselves as works of art, lest someone or something else do all the creating for us.

Even the full-fledged ironist, it follows, should examine the extent to which the social environment has shaped her own skeptical, ironic disposition. This inquiry cannot easily take place in isolation. It entails confronting and being confronted by those with whom one shares the world. For we find out who we really are only when we see what we say and do and when our beliefs, values, and actions are evaluated by others. Criticism delivers us perhaps the greatest opportunity for self-knowledge. Like Socrates, the ironist takes to heart the Delphic oracle's dictum to "Know thyself." And like Socrates, who spent his days in the Athenian *agora,* or public marketplace, probing the hearts and minds of his fellow citizens, the ironist largely comes to know herself through critical exchanges with others.

Politics demands action in the absence of firm foundations. To seek more than a "relative" validity for one's convictions, Isaiah Berlin writes, is perhaps a "deep and incurable metaphysical need." But to allow this necessarily unfulfilled need to thwart all practice, he insists, is "a symptom of an equally deep, and more dangerous, moral and political immaturity."[23] Fully ironic political theory evidences a similar immaturity. It stymies action through a never-ending self-questioning. On the other hand, fully ideological political theory amounts to little more than a ritual of self-confirmation. Political theorists, like citizens in general, must effectively balance themselves between the use of ironic and ideological lenses, which respectively expand and contract their breadth of vision.

Employing ideological lenses, the theorist authoritatively recommends the best means to view and comprehend the political world and thus encourages certain sorts of political commitment and action. Employing ironic lenses, the theorist points out that any number of perspectives might be employed and that no authoritative evaluation of their relative merits can be made, thus encouraging skeptical reserve and further reflection. Finding an appropriate balance between ideology and irony, active commitment and self-reflective contemplation, is the daunting task that has burdened political theorists from ancient times to the postmodern era.

Ideologies, we know, come in all shapes and sizes. They span the political spectrum from left to right and beyond. Likewise, irony is not unequivocally partisan. It does not promote any specific political orientation. On the one hand, the ironist's skepticism might point her toward a progressive politics that denies the prerogatives of authority. For authority is typically based on claims to knowledge or expertise. Irony, in this case, might serve as a democratic force that undermines imposed hierarchies and social stratifications. On the other hand, the ironist's skepticism might lean her toward a conservative politics that disparages the utopian pursuit of equality and shuns the illusion of progress. For this pursuit and illusion are typically grounded on faith in the stable goodness of the human heart and the power of the human mind. In this case, irony might become aligned with an elitism that looks down on those who retain naive moral beliefs and convictions. It is a fitting irony that irony itself remains politically ambiguous.

The Power of Words

The pen is said to be mightier than the sword. Generally we applaud the thought behind this aphorism, which celebrates reasoned persuasion above violent coercion. Nonetheless, the power of words and ideas, concepts and theories, is not always benign. And it is always dangerous. Language, especially when it is marshalled into political theory, is a worldly force.

Throughout history it has been recognized that language is indeed a powerful tool. A Spanish grammarian told Queen Isabella in 1492 that "language is the instrument of empire."[24] Language could be linked to empire building because of the power of the ideas that words form. To control language, it was assumed, is to control ideas and to control ideas is to control behavior. A few decades before the French Revolution, a scholar currying the favor of a ruler succinctly expressed this linkage:

> When you have thus formed the chain of ideas in the heads of your citizens, you will then be able to pride yourselves on guiding them and being their masters. A stupid despot may constrain his slaves with iron chains; but a true politician binds them even more strongly by the chain of their own ideas; it is at the stable point of reason that he secures the end of the chain; this link is all the stronger in that we do not know of what it is made and we believe it to be our own work; despair and time eat away the bonds of iron and steel, but they are powerless against the habitual union of ideas, they can only tighten it still more; and on the soft fibers of the brain is founded the unshakable base of the soundest of Empires.[25]

De Tracy had this sort of power in mind when he created his science of ideology.

Certainly this is the sort of power later ideologists sought. The Chinese communist leader Mao Tse-tung (1896–1975) did not believe that the pen was mightier than the sword, observing tersely that political power "grows out of the barrel of a gun." When you have got all the guns, he presumed with some justification, you can control all the pens. Once firmly in power, Mao put all the pens to work in a massive effort of public indoctrination called the Cultural Revolution (1966–69). Such indoctrination, euphemistically called reeducation and aptly described as brainwashing, was effectively based on the theory of ideology, as developed by de Tracy and modified by Marxists and Leninists. Mao wrote:

> China's 600 million people have two remarkable peculiarities: they are, first of all, poor, secondly blank. That may seem like a bad thing, but it is really a good thing. Poor people want change, want to do things, want revolution. A clean sheet of paper has no blotches, and so the newest and most beautiful words can be written on it, the newest and most beautiful pictures can be painted on it.[26]

This is the same sort of power over the human mind and will that B.F. Skinner had his behavioral technicians develop at Walden Two.

Importantly, ideology gains its power not so much by dictating to people how they should act but by telling them who they are. To tell people who they are, one must tell them where they belong. Sociologists observe that "all identifications take place within horizons that imply a specific social world.... Every name ... implies a designated

social location. To be given an identity involves being assigned a specific place in the world."[27] Identity is about social location. Ideologies
paint a picture of the world and situate us within it. Ideologies give us
identities, and tasks and duties to go with these, by defining our place
in nature, our role in society, and our mission in history.

Despite the relatively successful demonstrations of ideological indoctrination in this century, the power of ideas and words is limited.
Neither the language we use nor the ideologies we subscribe to wholly
determine our beliefs and behavior. Human beings have proven time
and again that they can successfully resist even the most devious and
coercive efforts to control their thoughts and actions. Societies, political theorists recognize, are arenas for competing and hybridized ideologies. No single ideological structure ever achieves complete control.[28]
Still, there is no doubt that ideology can be an oppressive force. In the
attempt to justify a particular social order or reordering, ideologies
claim incontestable truths as grounds for their principles and propositions. Incontestable truths are by definition not subject to democratic
debate. There is, then, something tyrannical about these truths.

With this in mind, Richard Rorty argues that theories that attempt
to ground themselves on incontestable truths, what Rorty calls metaphysical theories and what we have called ideologies, should be re-
served for private use. They are simply too dangerous for the public
world and ought to be restricted to individuals' efforts to regulate their
personal lives. Likewise, Rorty believes that ironic theories are equally
inappropriate for the public realm. Ironic theories, he maintains,
should also be used only to regulate one's personal life. They best serve
as antidotes for those infected with dangerous metaphysical or ideological beliefs. Though not as hazardous as metaphysical thinking, Rorty
concludes, ironic thinking is nonetheless "pretty much useless when it
comes to politics."[29] The public realm requires a much looser and more
tolerant ordering principle or "social glue" than metaphysics or ideology and a more stable, less ambiguous force to hold it together than
irony. Once we have dismissed both ideology and irony, Rorty suggests,
the only thing left to fall back on are the (liberal) social and political
traditions that we already practice. The social glue that holds the public
world together, then, is simply our "common vocabularies and common hopes," about which no unchanging rules can be written.[30]

There is a problem with Rorty's seemingly straightforward proposal. First, despite his reputation as a postmodernist, Rorty effectively
falls back on a dubious modernist dichotomy. He assumes that the
creation of identity is a private affair and that the regulation of interaction is the sole concern of politics. But the hard-and-fast distinction he

makes between the private realm and the public realm does not really exist. We do not and cannot operate with *fully* separate vocabularies for our personal and political lives. Even private identities are largely socially constructed. And when people enter the political world, they cannot simply abandon or ignore their private beliefs, commitments, relationships and values, though they may restrain their influence. What is public and what private is not an unproblematic distinction; it is highly contested terrain. We cannot help but bring ideological lenses into play when contesting this terrain, and we would be well advised to bring ironic lenses into play to temper our ideological predispositions.

The common hopes, vocabularies and traditions that Rorty would have us rely on to regulate our public lives, moreover, are themselves chock full of liberal concepts and orientations. The only way to become aware of these underlying ideological formations is critically to engage them. Such critical engagement, for better or worse, entails becoming aware of and further developing different sets of ideological and ironic lenses.

If the world would stand still, the ironic theorist might be able to fend off ideology indefinitely. But the world never stops moving, and it takes the theorist with it. If she chooses not to act, she nonetheless will be acted upon. Two possibilities present themselves. The theorist may become a passive passenger who naively or unconsciously reinforces the common vocabulary, the status quo, and the predominant ideology of the times. Alternatively, the theorist may actively and self-consciously engage in the construction and contestation of the mores that structure political life. This theoretical and inherently political action demands courage, for it cannot be grounded in certain knowledge. There is no substitute for reflective thought and measured judgment. The theorist must act when the justice of every action is precarious and the identities of both the self and others remain unstable.

Suggested Readings

Hannah Arendt. *The Life of the Mind*
Raymond Aron. *The Opium of the Intellectuals*
Daniel Bell. *The End of Ideology*
William E. Connolly. *The Terms of Political Discourse*
F.M. Cornford. *From Religion to Philosophy*
Dante Germino. *Beyond Ideology*
David Hume. *Hume's Moral and Political Philosophy*
Aldous Huxley. *Brave New World*
Arthur Koestler. *The Yogi and the Commissar*

V.I. Lenin. *What Is to Be Done?*
Karl Mannheim. *Ideology and Utopia*
George Orwell. *Nineteen Eighty-four*
Plato. *Apology, Euthyphro, Phaedrus, Republic,* and *Symposium*
Richard Rorty. *Contingency, Irony, and Solidarity*
George Rude. *Ideology and Popular Protest*
Judith Shklar. *Political Theory and Ideology*

Conclusion

et us summarize our theoretical voyage by reexamining the importance of political theory and paying heed to its inherent limitations. Our theoretical investigations have allowed us to describe, assess, explain, and judge the political world from various points of view. These investigations have been conducted under the auspices of a search for the nature of politics and its relation to the good life. This search led us to reflect on the exercise of power and the human capacity for reason, liberty, and justice. Such terms of political discourse prove to be highly contestable. Their meanings and uses are largely products of the conceptual lenses through which they are viewed. With this in mind, we employed many different lenses—scientific and interpretive, epistemological and ethical, methodological individualist and social structuralist, ancient, modern and postmodern, ideological and ironic—to frame the political world in different ways. In turn, we theorized our own complex and unstable identities as biological, cultural, racial, religious, sexual, economic, and ecological beings.

Confronted with the manifold mores that infuse political life and the multiple facets of our identities, we face the enduring challenge of theorizing the political world in order to understand our place within it and its place within us. Or do we? Edmund Burke wrote that "the bulk of mankind, on their part, are not excessively curious concerning any theories whilst they are really happy; and one sure symptom of an ill-conducted state is the propensity of the people to resort to them."[1] Burke suggests that theory is an affair of academics or armchair philosophers. He holds that most people most of the time do not concern themselves with political theory when things are not awry.

Burke may be right. Yet an atheoretical disposition might not be as politically benign as Burke believes it to be. Perhaps citizens *should* concern themselves more with theory, at least to the extent that it broadens their range of perspectives and illuminates the forces that structure their lives and shape their identities.

Human beings distinguish themselves from other animals by their reason. Political communities are held together by power and evaluate themselves according to various standards of justice. Individuals often value their freedom above all else. Such words as reason, power, justice, and freedom are the essentially contested concepts of political discourse. In concerning themselves with the meanings of these terms, political theorists are questioning and deliberating the concepts that structure collective life and shape individual identity.

Ideas matter. Victor Hugo once said that "there is one thing stronger than all the armies of the world: and that is an idea whose time has come." Yet ideas do not simply arrive in the world poised to accept positions of authority. They are often born as outcasts, see countless setbacks and reworkings, and must be argued for and fought over during long periods of cultivation before their "time" finally arrives. Many others languish in obscurity or are forever lost to memory. For all that, ideas can become powerful social and political agents.

As Max Weber attempted to demonstrate, ideas constitute "effective forces in history." Nevertheless, ideas do not have independent standing apart from the material conditions within which they develop. Employing a term coined by the German poet, novelist, and playwright Johann Goethe (1749–1832), Weber speaks of an "elective affinity" between particular ideas and their coexisting forms of social and political life. To say that there is an elective affinity between certain ideas and certain forms of social and political life is to say that there is a good probability, but no certainty, that particular forms of thought will develop out of and contribute toward the formation and maintenance of particular forms of social and political organization. Our aim as theorists, Weber insists, should not be to "substitute for a one-sided materialistic an equally one-sided spiritualistic causal interpretation of culture and of history."[2] Instead, we should seek understanding of the relationship between ideas and the concrete conditions of life that sustain them and that they, in turn, sustain.

This book is primarily concerned with thinking politics rather than doing politics, with theory rather than practice. Yet its underlying assumption is that the distinction between thinking and doing, theory and practice is, in political affairs, far from clear or categorical. Just as irony and ideology often go hand in hand, so theory and practice often prove inseparable. As political theorist Michael Sandel writes:

> Political philosophy seems often to reside at a distance from the world. Principles are one thing, politics another, and even our best efforts to 'live up' to our ideals typically founder on the gap between theory and practice. But if political philosophy is unrealizable in one sense, it is unavoidable in another. This is the sense in which philosophy inhabits the world from the start; our practices and institutions are embodiments of theory. To engage in a political practice is already to stand in relation to theory. For all our uncertainties about ultimate questions of political philosophy—of justice and value and the nature of the good life—the one thing we know is that we live *some* answer all the time.[3]

The answers that we cannot avoid living are written in the language of politics. Critically investigating that language—the task of political theory—is an indispensable part of any worthy political practice and, arguably, an indispensable part of the good life.

Our critical investigations as political theorists often leave us with few foundations on which to build. The methods and substance, means and ends, practices and principles of political theory remain susceptible to endless contestation. Postmodernists, for instance, might reject our basic definition of political theory as inquiry into "the nature of the good life." This normative definition arguably assumes that there is only one sort of good life to be lived. Too often, postmodernists warn, such singular formulations suppress difference. In this case, the presumption that we should all be living *the* good life might serve to privilege the norms of the powerful and exclude or constrain the beliefs and practices of others. Political theorists are always undermining one another's foundations.

Ludwig Wittgenstein (1889–1951), an Austrian philosopher, once wrote that philosophy consists in the bumps on the head one gets from butting up against the limits of language. He meant to say that language takes us so far in assessing the quandaries of life and that philosophic wonder and speculation results when certain of these quandaries are experienced as unresolvable. Political theory amounts to the bumps on the head that arise from battling with the essentially contested concepts of politics. They are worthy scars of battle. In large part, the metaphoric contusions sported by political theorists are received in an effort to avoid the real bumps to the head that would be suffered were blows exchanged instead of words in the ongoing effort to organize collective human life.

In *The Laws*, Plato warns of the problems faced in the attempt to establish a just city. "The real difficulty," the Athenian speaker in the dialogue states, "is to make political systems reflect in practice the trouble-free perfection of theory."[4] Practicing what you preach, having one's political life conform to one's political beliefs, is indeed a difficult task. Yet theory itself is hardly trouble-free. As any ironist knows, it is never perfect. Theories reflect the ambiguities, tensions, and shortcomings inherent in human life. Those ambiguities, tensions and shortcomings are perhaps easier to negotiate and manipulate in the mind or on paper than in the public forum, but they do not for that reason disappear.

The problem is twofold. The world is complex and any theoretical attempt to capture it completely necessarily falls short. In turn, to understand social and political life one must become part of it. This participation in worldly affairs leads one to adopt interests and identities that color one's understanding. Without this coloring, the world would remain invisible to us. Yet this coloring often obscures as much as it reveals. William James observed that "a great many people think they are thinking, when they are merely rearranging their prejudices." Despite a theorist's most diligent effort at critical self-reflection, there is no guarantee that his or her thinking does not largely consist in the rearrangement of biases born of particular interests and identities.

Ideology, the systematic ordering of socially generated biases, plays an important role in channeling thoughts and actions. It is probably impossible to become fully conscious of this ideological channeling in one's life or to put a complete stop to it. Political theorists are certainly not immune to its force. They do not occupy a privileged vantage point from which neutral descriptions and explanations of an objective political reality might be obtained. Instead, they speak from particular points of view. In their work, theorists evidence the effects that power has had upon them. They also actively vie for and exercise power themselves. Theorists are invested in the world, and much of their insight derives from this investment.

Ideological predispositions may and should be challenged by self-reflective thought. The result of this challenge, however, is not unassailable political knowledge. Instead, one is left with a more informed understanding tempered by ironic reserve. Irony stimulates the opportunity, and suggests the responsibility, to see the world from many different points of view. Gaining multiple perspectives facilitates the task political theorists have taken on since the time of Plato, namely, exploring the relationship between the just soul and the just state. Learning about justice in the absence of certain knowledge is a daunting task to be sure. Yet viewing the world from the standpoint of others facilitates the effort to discover what each of them is due.

T.H. Huxley (1825–95), a biologist and advocate for Darwin's theories, once remarked that the utopian notion of taking from each according to his or her ability and giving to each according to his or her needs is actually well fulfilled in a hive of bees.[5] Among societies of humans, of course, the ideal is a good deal more difficult to attain. In human societies, one is confronted with the needs and abilities of individuals rather than of classes or castes of identical people. Rendering justice to individuals is indeed a formidable challenge.

The classical understanding of justice—rendering each his or her due—was formulated at the very dawn of political theory, nearly two and a half millennia ago. It has been vigorously debated ever since. The task facing political theorists today is to understand and explain how the contestable demands of justice are best incorporated into contemporary life. Diligent efforts to take on this crucial task ensure that political theory will never slip into its twilight.

Notes

Introduction

1. Clifford Geertz, "Blurred Genres: The Refiguration of Social Thought," in *Local Knowledge* (New York: Basic Books, 1983), 19–35.

Chapter 1

1. Quoted in John G. Gunnell, *The Descent of Political Theory: The Genealogy of an American Vocation* (Chicago: University of Chicago Press, 1993), 21.

2. Sheldon Wolin, "Political Theory as a Vocation," *American Political Science Review* 63 (1969): 1064.

3. See Karl Popper, *The Logic of Scientific Discovery* (New York: Basic Books, 1959), and *Conjectures and Refutations* (New York: Basic Books, 1962).

4. Claude Henri de Saint-Simon, *Social Organization, the Science of Man, and Other Writings*, trans. Felix Markham (New York: Harper Torchbooks, 1964), 39–40.

5. John Stuart Mill, *Collected Works* (Toronto: University of Toronto Press, 1974), 8:833.

6. James Shotwell, quoted in Bernard Crick, *In Defense of Politics*, 4th ed. (Chicago: University of Chicago Press, 1992), 95–96.

7. Robert Michels, *Political Parties: A Sociological Study of the Oligarchical Tendencies of Modern Democracy*, trans. Eden and Cedar Paul (New York: Dover Publications, 1915), viii, 401.

8. Max Weber, *The Methodology of the Social Sciences* (New York: Free Press, 1949).

9. Max Weber, *The Protestant Ethic and the Spirit of Capitalism*, trans. Talcott Parsons (New York: Scribner's, 1958), 98.

10. Weber, *The Protestant Ethic*, 233.

11. See Charles Taylor, "Interpretation and the Sciences of Man," in *Philosophical Papers* (Cambridge: Cambridge University Press, 1985, 2:15–57; also found in Fred Dallmayr and Thomas McCarthy, eds., *Understanding and Social Inquiry* (Notre Dame: University of Notre Dame Press, 1977), 101–31.

12. Quoted in Charles R. Bambach, *Heidegger, Dilthey, and the Crisis of Historicism* (Ithaca: Cornell University Press, 1995), 161.

13. Hans-Georg Gadamer, *Truth and Method* (New York: Crossroad, 1975), 358.

14. Hans-Georg Gadamer, "The Universality of the Hermeneutical Problem," *Philosophical Hermeneutics* (Berkeley: University of California Press, 1976), 9.

15. Gadamer, *Truth and Method*, 238.

16. Ibid., 273.

17. Hans-Georg Gadamer, *Reason in the Age of Science*, trans. Frederick Lawrence (Cambridge: MIT Press, 1981), 109–10.

18. Leo Strauss, *What Is Political Philosophy and Other Studies* (Westport, Conn.: Greenwood Press, 1959), 21.

19. Thomas Jefferson's letter to William Charles Jarvis, September 28, 1820, in Paul Leicester Ford, ed., *The Writings of Thomas Jefferson*, vol. 10 (New York: G.P. Putnam's Sons, 1899).

20. Quentin Skinner, "Meaning and Understanding in the History of Ideas," *History and Theory* 8, no. 1 (1969): 52–53.

Chapter 2

1. See Donald Griffin, *Animal Minds* (Chicago: University of Chicago Press, 1992), 219. For an account of the limitations of animal language, see Steven Pinker, *The Language Instinct* (New York: Morrow, 1994).

2. See Daniel C. Dennett, *Darwin's Dangerous Idea: Evolution and the Meanings of Life* (New York: Simon and Schuster, 1995), 379.

3. St. Augustine, *The City of God* (New York: Penguin, 1972), 596.

4. St. Thomas Aquinas, *The Political Theories of St. Thomas Aquinas*, ed. Dino Bigongiari (New York: Hafner Press, 1953), 180.

5. Thomas Paine, *The Rights of Man* (Garden City, N.Y.: Doubleday, 1961), 398–99.

6. Alexander Hamilton, James Madison, and John Jay, *The Federalist Papers* (New York: Mentor, 1961), 79.

7. Thomas Hobbes, *Leviathan*, ed. C.B. Macpherson (New York. Penguin, 1968), 261.

8. Ibid., 186.

9. Thucydides, *The Peloponnesian War* (New York: Modern Library, 1951), 334, 331.

10. Pinker, *The Language Instinct*, 430.

11. A similar expression was employed by Edward O. Wilson in *On Human Nature* (Cambridge: Harvard Univesity Press, 1978), 78–79.

12. Roger D. Masters, *The Nature of Politics* (New Haven: Yale University Press, 1989), 26.

13. Cited in ibid., 35.

14. Aristotle, *Nichomachean Ethics* (1160–1161), trans. Terence Irwin (Indianapolis: Hackett Publishing, 1985), 224–32. See also Larry Arnhart, "The New Darwinian Naturalism in Political Theory," *American Political Science Review* 89 (June 1995): 390.

15. Melvin Konner, *The Tangled Wing: Biological Constraints on the Human Spirit* (New York: Holt, Rinehart and Winston, 1982), 111. See also James Q. Wilson, *The Moral Sense* (New York: Free Press, 1993), 165–90.

16. Gerald Edelman, *Bright Air, Brilliant Fire: On the Matter of the Mind* (New York: Basic Books, 1992), 166.

17. What Richard Dawkins calls *memes*, Wilson and Lumsden have called *culturgens*. See Richard Dawkins, *The Selfish Gene*, new ed. (Oxford: Oxford University Press, 1989). Charles Lumsden and Edward O. Wilson, *Genes, Mind, and Culture: The Coevolutionary Process* (Cambridge: Harvard University Press, 1981).

18. See Masters, *The Nature of Politics*, 109.

19. Dawkins, *The Selfish Gene*, 192.

20. Ibid., 199.

21. The term "reaction range" is George Gaylord Simpson's. Likewise, Theodosius Dobzhansky speaks of heredity not as determining ready-made physical traits or behaviors but as a force establishing a "norm of reaction" to given environments. Both Simpson and Dobzhansky are cited in Masters, *The Nature of Politics*, 121.

Chapter 3

1. Bertrand Russell, *Power: A New Social Analysis* (New York: Barnes and Noble, 1962), 9–10.

2. Thomas Hobbes, *Leviathan*, ed. C.B. Macpherson (New York: Penguin, 1968), 150.

3. See Hannah Arendt, *The Human Condition* (Chicago: University of Chicago Press, 1958), 200–205; and Michel Foucault, "The Subject and Power," in Hubert L. Dreyfus and Paul Rabinow, *Michel Foucault: Beyond Structuralism and Hermeneutics*, 2d ed. (Chicago: University of Chicago Press, 1983).

4. Niccolò Machiavelli, *The Prince and the Discourses* (New York; Random House, 1950), 44, 61–62.

5. R.J. Rummel, "War Isn't This Century's Biggest Killer," *Wall Street Journal*, 7 July 1986, 12.

6. Emma Goldman, "Anarchism: What It Really Stands For," in *Anarchism and Other Essays* (New York: Dover, 1969), 50.

7. Robert Dahl, *Democracy and Its Critics* (New Haven: Yale University Press, 1989), 50.

8. Max Weber, *From Max Weber: Essays in Sociology*, trans. H.H. Gerth and C. Wright Mills (New York: Oxford University Press), 1958, 120–21.

9. Hobbes, *Leviathan*, 227, 232.

10. Quoted in Bertrand de Jouvenal, *On Power: The Natural History of Its Growth* (Indianapolis: Liberty Fund, 1993), 36.

11. See Arendt, *The Human Condition*, 202.

12. *Public Citizen*, January/February 1996, 6.

13. Bernard Crick, *In Defense of Politics*, 4th ed. (Chicago: University of Chicago Press, 1992), 20.

14. Quoted in Jay M. Shafritz, *The HarperCollins Dictionary of American Government and Politics* (New York: HarperCollins, 1993), 368.

15. Ambrose Bierce, *The Devil's Dictionary (1906)*, quoted in Shafritz, *HarperCollins Dictionary of American Government and Politics*, 369.

16. See, for example, Sidney Verba, Norman Nie, and Jae-on Kim, *Participation and Political Equality: A Seven-Nation Comparison* (Cambridge: Cambridge University Press, 1978), 46–48.

17. Crick, *In Defense of Politics*, 151.

18. Ibid., 130.

19. Antonio Gramsci, *Selections from the Prison Notebooks*, ed. and trans. Quintin Hoare and Geoffrey Smith (New York: International Publishers, 1971), 244.

Chapter 4

1. Quoted in Peter Coveney and Roger Highfield, *The Arrow of Time* (New York: Fawcett Columbine, 1990), 49.

2. Voltaire, *Lettres Philosophiques*, XII, *Œuvres Complètes* (Paris: Garnier, 1879), 22:118.

3. René Descartes, *A Discourse on Method*, trans. E. Haldane and G. Ross (New York: Washington Square Press, 1965), 89, 117.

4. Harold Lasswell, *Politics: Who Gets What, When, and How* (New York: Meridian Books, 1958).

5. Alasdair MacIntyre, *A Short History of Ethics* (New York: Macmillan, 1966), 187.

6. Quoted in Anthony Giddens, *Capitalism and Modern Social Theory: An Analysis of the Writings of Marx, Durkheim, and Weber* (Cambridge: Cambridge University Press, 1971), 88.

7. Émile Durkheim, *The Division of Labor in Society*, trans. George Simpson (New York: Free Press, 1933), 350.

8. Pierre Bourdieu and Loic J.D. Wacquant, *An Invitation to Reflexive Sociology* (Chicago: University of Chicago Press, 1992), 113.

9. See, for example, Claude Lévi-Strauss, *The Savage Mind* (London: Weidenfeld and Nicolson, 1966), and *Structural Anthropology* (New York: Basic Books, 1963).

10. Immanuel Kant, *Critique of Pure Reason*, trans. Norman Kemp Smith (New York: St. Martin's Press, 1929), 59.

11. See, for example, Louis Althusser, *For Marx* (New York: Vintage Books, 1969).

12. See Claude Lévi-Strauss, "Reflections on Liberty," in *The View from Afar*, trans. Joachim Neugroschel and Phoebe Hoss (New York: Basic Books, 1985), 279–88.

13. Anthony Giddens, *Central Problems in Social Theory* (Berkeley: University of California Press, 1979).

14. Bourdieu and Wacquant, *An Invitation to Reflexive Sociology*, 133.

15. See, for instance, Jacques Derrida, *Writing and Difference*, trans. Alan Bass (Chicago: University of Chicago Press, 1978).

16. Richard J. Bernstein, *The New Constellation: The Ethical-Political Horizons of Modernity/Postmodernity* (Cambridge: MIT Press, 1991), 8.

17. For a good discussin of some of these thinkers' relation to postmodernism, see Steven Best and Douglas Kellner, *Postmodern Theory: Critical Investigations* (New York: Guilford Press, 1991).

18. Friedrich Nietzsche, *On the Genealogy of Morals*, trans. Walter Kaufmann (New York: Vintage, 1967), 119.

19. Richard Rorty, *Contingency, Irony, and Solidarity* (Cambridge: Cambridge University Press, 1989), xiii.

20. See Jean Baudrillard, *Jean Baudrillard: Selected Writings*, ed. Mark Poster (Cambridge: Polity Press, 1988).

21. Craig Reinarman, *American States of Mind: Political Beliefs and Behavior among Private and Public Workers* (New Haven: Yale University Press, 1987), 221.

22. Murray Edelman, *The Symbolic Uses of Power* (Urbana: University of Illinois Press, 1964), 172–73.

23. Charles E. Lindblom, *Inquiry and Change: The Troubled Attempt to Understand and Shape Society* (New Haven: Yale University Press, 1990), 89.

24. Antonio Gramsci, *Selections from the Prison Notebooks of Antonio Gramsci*, ed. and trans. Q. Hoare and G.N. Smith (New York: International Publishers, 1971).

25. Wilson Bryan Key, *Subliminal Seduction: Ad Media's Manipulation of a Not So Innocent America* (Englewood Cliffs, N.J.: Prentice Hall, 1973), 70.

26. One of the more seminal works in the study of political culture is Gabriel Almond and Sidney Verba, *The Civic Culture* (Boston: Little, Brown, 1963).

27. Edelman, *The Symbolic Uses of Politics*, 172–73.

28. See James Burnham, *The Machiavellians* (New York: John Day, 1943); and C. Wright Mills, *The Power Elite* (New York: Oxford University Press, 1959).

29. Robert Solomon, "Nietzsche, Postmodernism, and Resentment: A Genealogical Hypothesis," in *Nietzsche as Postmodernist: Essays Pro and Contra*, ed. C. Koelb (Albany: SUNY, 1990), 292.

30. K. Katherine Hayles, "Searching for Common Ground," in *Reinventing Nature: Responses to Postmodern Deconstruction*, ed. Michael E. Soulé and Gary Lease (Washington, D.C.: Island Press, 1995), 47.

31. Michel Foucault, *Discipline and Punish: The Birth of the Prison*, trans. Alan Sheridan (New York: Vintage Books, 1977), 26.

32. Michel Foucault, *The History of Sexuality*, vol. 1, *An Introduction*, trans. Robert Hurley (New York: Vintage Books, 1978), 88–89.

33. Alexis de Tocqueville, *Democracy in America* (New York: Vintage Books, 1959), 1:273–74.

34. Foucault, *The History of Sexuality*, 94–95.

35. Michel Foucault, *The Order of Things: An Archaeology of the Human Science* (New York: Vintage Books, 1970), xiii–xiv.

36. Michel Foucault, *Power/Knowledge: Selected Interviews and Other Writings, 1972–1977*, ed. Colin Gordon (New York: Pantheon Books, 1977), 98.

37. Jürgen Habermas, "The Genealogical Writing of History: On Some Aporias in Foucault's Theory of Power," *Canadian Journal of Political and Social Theory* 10 (1986): 7. See also Nancy Fraser, "Foucault on Modern Power: Empirical Insights and Normative Confusions," *Praxis International* 1 (1981): 2762–87.

38. Michel Foucault, "The Subject and Power," in Hubert L. Dreyfus and Paul Rabinow, *Michel Foucault: Beyond Structuralism and Hermeneutics*, 2d ed. (Chicago: University of Chicago Press, 1983), 220.

39. For an account of the postmodern "responsibility to otherness" versus the modern "responsibility to act," see Stephen K. White, *Political Theory and Postmodernism* (Cambridge: Cambridge University Press, 1991).

40. B.F. Skinner, *Walden Two* (New York: Macmillan, 1948).

41. B.F. Skinner, *Beyond Freedom and Dignity* (New York: Vintage, 1971), 191, 205–6.

42. Michel Foucault, "On the Genealogy of Ethics: An Overview of Work in Progress," in Dreyfus and Rabinow, *Michel Foucault*, 232.

43. Jean-François Lyotard, *The Postmodern Condition: A Report on Knowledge*, trans. G. Bennington and B. Massumi (Minneapolis: University of Minnesota Press, 1984), xxiv.

44. Werner Heisenberg, *Physics and Philosophy* (New York: Harper & Row, 1971), 58.

45. Michel Foucault, *Language, Counter-Memory, Practice*, ed. Donald Bouchard (Ithaca: Cornell University Press, 1977), 151.

46. Michael Walzer, "The Communitarian Critique of Liberalism," *Political Theory* 18 (February 1990): 21.

47. Bernard Crick, *In Defense of Politics*, 4th ed. (Chicago: University of Chicago Press, 1992), 171.

48. Ibid., 272.

Chapter 5

1. Thomas Jefferson, *Thomas Jefferson on Democracy* (New York: Mentor, 1939), 13.

2. Craig Calhoun, "Social Theory and the Politics of Identity," in *Social Theory and the Politics of Identity*, ed. Craig Calhoun (Cambridge: Blackwell, 1994), 3.

3. Steven Best and Douglas Kellner, *Postmodern Theory: Critical Investigations* (New York: Guilford Press, 1991), 205.

4. Quoted in Anthony Pagden, *European Encounters with the New World* (New Haven: Yale University Press, 1993), 19.

5. See *Journals and Other Documents on the Life and Voyages of Christopher Columbus*, trans. and ed. by Samuel Eliot Morison (New York: Heritage Press, 1963).

6. Tzvetan Todorov, *The Conquest of America*, trans. Richard Howard (New York: Harper & Row, 1984), 3.

7. Quoted in Pagden, *European Encounters with the New World*, 20, 97.

8. Wayne Moquin and Charles Van Doren, eds., *Great Documents in American Indian History* (New York: Praeger, 1973), 104–5.

9. Alexis de Tocqueville, *Democracy in America* (New York: Vintage Books, 1959), 349.

10. Russell Thornton, *American Indian Holocaust and Survival: A Population History since 1492* (Norman: University of Oklahoma Press, 1987), xv–xvi.

11. Cited in Wub-e-ke-niew, *We Have the Right to Exist: A Translation of Aboriginal Indigenous Thought* (New York: Black Thistle Press, 1995), 130.

12. Clark Wissler, *Indians of the United States*, rev. ed. (New York: Doubleday, 1966).

13. Jefferson, *Thomas Jefferson on Democracy*, 106–7.

14. Jared Diamond, *The Third Chimpanzee: The Evolution and Future of the Human Animal* (New York: HarperCollins, 1992), 308.

15. Quoted in Robert McHenry and Charles Van Doren, eds., *A Documentary History of Conservation in America* (New York: Praeger, 1972), 186.

16. Moquin and Van Doren, eds., *Great Documents in American Indian History*, 236–37.

17. Native American Scholarship Fund newsletter, 25 September 1995.

18. Wub-e-ke-niew, *We Have the Right to Exist*, 35, 71–73.

19. Ibid., 74, 218.

20. Vernon Van Dyke, *Ideology and Political Choice: The Search for Freedom, Justice, and Virtue* (Chatham, N.J.: Chatham House, 1995), 66–67.

21. See Douglas S. Massey and Nancy A. Denton, *American Apartheid: Segregation and the Making of the Underclass* (Cambridge: Harvard University Press, 1993).

22. J. Donald Moon, *Constructing Community: Moral Pluralism and Tragic Conflicts* (Princeton: Princeton University Press, 1993), 185.

23. Plato, *Republic* (344c), in *The Collected Dialogues of Plato*, ed. Edith Hamilton and Huntington Cairns (Princeton: Princeton University Press, 1989), 594.

24. Sheldon Wolin, "What Revolutionary Action Means Today," in Chantal Mouffe, ed., *Dimensions of Radical Democracy: Pluralism, Citizenship, Community* (London: Verson, 1992), 251–52.

25. Alasdair MacIntyre, *A Short History of Ethics* (New York: Macmillan, 1966), 187.

26. Calhoun, "Social Theory and the Politics of Identity," 10.

27. Kate Millett, *Sexual Politics* (Garden City, N.Y.: Doubleday, 1970).

28. Jody Newman, "Perception and Reality: A Study Comparing the Success of Men and Women Candidates" (Executive Summary). National Women's Political Caucus, 1994.

29. Jean Bethke Elshtain, *Public Man, Private Woman: Women in Social and Political Thought*, 2d ed. (Princeton: Princeton University Press, 1993), 357–58.

30. Bernard Crick, *In Defense of Politics*, 4th ed. (Chicago: University of Chicago Press, 1992), 84.

31. See Peter Bachrach and Morton S. Baratz, "Two Faces of Power," *American Political Science Review* 56 (1962): 947–52.

32. John Stuart Mill, *Three Essays* (Oxford: Oxford University Press,

1975), 451.

33. Quoted in Nancy McGlen and Karen O'Connor, *Women's Rights: The Struggle for Equality in the Nineteenth and Twentieth Centuries* (New York: Praeger, 1983), 1.

34. See Robert Dahl, *Democracy and Its Critics* (New Haven: Yale University Press, 1989), 232–43.

35. *Philadelphia Inquirer,* 13 August 1995, E3.

36. *Women Action Coalition Stats: The Facts about Women* (New York: New Press, 1993), 59.

37. Cited in Jay M. Shafritz, *The HarperCollins Dictionary of American Government and Politics* (New York: HarperCollins, 1993), 374.

38. Timothy Wirth, former Colorado senator and U.S. undersecretary of state for global affairs, quoted in *Sierra,* September/October 1995, 79.

39. UN Human Development Report, *Philadelphia Inquirer,* 19 August 1995, A5. See also Ruth Leger Sivard, *Women … A World Survey* (Washington, D.C.: World Priorities, 1985).

40. For a vivid account of the state of many of America's schools, see Jonathan Kozol, *Savage Inequalities: Children in America's Schools* (New York: Crown, 1991).

41. The 1995 UN Human Development Report, cited in the *ZPG Reporter,* November/December 1995, 2. See also *Women Action Coalition Stats,* 49.

42. Shulamith Firestone, *The Dialectic of Sex* (New York: Bantam Books, 1970), 198–99.

43. See Susan Brownmiller, *Against Our Will: Men, Women, and Rape* (New York: Simon and Schuster, 1975).

44. Mary Daly, *Gyn/Ecology: The Meta-Ethics of Radical Feminism* (Boston: Beacon Press, 1978), 39.

45. See Elizabeth Cady Stanton, Susan Anthony, and Matilda Gage, eds., *History of Woman Suffrage,* 3 vols. (Rochester: Charles Mann, 1881–91); and Susan Anthony and Ida Harper, eds., *History of Woman Suffrage,* vol. 4 (Indianapolis: Hollenbeck Press, 1902).

46. Marcel Griaule, quoted in Marimba Ani, *Yurugu: An African-Centered Critique of European Cultural Thought and Behavior* (Trenton: African World Press, 1994), 532.

47. Carole Pateman, *The Sexual Contract* (Stanford: Stanford University Press, 1988), 231.

48. Carol Gilligan, *In a Different Voice: Psychological Theory and Women's Development* (Cambridge: Harvard University Press, 1982), 6.

49. For a discussion of the accommodation between theories of the morality of rights and the morality of care, see Seyla Benhabib, "The Generalized and the Concrete Other: The Kohlberg-Gilligan Controversy and Feminist Theory," in *Feminism as Critique: On the Politics of Gender,* ed. Seyla Benhabib and Drucilla Cornell (Minneapolis: University of Minnesota Press, 1987), 77–95.

50. Mary Belenky et al., *Women's Ways of Knowing: The Development of Self, Voice, and Mind* (New York: Basic Books, 1986).

51. Nancy Chodorow, *Feminism and Psychoanalytic Theory* (New Haven: Yale University Press, 1989), 44. See also Nancy Chodorow, *The Reproduction of Mothering: Psychoanalysis and the Sociology of Gender* (Berkeley: University of California Press, 1978). For a related thesis, see Dorothy Dinnerstein, *The Mermaid and the Minotaur* (New York: Harper Colophon, 1976).

52. Simone de Beauvoir, *The Second Sex* (New York: Vintage Press, 1973), 301.

53. Mary Daly's *Gyn/Ecology* and Susan Griffin's *Woman and Nature: The Roaring Inside Her* (New York: Harper & Row, 1978), for example, have been criticized for their essentialist linkage of women and nature. See Alison Jaggar, *Feminist Politics and Human Nature* (Totowa, N.J.: Rowman and Allanheld, 1983).

54. Hester Eisenstein, *Contemporary Feminist Thought* (Boston: G.K. Hall, 1983), 132.

55. Mill, *Three Essays*, 451.

56. For a discussion of the types of feminism, see Alison Jagger and Paula Rothenberg, *Feminist Frameworks: Alternative Theoretical Accounts of the Relations between Women and Men* (New York: McGraw-Hill, 1978).

57. Carole Pateman, *The Problem of Political Obligation: A Critique of Liberal Theory* (Cambridge, England: Polity Press, 1985), 189.

58. John Rawls, *A Theory of Justice* (Cambridge: Harvard University Press, 1971).

59. Myra Marx Ferree, "The Political Context of Rationality," in *Frontiers of Social Movement Theory*, ed. Aldon Morris and Carol McClurg Mueller (New Haven: Yale University Press, 1992), 36.

60. Susan Moller Okin, "Gender Inequality and Cultural Differences," *Political Theory* 22 (February 1994): 5–24.

61. Allison Pearson, "Feminism with a Friendly Face," *World Press Review*, February 1994, 38–39.

62. See Linda Nicholson, "Feminism and Marx: Integrating Kinship with the Economic," in Benhabib and Cornell, *Feminism as Critique*, 18.

63. See, for instance, Nancy Hartsack, *Money, Sex, and Power: Toward a Feminist Historical Materialism* (Boston: Northeastern University Press, 1983).

64. Karl Marx, "Contribution to the Critique of Hegel's *Philosophy of Right:* Introduction," in *The Marx-Engels Reader*, 2d ed., ed. Robert C. Tucker (New York: Norton, 1978), 54.

65. Ibid.

66. Ibid., 64.

67. Karl Marx and Friedrich Engels, "Manifesto of the Communist Party," in *The Marx-Engels Reader*, 484.

68. Karl Marx, "The German Ideology," in *The Marx-Engels Reader*, 150.

69. Ibid., 155.

70. Karl Marx, "Critique of the Gotha Program," in *The Marx-Engels Reader*, 530–31.

71. Karl Marx, *Writings of the Young Marx on Philosophy and Society*, trans. L. Easton and K. Guddat (Garden City, N.Y.: Doubleday, 1967), 39.

72. Friedrich Engels, "Preface to the German Edition [of the Communist

Manifesto] of 1883," in *The Marx-Engels Reader*, 472.

73. Marx, "The German Ideology," 160.

74. Michael Bakunin, *Bakunin on Anarchism*, ed. Sam Dolgoff (Montreal: Black Rose Books, 1980), 331.

75. Karl Marx, *Selected Writings*, ed. David McLellan (Oxford: Oxford University Press, 1977), 563.

76. Marx, "The German Ideology," 165.

77. Karl Marx, "Theses on Feuerbach," in *The Marx-Engels Reader*, 144.

78. See, for example, Michael Ryan, *Marxism and Deconstruction: A Critical Articulation* (Baltimore: Johns Hopkins University Press, 1982), and *Politics and Culture: Working Hypotheses for a Post-Revolutionary Society* (Baltimore: Johns Hopkins University Press, 1989).

79. Ernesto Laclau and Chantal Mouffe, *Hegemony and Socialist Strategy: Towards a Radical Democratic Politics* (London: Verso, 1985), 176.

80. Ernesto Laclau and Chantal Mouffe, "Post-Marxism without Apologies," *New Left Review* 166 (November/December 1987): 79–106.

81. Ralph Miliband, *The State in Capitalist Society* (New York: Basic Books, 1969), 265–66.

82. Ralph Miliband, *Marxism and Politics* (Oxford: Oxford University Press, 1977), 189–90.

83. J. Donald Moon, *Constructing Community: Moral Pluralism and Tragic Conflicts* (Princeton: Princeton University Press, 1993), 69–70.

84. Karl Marx, "Economic and Philosophic Manuscripts of 1844," in *The Marx-Engels Reader*, 87.

85. R.H. Tawney, *Equality*, 4th ed. (London: Unwin, 1964), 57.

Chapter 6

1. Plato, *Gorgias* (464b), in *The Collected Dialogues of Plato*, ed. Edith Hamilton and Huntington Cairns (Princeton: Princeton University Press, 1989), 246.

2. Plato, *Timaeus* (87b), in *Collected Dialogues*, 1207.

3. See Martha C. Nussbaum, *The Therapy of Desire: Theory and Practice in Hellenistic Ethics* (Princeton: Princeton University Press, 1994).

4. Plato, *Republic* (592b), trans. Allan Bloom (New York: Basic Books, 1968), 275. In *Collected Dialogues*, 819.

5. Plato, *Symposium* (204a), in *Collected Dialogues*, 556.

6. Plato, *Phaedo* (84a), in *Collected Dialogues*, 67.

7. Plato, "Letter VII" (343e), in *Collected Dialogues*, 1591.

8. Plato, *Phaedrus* (271b), in *Collected Dialogues*, 516.

9. Plato, *Republic* (368a), in *Collected Dialogues*, 614.

10. Plato, *Phaedrus* (249e–250a), in *Collected Dialogues*, 496.

11. Ibid., 522–23.

12. Plato, *Republic* (532c), in *Collected Dialogues*, 764.

13. Ibid., 701.

14. Plato, *The Laws* (942), in *Collected Dialogues*, 1488–89.

15. Ibid., 1235.

16. Baron de Montesquieu, *The Spirit of the Laws*, trans. Thomas Nugent (New York: Hafner Press, 1949), 326.

17. Quoted in Bertrand de Jouvenal, *On Power: The Natural History of Its Growth* (Indianapolis: Liberty Fund, 1993), 326.

18. Plato, *Phaedrus* (266b), in *Collected Dialogues*, 512.

19. Plato, *Phaedo* (89d–e), in *Collected Dialogues*, 71–72.

20. Thomas Jefferson, *Thomas Jefferson on Democracy* (New York: Mentor, 1939), 168.

21. See Orlando Patterson, *Freedom: Freedom in the Making of Western Culture*, vol. 1 (New York: Basic Books, 1991).

22. G.W.F. Hegel, *The Philosophy of History*, trans. J. Sibree (New York: Dover, 1956), 19.

23. A.J. Carlyle, *Political Liberty: A History of the Conception in the Middle Ages and Modern Times* (Westport, Conn.: Greenwood Press, 1941), vii.

24. Patterson, *Freedom*, 402–3.

25. Edmund Burke, *Selected Writings of Edmund Burke*, ed. W.J. Bate (Westport, Conn.: Greenwood Press, 1960), 211.

26. Michel de Montaigne, "Of Moderation," in *The Complete Essays of Montaigne*, trans. Donald Frame (Stanford: Stanford University Press, 1985), 146.

27. Montesquieu, *The Spirit of the Laws*, 150.

28. G.W.F. Hegel, *Hegel's Philosophy of Mind*, trans. William Wallace and A.V. Miller (Oxford: Clarendon Press, 1971), 239.

29. Isaiah Berlin, "Two Concepts of Liberty," in *Four Essays on Liberty* (Oxford: Oxford University Press, 1969), 119.

30. John Stuart Mill, *On Liberty* (Indianapolis: Bobbs-Merrill, 1956), 13.

31. A.V. Dicey, *Law and Public Opinion in England during the Nineteenth Century* (London: Macmillan, 1962), 146. Quoted in Vernon Van Dyke, *Ideology and Political Choice: The Search for Freedom, Justice, and Virtue* (Chatham, N.J.: Chatham House, 1995), 24.

32. Mill, *On Liberty*, 13.

33. John Locke, *Two Treatises of Government*, ed. Peter Laslett (New York: Cambridge University Press, 1960), 336–37.

34. Jean-Jacques Rousseau, *The Social Contract and Discourses*, trans. G.D.H. Cole (London: J.M. Dent and Sons, 1973), 178.

35. Ibid., 240.

36. Berlin, "Two Concepts of Liberty," 131.

37. Rousseau, *The Social Contract and Discourses*, 47.

38. Ibid., 165.

39. Jean-Jacques Rousseau, "On Public Happiness," *Œuvres Complètes* (Pleide, 1964), 3:510, 881.

40. Berlin, *Four Essays on Liberty*, 138, 141.

41. Bruce Bower, "Growing up Poor," *Science News* 146 (9 July 1994): 24–25.

42. J.L. Brown, "Hunger in the U.S.," *Scientific American* (February 1987), 37–41. A UNICEF report released in June 1996 confirms Brown's figures.

43. Benjamin Barber, *Strong Democracy: Participatory Politics for a New Age* (Berkeley: University of California Press, 1984), xvi.

44. See, for instance, Gary Frank Reed, "Berlin and the Division of Liberty," *Political Theory* 8 (1980): 376.

45. Quoted in James Boswell, *The Life of Samuel Johnson* (New York: Penguin Books, 1979), 140.

46. John Locke, *A Letter Concerning Toleration*, 2d ed. (Indianapolis: Bobbs-Merrill, 1955), 17.

47. Isaiah Berlin, "Philosophy and Life: An Interview," *New York Review of Books*, 28 May 1992, 52–53.

48. Quoted in Anthony Giddens, *Capitalism and Modern Social Theory: An Analysis of the Writings of Marx, Durkheim, and Weber* (Cambridge: Cambridge University Press, 1971), 117.

49. William E. Connolly, *Identity/Difference: Democratic Negotiations of Political Paradox* (Ithaca: Cornell University Press, 1991), 29.

50. Benjamin Constant, "The Liberty of the Ancients Compared with That of the Moderns: Speech Given at the Athènée Royal in Paris," in *Political Writings*, ed. Biancamaria Fontana (Cambridge, 1988), 310–11, quoted in Stephen Macedo, *Liberal Virtues: Citizenship, Virtue, and Community in Liberal Constitutionalism* (Oxford: Clarendon Press, 1990), 9.

51. John Locke, *Two Treatises of Government*, ed. Peter Laslett (Cambridge: Cambridge University Press, 1960), 336–39.

52. I examine the political relevance of Heidegger's understanding of freedom in *Timely Meditations: Martin Heidegger and Postmodern Politics* (Princeton: Princeton University Press, 1995).

53. Hannah Arendt, *Between Past and Future* (New York: Penguin Books, 1968), 164–65.

54. Thomas A. Spragens, *Reason and Democracy* (Durham: Duke University Press, 1990), 255.

55. Macedo, *Liberal Virtues*, 38.

56. Ibid., 46, 50.

57. Michel Foucault, *The Foucault Reader*, ed. Paul Rabinow (New York: Pantheon Books, 1984), 249.

58. Locke, *Two Treatises of Government*, 348.

59. Rousseau, *The Social Contract and Discourses*, 178.

60. Foucault, *The Foucault Reader*, 249.

61. William E. Connolly, *The Terms of Political Discourse*, 3d ed. (Princeton: Princeton University Press, 1993), 1.

62. See, for instance, Sara Ruddick, "Remarks on the Sexual Politics of Reason," in *Women and Moral Theory*, ed. Eva Kittay and Kian Meyers (Savage, Md.: Rowman and Littlefield, 1987), and *Maternal Thinking* (Boston: Beacon Press, 1989); Roslyn Bologh, *Love or Greatness: Max Weber and Masculine Thinking—A Feminist Inquiry* (London: Unwin Hyman, 1990), esp. 240–65; and Susan Moller Okin, *Justice, Gender, and the Family* (New York: Basic Books, 1989), esp. 41–73.

63. Marimba Ani, *Yurugu: An African-Centered Critique of European Cultural Thought and Behavior* (Trenton: African World Press, 1994), 107.

64. Charles A. Reich, *The Greening of America* (New York: Bantam Books, 1970), 381, 415.

65. See Jürgen Habermas, *Theory of Communicative Action*, vol. 1: *Reason and the Rationalization of Society*, and vol. 2: *Lifeworld and System: A Critique of Functionalist Reason*, trans. Thomas McCarthy (Boston: Beacon Press, 1984 and 1987).

66. John Maynard Keynes, *General Theory of Employment, Interest, and Money*, 1936. Quoted in Charles Birch and John Cobb, *The Liberation of Life: From the Cell to the Community* (Cambridge: Cambridge University Press, 1981), 265.

67. John S. Dryzek, *Rational Ecology: Environment and Political Economy* (New York: Basil Blackwell, 1987), 55.

68. Max Weber, *The Protestant Ethic and the Spirit of Capitalism*, trans. Talcott Parsons (New York: Scribner's, 1958), 26.

69. See Rogers Brubaker, *The Limits of Rationality: An Essay on the Social and Moral Thought of Max Weber* (London: George Allen and Unwin, 1984).

70. Weber, *The Protestant Ethic*, 194.

71. Max Weber, *The Sociology of Religion*, trans. Ephraim Fishcoff (Boston: Beacon Press, 1963), 22.

72. Max Weber, *From Max Weber: Essays in Sociology*, trans. H.H. Gerth and C. Wright Mills (New York: Oxford University Press, 1958), 293.

73. Weber, *The Protestant Ethic*, 115.

74. Ibid., 166.

75. On the identification of rationality with economic thought and activity, see Spragens, *Reason and Democracy*, 176; Nancy Holmstrom, "Rationality and Moral/Political Decisions," in *Rationality in Thought and Action*, ed. Martin Tamny and K.D. Irani (Westport, Conn.: Greenwood Press, 1986); David Gauthier, "Reason and Maximization," *Canadian Journal of Philosophy* 4, no. 3 (March 1975); A.K. Sen, "Rational Fools: A Critique of the Behavioural Foundations of Economic Theory," *Philosophy and Public Affairs* 6, no. 2 (Summer 1977); and Frederic Schick, *Having Reasons: An Essay on Rationality and Sociality* (Princeton: Princeton University Press, 1983).

76. See, for example, Lewis Mumford, *The Myth of the Machine: Technics and Human Development* (San Diego: Harcourt Brace Jovanovich, 1967), 270–81.

77. Weber, *The Protestant Ethic*, 284.

78. Brian Barry, *Sociologists, Economists, and Democracy* (Chicago: University of Chicago Press, 1978), 31.

79. Anthony Downs, *An Economic Theory of Democracy* (New York: Harper & Brothers, 1957), 5.

80. Ron Rogowski, "Rationalist Theories of Politics: A Midterm Report," *World Politics* 30 (1978): 299. See also Todd Sandler, *Collective Action: Theory and Applications* (Ann Arbor: University of Michigan Press, 1992), 4.

81. Herbert Simon, *Administrative Behavior*, 3d ed. (New York: Free Press, 1976), xxviii.

82. Downs, *Economic Theory of Democracy*, 5; italics added.

83. Rogowski, "Rationalist Theories of Politics," 300.

84. Herbert Simon, "Human Nature in Politics: The Dialogue of Psychology with Political Science," *American Political Science Review* 79 (1985): 297.

85. James March and Herbert Simon, *Organizations* (New York: Wiley, 1958), 21.

86. James March, "Bounded Rationality and the Engineering of Choice," *Bell Journal of Economics*, 1978; also see James March and J. Olson, *Ambiguity and Choice in Organizations* (Bergen: Universitätsforlaget, 1976).

87. Timothy O'Riordan, "Attitudes, Behavior, and Environmental Policy Issues," in *Human Behavior and Environment*, ed. Irwin Altman and Joachim Wohlvill (New York: Plenum Press, 1976), 1:1–36.

88. David Hume, *Hume's Moral and Political Philosophy*, ed. Henry Aiken (New York: Macmillan, 1948), 25.

89. Bertrand Russell, *Human Society in Ethics and Politics* (London: Allen and Unwin, 1954), viii.

90. Herbert Simon, *Reason in Human Affairs* (Stanford: Stanford University Press, 1983), 7–8.

91. Jean-Pierre Vernant, *The Origins of Greek Thought* (Ithaca: Cornell University Press, 1982), 130.

92. Joseph Dunne, *Back to the Rough Ground: "Phronesis" and "Techne" in Modern Philosophy and in Aristotle* (Notre Dame: University of Notre Dame, 1993), 263.

93. Hannah Arendt, *The Human Condition* (Chicago: University of Chicago Press, 1958), 184.

94. Ibid., 206. See also Dana Villa, "Beyond Good and Evil: Arendt, Nietzsche, and the Aestheticization of Political Action," *Political Theory* 20 (May 1992): 274–308.

95. Quoted in Jonathan Schell, *The Fate of the Earth* (New York: Avon, 1982), 109.

96. J. Peter Euben, *The Tragedy of Political Theory* (Princeton: Princeton University Press, 1990), 9.

97. Aristotle, *Nichomachean Ethics* (1140b), trans. Terence Irwin (Indianapolis: Hackett, 1985), 154.

98. For discussion of the political nature of dialogue and the dialogic nature of politics, see Hans-Georg Gadamer, *Truth and Method* (New York: Crossroad Publishing, 1985); and M.M. Bakhtin, *The Dialogic Imagination* (Austin: University of Texas Press, 1981).

99. Jürgen Habermas, *Toward a Rational Society*, trans. Jeremy Shapiro (Boston: Beacon Press, 1970), 118.

100. See Karl Popper, *The Logic of Scientific Discovery* (New York: Basic Books, 1959), and *Conjectures and Refutations* (New York: Basic Books, 1962).

101. Joseph Schumpeter, *Capitalism, Socialism, and Democracy*, 2d ed. (New York: Harper & Row, 1950).

102. See Bruce Mayhew, "Structuralism vs. Individualism," *Social Forces* 59 (1980): 335–75.

103. Albert O. Hirschman, *Shifting Involvements: Private Interest and Public Action* (Princeton: Princeton University Press, 1982), 85–88.

104. Frederick W. Allen and Roy Popkin, "Environmental Polls: What They Tell Us," *EPA Journal* 14, no. 6 (July/August 1988): 10. See also John Gillroy and Robert Shapiro, "The Polls: Environmental Protection," *Public Opinion Quarterly* 50 (1986): 270–79.

105. See Douglass North, *Institutions, Institutional Change, and Economic Performance* (Cambridge: Cambridge University Press, 1990).

106. Joseph M. Petulla, *American Environmentalism: Values, Tactics, Priorities* (College Station: Texas A & M University Press, 1980), 91.

107. Al Gore, *Earth in the Balance: Ecology and the Human Spirit* (Boston: Houghton Mifflin, 1992), 170.

108. Robert L. Heilbroner, *An Inquiry into the Human Prospect: Looked at Again for the 1990s* (New York: Norton, 1991), 138.

109. John S. Dryzek, *Rational Ecology: Environment and Political Economy* (New York: Basil Blackwell, 1987), 56.

110. Theodore Roszak, *The Voice of the Earth* (New York: Simon and Schuster, 1992), 249–50.

111. Ben Bolch and Harold Lyons, *Apocalypse Not: Science, Economics, and Environmentalism* (Washington, D.C.: Cato Institute, 1993), viii.

112. David W. Orr, *Ecological Literacy: Education and the Transition to a Postmodern World* (Albany: SUNY Press, 1992), 181–82.

113. Dryzek, *Rational Ecology,* 58–59.

114. Sandler, *Collective Action,* 3.

115. See, for example, Warwick Fox, *Toward a Transpersonal Ecology: Developing New Foundations for Environmentalism* (Boston: Shambhala, 1990); and Paul Wapner, *Environmental Activism and World Civic Politics* (Albany: SUNY Press, 1996).

116. See Clive L. Spash, "Economics, Ethics, and Long-Term Environmental Damages," *Environmental Ethics* 15 (Summer 1993): 118, 127, 128.

117. *Earth Island Journal,* Fall 1995, 19.

118. Lester Milbrath, "Environmental Understanding: A New Concern for Political Socialization," in *Political Socialization: Citizenship, Education, and Democracy,* ed. Orit Ichilov (New York: Teachers College Press, 1990), 292. Milbrath takes his axiom from Barry Commoner, whose formulation is, "You can't do just one thing" (*The Closing Circle* [New York: Bantam, 1972], 29).

119. David Harvey, *The Condition of Postmodernity: An Enquiry into the Origins of Cultural Change* (Cambridge: Blackwell, 1989), 218.

120. Orr, *Ecological Literacy,* 10–11.

Chapter 7

1. Francis Bacon, *Selected Writings,* ed. H.G. Dick (New York: Randon House, 1955), 435.

2. Francis Bacon, *The Advancement of Learning* (London, 1974), bk. 2, sec. 23.49, quoted in Stephen Macedo, *Liberal Virtues: Citizenship, Virtue, and Community in Liberal Constitutionalism* (Oxford: Clarendon Presss, 1990), 43.

3. Karl Marx, "The German Ideology," in *The Marx-Engels Reader,* 2d ed., ed. Robert C. Tucker (New York: Norton, 1978), 154–55.

4. V.I. Lenin, "What Is to Be Done," in *The Lenin Anthology*, ed. Robert C. Tucker (New York: Norton, 1975), 28–29.

5. Michael Freeden, "Editorial," *Journal of Political Ideologies* 1 (February 1996): 9.

6. Francis Fukuyama, *The End of History and the Last Man* (New York: Free Press, 1992).

7. Karl Mannheim, *Ideology and Utopia: An Introduction to the Sociology of Knowledge*, trans. Louis Wirth and Edward Shils (New York: Harcourt, Brace, 1936), 154–55, 161.

8. William E. Connolly, *The Terms of Political Discourse*, 3d ed. (Princeton: Princeton University Press, 1993), 180.

9. Aldous Huxley, *Brave New World* (London: Granada Publishing, 1932); and George Orwell, *Nineteen Eighty-four* (New York: Penguin Books, 1949).

10. George Orwell, "Politics and the English Language," in *A Collection of Essays* (Garden City, N.Y.: Doubleday, 1954).

11. Connolly, *The Terms of Political Discourse*, 227.

12. See Richard Rorty, *Contingency, Irony, and Solidarity* (Cambridge: Cambridge University Press, 1989).

13. See Leslie Paul Thiele, "Out from the Shadows of God: Nietzschean Skepticism and Political Practice," *International Studies in Philosophy* 27, no. 3 (August 1995): 55–72.

14. Michel Foucault, *Foucault Live: Interviews, 1966–84*, trans. John Johnston (New York: Semiotext(e), 1989), 79.

15. Quoted in William Connolly, "The Irony of Interpretation," in *The Politics of Irony*, ed. Daniel W. Conway and John E. Seery (New York: St. Martin's Press, 1992), 144.

16. Leo Strauss, *What is Political Philosophy and Other Studies* (Westport, Conn.: Greenwood Press, 1959), 38.

17. Plato, *Phaedrus* (275c), in *The Collected Dialogues of Plato*, ed. Edith Hamilton and Huntington Cairns (Princeton: Princeton University Press, 1989), 521.

18. Plato, *Phaedrus* (275e), in *Collected Dialogues*, 521.

19. Plato, *Seventh Letter* (343), in *Collected Dialogues*, 1590.

20. Hannah Arendt, *The Life of the Mind* (New York: Harcourt Brace Jovanovich, 1978), 177.

21. Vernon Van Dyke, *Ideology and Political Choice: The Search for Freedom, Justice, and Virtue* (Chatham, N.J.: Chatham House, 1995), 2.

22. Friedrich Nietzsche, *Daybreak: Thoughts on the Prejudices of Morality*, trans. R.J. Hollingdale (Cambridge: Cambridge University Press, 1982), 76–77.

23. Isaiah Berlin, *Four Essays on Liberty* (Oxford: Oxford University Press, 1969), 172.

24. Quoted in Anthony Pagden, *European Encounters with the New World* (New Haven: Yale University Press, 1993), 118.

25. J.M. Servan, *Discours sur l'administration de la justice criminelle*, 1767, quoted in Michel Foucault, *Discipline and Punish: The Birth of the*

Prison (New York: Vintage, 1977), 102–3.

26. Quoted in Stuart R. Schram, *The Political Thought of Mao Tse-Tung*, rev. ed. (New York: Praeger, 1969), 352.

27. Peter L. Berger and Thomas Luckmann, *The Social Construction of Reality: A Treatise on the Sociology of Knowledge* (New York: Doubleday, 1966), 132.

28. Freeden, "Editorial," 10.

29. Rorty, *Contingency, Irony, and Solidarity*, 83.

30. Ibid., 86.

Conclusion

1. Edmund Burke, *Selected Writings of Edmund Burke*, ed. W.J. Bate (Westport, Conn.: Greenhaven Press, 1960), 211–12.

2. Max Weber, *The Protestant Ethic and the Spirit of Capitalism*, trans. Talcott Parsons (New York: Scribner's, 1958), 183.

3. Michael Sandel, "The Procedural Republic and the Unencumbered Self," in *Communitarianism and Individualism*, ed. Shlomo Avineri and Avner de-Shalit (Oxford: Oxford University Press, 1992), 12.

4. Plato, *The Laws* (636a), trans. Trevor Saunders (New York: Penguin Books, 1970), 61; in *Collected Dialogues*, 1236.

5. T.H. Huxley, *Evolution and Ethics* (Princeton: Princeton University Press, 1989), 82.